Regulating Social Media in China

This book is part of the Peter Lang Media and Communication list.
Every volume is peer reviewed and meets
the highest quality standards for content and production.

PETER LANG
New York • Bern • Berlin
Brussels • Vienna • Oxford • Warsaw

Bei Guo

Regulating Social Media in China

Foucauldian Governmentality and the Public Sphere

PETER LANG
New York • Bern • Berlin
Brussels • Vienna • Oxford • Warsaw

Library of Congress Cataloging-in-Publication Data

Names: Guo, Bei, author.
Title: Regulating social media in China: Foucauldian governmentality
and the public sphere / Bei Guo.
Description: New York: Peter Lang, 2018.
Includes bibliographical references.
Identifiers: LCCN 2018014109 | ISBN 978-1-4331-5271-9 (hardback: alk. paper)
ISBN 978-1-4331-5708-0 (ebook pdf) | ISBN 978-1-4331-5709-7 (epub)
ISBN 978-1-4331-5710-3 (mobi)
Subjects: LCSH: Internet—Social aspects—China.
Internet—Government policy—China.
Social media—China.
Social media—Government policy—China.
Classification: LCC HN740.Z9 I56737 2018 | DDC 302.23/10951—dc23
LC record available at https://lccn.loc.gov/2018014109
DOI 10.3726/b14041

Bibliographic information published by **Die Deutsche Nationalbibliothek**.
Die Deutsche Nationalbibliothek lists this publication in the "Deutsche
Nationalbibliografie"; detailed bibliographic data are available
on the Internet at http://dnb.d-nb.de/.

29 Broadway, 18th floor, New York, NY 10006
www.peterlang.com

TABLE OF CONTENTS

ACKNOWLEDGEMENTS

This book began as a doctoral research project at the University of Adelaide, and that long PhD journey does have particular meanings in my life. I suffered the great loss of my father and welcomed the birth of my son during that time. Fortunately, many people have offered considerable support and help to me both in study and life. Therefore, I would like to thank colleagues, friends and family members who supported me in different ways in the process of conducting this research and the production of this book.

My most profound thanks go to Associate Professor Peter C. Pugsley and Dr. Ying Jiang, for their patiently listening to my plans, constantly encouraging me and offering me advice when I was in need. I have benefited tremendously from their excellent academic guidance. I have also been enriched by many scholars in the Department of Media at the University of Adelaide, whose comments, inspiration and support made me feel encouraged in this big environment. I'm grateful to my colleagues and friends, who have offered generous support during the journey, Dr. Weiming Zhang, Dr. Minghua Wu and Dr. Margarita Flabouris. Their help and friendship to me is unforgettable.

Special gratitude goes to colleagues in the School of Journalism and Communication at Shaanxi Normal University in China. Sincere thanks also go to Editor Farideh Koohi-Kamali, Editorial Assistant Megan Madden and

Commissioning Editor Na Li at Peter Lang, for the patient and considerable support making this work finally came to fruition.

My heartfelt thanks go to my parents, for their unconditional love, understanding and encouragement during my growth. They do not only play the role of parents in my life, but also mentors and friends to me. Thanks go to my parents in law, who gave me great support during my difficulties and helped me to look after my son. Finally, I owe an enormous debt of gratitude to my husband, Liang Yan, who embarked on his own PhD journey together with me, while always giving me care, love and tremendous support whenever I was in need.

ABBREVIATIONS

China Internet Network Information Centre (CNNIC)
China Central Television (CCTV)
Chinese Communist Party (CCP)
Human Flesh Search Engine (HFSE)
Internet Content Provider (ICP)
Non-Government Organizations (NGO)
World Health Organization (WHO)
People's Daily Public Opinion Monitoring (PDPOM)

· 1 ·

INTRODUCTION

Online activism is a microcosm of China's new citizen activism, and it is one of its most vibrant currents. In this sense, online activism marks the expansion of a grassroots, citizen democracy. It is an unofficial democracy because the initiatives, both in thinking and action, come from citizens. (Yang 2009, p. 223)

Aims of the Research

The advent of the internet has made the Chinese communication landscape more vibrant and complex. China had long been criticized for its strict information control and internet censorship. However, the Chinese authorities were quick to seize the advent of the internet to deliver the benefits of the information revolution which they saw as crucial to China's modernization and the rise of China in the international community, despite the clear potential threats to longstanding information regulation. This dynamic is reflected in current scholarship, with some scholarly works focusing on the Chinese government's continuing rigid censorship to maintain the status quo and ensure state security, particularly through the various measures taken by the government to reinforce internet control (MacKinnon 2008). Others show interest in online activism and smart strategies used to counter censorship against political participation (Yang 2009). The most contested question in the existing literature since the arrival of the internet relates to its role in Chinese state-society relations, and whether the internet and its related technologies represent a crucial step in the development of civil society. The internet, after all, is said to carry the potential for the development of a public sphere, and even the eventual democratization of China (Rosen 2010). In recent years a number of technology-driven revolutions have taken place across the world, with many Western media reports and scholarly works placing a great deal of emphasis on the political implications of the internet in China; as elsewhere, the thriving use of the internet and new communication technology has given birth to the myth of cyber democracy.

Weibo, a Chinese microblogging platform that combines the features of Twitter and Facebook, has channeled new energy into the Chinese social media landscape. The anticipated political significance of the internet has been intensified by Weibo, with its unique functions of allowing real-time communication and the attraction of wide audiences. Weibo has quickly become the most powerful form of social media in China, and it has brought a number of significant changes to the Chinese media and society. According to the China Internet Network Information Centre, the total number of Weibo users comprises 40.9 percent of the total internet population by end of 2017 (CNNIC 2018). Just as the arrival of the internet in China had challenged official information control, Weibo's revolutionary potential lay in its opportunities for citizen and social activism, requiring new responses from the government. This has been especially the case in the public opposition to government corruption in recent years (Diamond 2010). Consequently, Weibo has indeed posed a new and serious challenge to official information control. A common assumption is that the rise of social media will have the potential to undermine China's Party controls. The particular threats Weibo invokes can be attributed to a number of factors: greater user participation, instantaneous communications drawing on citizen witnessing of events and its potential for the subversive exchange of information within 140 Chinese characters. With their enriched meanings as singular or part-word forms, Chinese characters have the potential to convey multiple meanings compared with English letters (Tong & Lei 2013). Many scholars declare that Weibo is able to create a more democratic communication space in Chinese society. This book, however, develops a more nuanced and critical perspective about the common equation of Weibo and democratic communication and argues that these discussions underestimate the Chinese government's skills in managing this new technology and oversimplify China's sophisticated internet culture. In other words, China is pursuing a distinctive response to Weibo based on a sophisticated and constantly evolving relationship between the Chinese government and the medium of Weibo.

Previous studies have documented the Chinese authorities' success in the historical management and control of information in the mass media. However, in the internet era, particularly in the Weibo era, will the government be as successful in controlling the flow of information as before? If so, how? While the significant role that the Chinese government has played in expanding the internet in China is rarely explored, this study aims to examine the Chinese government's simultaneous efforts to strengthen the scope of the internet, along with its governance and at the same time to fulfill the official political agenda, particularly through managing Weibo and in the way it deals with politically sensitive events.

Efforts to control internet information in the past have been characterized by mechanisms such as the state-controlled blocking of sites that became widely known as the "Great Firewall of China". Many scholars from various disciplines have established how this technical solution, together with other containment strategies, including specific laws and regulations, have helped the Chinese government to successfully maintain control over the internet (Boas 2006; Bandurski 2010; MacKinnon 2008). However, with the fast development of recent technologies, especially in the Weibo era, it is now almost impossible for the Chinese government to overtly shut down access to information and to block outside threats, simply by using the Great Firewall. This research newly contends that Chinese regulatory strategies have evolved far beyond these straightforward, often punitive measures of the past, and have become varied and multiple, strategic, sophisticated and successful.

The social media industry in China is dynamic and rapidly evolving. Scholarly analysis therefore needs to understand the impact of China's new social media applications and the efforts of the Chinese authorities to control them. Some scholars view the way an authoritarian regime embraces and adjusts to the changes brought by digital communications as "networked authoritarianism", where the ruling Party still remains in control while allowing a range of conversations to take place (MacKinnon 2011; Hassid 2012). This book acknowledges that the Chinese government does not exert complete control over Weibo, instead, adopting a proactive attitude by allowing selective freedoms. In contrast to an extreme view of the false dichotomy between an ideal freedom and total control on Weibo, a space in which much scholarship currently takes place, the reality is that the Chinese government has been successful in both opening up the Weibo platform for public discussion, while also retaining the ability to regulate Weibo. This book argues that both the opening up and closing down of information occurs on Weibo, sometimes simultaneously, but always strategically, as the later case study chapters illustrate. This formulation should be understood as a new type of governance, with the ultimate outcome always to sustain government control. In other words, the political implications of Weibo cannot be understood solely by looking at users' participatory practices, but should be revisited to consider the networked conditions that enable it. It is too simplistic a question to focus only on whether or not Weibo expands public communication as a basis for political reform; a more significant focus considers how the state accommodates and manages the openness of public expression on Weibo for its own purposes.

By providing an outlet for increasingly information-rich and contentious public expression, the Chinese government has developed updated versions of regulation through selective and targeted responses or by subtly using the medium to deliberately set the public agenda on certain issues. This is not to say that the authorities have abandoned their more overt control measures, including coercion, censorship and persuasion to make sure that events conform to the political agenda. Rather, the new spectrum of strategic and subtle government controls of public expression and thought on Weibo confirms that Weibo represents its most serious challenge to date, requiring different and highly skilled management. As a result, the rise of Weibo has not fundamentally undermined the party-state's control, but rather, served as a new tool for building consensus and fulfilling the interests of various sectors.

This book therefore examines the dialogues appearing on Weibo as a complex picture based on interaction and constant negotiation between public expression and official control. In addition to elaborating this paradoxical picture, the study argues that in this practice, the Chinese government is more successful and effective in attaining its intended goals to bolster its legitimacy, and that this has been largely overlooked by scholars to date. This book highlights the central role of the Chinese government in developing such a method for dealing with ever-evolving Weibo dynamics.

The arguments raised in this book situate the negotiated relationship between the Chinese authorities and Weibo within the larger historical context of the public sphere, where new technologies provide information and tools that may extend the role of the public in the social and political arena.

The introduction of Weibo has indeed provided an unprecedented communications space for ordinary people, allowing wide participation and freer expression, particularly in recent years. With a number of social problems and expressions of social dissatisfaction in the wake of China's huge economic success (which has been profitable for some individuals while excluding others), this platform has been a particularly important and valuable public forum. Therefore, this book does not deny the active public participation of ordinary people through communication on Weibo; rather, it fully acknowledges the increased power of ordinary people in this process. However, instead of exaggerating its transformative power, this study holds the position that the landscape of government-regulated Weibo communication is complex and still evolving. It is therefore too early to draw conclusions about increased public participation through what Diamond (2010) dubbed "liberation technology" and democratic communication and action, as the Chinese government is keeping pace with rapid technological development and adapts quickly in building capacity to shape digital communications and to consolidate its control. As Diamond (2010) argues, "it is not technology, but people, organizations, and governments that will determine who prevails" (ibid., p. 82). In considering the democratic role of the internet, other factors including socio-cultural context and political context should be taken into consideration (Lagerkvist 2006, p. 18). Therefore, this study focuses more upon the changing and evolving regulatory strategies from the authorities in the face of Weibo's dynamic development, so illustrating the role of the Chinese government as it plays in the Weibo version of a public sphere.

The concept of the "public sphere", on the one hand, can be understood in daily practice as information being circulated in public; on the other hand, it is also a well-developed concept of "how democratic culture should work" (Mckee 2005). It has a more significant and specific meaning in the Chinese context, where the Chinese government has long enjoyed monopolistic control over information. Thus Weibo, with its inherently anti-control nature, is an extremely effective channel for spreading information. A careful empirical examination is needed of the extent to which government intervention affects the formulation of different public spheres and as well, of the distinct types of public spheres that exist in Weibo communication space. Given the ongoing and ever more sophisticated government controls, we should bear in mind that no matter how powerful Weibo appears to be, it cannot totally detach its users from government oversight.

A central focus of this book is on the "negotiation" among the players in Chinese governmental control structures and those in the potential Weibo public sphere. The advent of Weibo has required that the responses of the government are agile and fluid. The government calculations behind the scenes as to how to respond to and manage information flow on Weibo have opened the door for a more fluid interconnection in the process of regulation. This is an element in how the Chinese government is necessarily evolving and adapting within global communications, as well as internally. Hence, this book offers a critical perspective in answering the question of how Weibo is changing China while the leadership maintains official control of the medium. This formulation of the relationship between Weibo and its government regulators differs from, and extends, the current scholarship that considers Weibo's power from two extreme perspectives, as either a freely expanding space beyond the reach of political authority or as heavily stifled by government control. The key differences in the perspective explored in this book will be examined in chapter two, in which the government's adaptive mechanisms and techniques for control in the Weibo era are described in detail. Here, the study adopts a theoretical approach based on the Foucauldian notion of governmentality that proposes "strategies to govern through the desires of individuals" (Sigley 2006), and the theoretical concept of the public sphere as formulated by Habermas, that suggests a space of communication in which a number of issues can be discussed without government interventions. While the ideas of governmentality and public sphere would seem to be in opposition, the reason for drawing on both theoretical constructs is to better analyze a "mediated" version of the public sphere in China, which remains an authoritarian state that is nevertheless home to one of the most diverse media environments in the world. These two theoretical foundations acknowledge that the Chinese government itself has played an important role in shaping a version of a mediated public sphere that has emerged. This study argues that the rise of Weibo, however, has provided a specific stimulus for the emergence of multiple mediated public spheres. To some extent, the Chinese state plays a role in both forming and inhibiting the growth of these mediated public spheres in China.

This approach builds on current scholarship that attempts to move beyond the simplistic examination of the positive benefits of the new media technologies for future democratization or internet regulation in China (Yang 2009; MacKinnon 2008). Moreover, the application of this approach allows a more nuanced interpretation of the manner in which the free space on Weibo is indeed carefully balanced by the Chinese government. This book provides a systematic framework for how regime structures have successfully managed public sphere discourses in China, while ultimately shaping public discourses to facilitate control. This governmentality approach goes beyond what scholars have described as the Chinese government's attitude towards social media, which they have summarized as one of "deep ambivalence" (Qian & Bandurski 2010; Xiao 2011), however this book does not purport to hold all the answers to the question of ambivalence. Instead, it puts forward an original position on how Weibo is regulated, shaped and governed, strategically, through the framework of governmentality. Therefore, the theory of governmentality will be applied to make sense of the Chinese government's approach towards the management of social media regulation.

As noted, the analysis contained in this book also draws on the theory of the public sphere, as formulated by Jurgen Habermas. In this way, this study not only closely examines both the specific programs and tactics the Chinese government employs to accomplish its management goals, but more significantly, the more subtle and often invisible controls it uses to regulate social media through allowing an impression of new freedom. Hence, this study first aims to present an analysis of how various government intentions are enabled in the Weibo version of a public sphere, and second, how the Chinese government employs particular strategies in curtailing the democratic role that Weibo plays in the Chinese context. The ultimate research aims are not only to fill the gap between the normative Western assumptions about the effects of Chinese social media power, with its specific Chinese characteristics based on China's unique socio-cultural context, but also to argue that the Chinese state demonstrates an overall strategy for its regulation. This strategy is well documented through examples on Weibo, presenting the most significant challenge to the authorities of all Chinese social media, and currently enjoying greater freedom than other forms of social media. More importantly, this research documents key examples of the overall Chinese strategy for the regulation of Weibo without overt censorship, through its subtle and astute embrace of various forms of governance in order to publicly balance control and freedom, as expressed in terms of the people's will.

Through examining different actors playing in the Weibo sphere, using the Foucauldian governmentality framework, this study contributes a novel perspective on the political implications of Weibo in China, through its focus on the Chinese government's role in a changing media environment. It demonstrates how China, as an authoritarian country, responds to its citizens' voracious hunger for information and regulates this by carefully adopting both liberal and authoritarian techniques. The combination of both opening and closing access to information in a version of a public sphere on Weibo reflects the Chinese government's national strategy and overall planning from a macro state perspective in the regulation of social media.

Key Terms in Use in This Book

There are several definitions in this book that are important to clarify. The first is "Chinese government" or "Chinese authorities", terms that are frequently used, because government can refer to different levels, such as the local prefecture, city or provincial level, or the national level. In *Technological Empowerment: The Internet, State and Society in China*, Yongnian Zheng (2008) makes the point that whether online activism succeeds depends on its scope and focus. For example, anti-corruption cases could always gain attention from the public, and they always take place at the local level. This book principally locates its examination of Weibo's political implications against the background of the Chinese government's overall calculations of control at the national level. It therefore confines the scope of discussion of the Chinese government to the national level. "Chinese local government" will be used only in relation to a specific local prefecture, city or to provincial governments.

In this book, the term Weibo refers to Sina Weibo, rather than the other service providers, Tencent Weibo and Sohu Weibo.

There are already a large number of scholarly works which discuss the current functioning of the public sphere in different media, including Weibo. This book extends these discussions by asking, first, whether the version of a mediated public sphere as formulated in this study, is evolving on Weibo within a specifically Chinese context. If so, what is the role of the Chinese government in overseeing the Weibo version of a public sphere or public spheres? Is that role also evolving?

The concept of the public sphere has a well-developed meaning in media and cultural studies. Defined in the work of German philosopher, Jurgen Habermas (which will be explained in detail in Chapter Two), the public sphere is "A domain of social life where such a thing as public opinion can be formed [where] citizens …deal with matters of general interest without being subject to coercion …[to] express and publicize their views" (Habermas

1997, p. 105). Habermas provides a version of the ideal public sphere, which is free from government intervention, commercialization and sensationalism. Rejecting the view of ideal public sphere, this book takes a postmodern view in acknowledging that there are many types or versions of public sphere existing on Weibo, which the book considers holistically when evaluating their collective impact.

The term patriotism, which is used in a case study chapter, does not refer to earlier historical versions of nationalism inspired by foreign invasion or territory conflicts among countries, including China. Instead, in this book, this term is used to describe the concern for the people's sense of national identity in contemporary China, particularly within the context of the global rise of China. Simply put, an illustrative case study deals with a natural response or reaction when ordinary Chinese feel a sense of embarrassment or disgrace in the international context.

Background and Significance

Weibo has greatly accelerated the expansion of freedom of speech in China and thus has the emancipatory potential to promote citizen activism; however, it is necessary to take a cautious approach in evaluating Weibo's political impact in the specific Chinese socio-cultural context. Weibo's success in recent years as a public space for greater citizen-to-citizen communication has been affirmed by the fact that many major events were first exposed on Weibo. In such cases, after a series of widespread and often heated online discussions, an event will then become a virtual public event, which places intense pressure on the authorities and pushes the latter to respond through existing policies or practices, which can lead to change. To some extent then, Weibo is able to alter the progress of events. There are many examples of this, and a number of them concern illegal behavior by privileged people, who in the past would have been protected from public exposure. In acknowledging Weibo's tremendous power in this respect, instead of adopting the conventional approach of direct opposition, the Chinese government selectively guides or shapes the unfolding of, and responses to, certain incidents according to its own aims.

Some scholars take this from a very optimistic attitude towards the internet and Weibo and its potential for transformative power (Xiao 2011; Yang 2009), and others go even further, illustrating typologies of different kinds of public spheres on Weibo through the lens of cultural differences or specific media event characteristics (Rauchfleisch & Schäfer 2014); still other scholars have been primarily concerned with continuing censorship in China as the main obstacle to free public debate. Among these examples of overt censorship, the most notable is the Great Firewall, which is used to block unwanted information or webpages, such as Facebook and Twitter from being accessible to users in China (MacKinnon 2011). In addition, internet content providers such as the Sina Company, which is the host company of Sina Weibo, are required to overtly comply with the government's information regulations, either by using a blacklist to automatically censor information or by employing a large number of human censors to delete information manually (Fu, Chan & Chau 2013). In sum, all of these views of Weibo confirm that the government is now more present on Weibo than ever before, while at the same time, taking up new and much more sophisticated macro governance strategies in response to Weibo than either of the two sets of scholarly responses outlined have considered (Sullivan 2014; Noesselt 2013). This book closely examines both the specific programs and tactics the Chinese government employs to accomplish its public information management goals and even more significantly, the more subtle and often invisible controls it uses to regulate social media, while allowing a superficial impression of freedom.

In the past, there has been a scholarly recognition of longstanding and specific censorship practices in relation to Chinese blogs or microblogs (King, Pan & Roberts 2013; MacKinnon 2008; Fu, Chan & Chau 2013). These studies, however, have focused mainly on the impact of censorship or the empirical practice of censorship, both of which merely take censorship practices for granted. This current research, however, presents a new approach to understanding the censorship characteristics and the reasons behind new strategies for regulation of Weibo by the Chinese authorities, which reveal the changing and indirect censorship technologies developed to address it. Finally, the directness of past state measures to control the internet is contrasted with the present government's more strategic control measures in contemporary times.

The transformation of Chinese statecraft from a relatively simple and coercive set of measures to a more complex approach has coincided with the overall planning attitude and the current leadership's inclusive reaction to new media. The use of these new tactics aims to guide public opinion to promote social harmony, which is an important national goal for China's leadership. The concept of a harmonious society marks a shift from the purely economic-centered development of the past to a more people-centered sustainable development, as viewed by the international community. The flow of information is no longer simply blocked or censored as the only means of regulating public expression, although that still happens. Instead, the government allows a degree of online citizen communication and unfettered personal expression, while keeping a close eye on any signs of social unrest or the possibility of collective action which may arise in response (King, Pan & Roberts 2013). Such manipulation of free expression indicates a clear evolution in government thinking about regulation. Weibo has been instrumental in requiring such an evolution in approach, if social stability is to be ensured. However, this book argues that it is far too soon to assume that increased participation and public expression on social media will correlate with increased personal power for citizens, or even lead to democracy. While this book acknowledges Weibo's power, it nonetheless refutes an intrinsic connection between greater participation and a democratic politics. The possibility of such a connection is questioned by Yeo and Li (2012, p. 8) who suggest that:

> In today's context, political authority is ontogenetic while the cyberspace is phylogenetic. The health of human society depends on the balance between the two. When they are out of balance, the body politic falls sick with catastrophic consequences.... Too much intervention is as bad as too little. Constant monitoring is necessary so that one knows when and how much to intervene. The word in Chinese is *tiao*, which means continuous tuning of a complex system.

This transformation has also had a major effect on the role of traditional forms of the media. The traditional mass media in China is directly controlled by political power and its related economic players, which stands in contrast to the liberation of online expression through social media platforms, particularly Weibo, giving direct voice to citizens. Scholars have, however, in the Chinese context, established that the specific relationship between online media and traditional mass media could be described as complementary from the authorities' point of view; when a breaking story first appears online it is then picked up by the mass media.

Among the few scholarly works to have paid attention to the more complex relationship between the Chinese state, new media technology and democratization in China, several (Zheng 2008; MacKinnon 2011; Jiang 2012) highlight the success or failure of online activism in China under different circumstances. In other words, the rise of online activism alone cannot necessarily be considered as a sign of a linear, expanding democracy. A key element missing from these earlier discussions is a comprehensive understanding of "how" the intentions and strategies of government are adopted in response to politically sensitive topics, and then skillfully applied to manage China's social media approaches to these topics. The examination in this research of the political implications of Weibo aims to go further, by identifying how the authoritarian state of China first deliberates on these political implications and then strategically intervenes in a manner that both allows an opening of public discourse on Weibo, while ultimately bolstering the CCP's legitimacy.

This book probes a new phenomenon based on recent observations of cultural and political incidents on Weibo. As Lagerkvist noted in the analysis of China's internet, state regulation and social freedom have adapted together in China (Lagerkvist 2006). What distinguishes Weibo from the larger internet is its unprecedented influence in China, so requiring from the authorities a more proactive and international regulatory method in order to regulate Weibo. These changes or trends are newly shown on Weibo, especially in the area of political incidents, an area with little systematic and theoretical analysis in the past.

From a theoretical perspective, governmentality studies have been widely applied in a non-Western context, including China (Sigley 2004, 2006; Jiang 2012), only by addressing cultural and economic perspectives. This study provides an original analysis of governmentality in the Chinese political sphere, the first such systematic and detailed analysis. This will also allow readers to critically rethink the governmental role in social media regulation, and in addition, to re-evaluate Weibo's potential democratizing power in the Chinese context. Hence, this book will present the full and complex picture of the Weibo sphere and the resulting "negotiations" between the Chinese authorities and Weibo users. In this way, this study not only plays a crucial role in examining the political implications of Weibo in China, but also makes a contribution to existing scholarship in illuminating more fully the strategies and techniques in play in the CCP's responses to Weibo. These changes are fundamental in understanding the attitude of the CCP towards any new technologies in the rise of China, although the regulatory measures are still evolving and in transition.

Historically, the language used to describe earlier governmental interventions in this area was expressed in black and white terms: "propaganda" or "thought management" (Brady 2012) in controlling people's minds, especially during the Mao years, with the publication of Quotations from Chairman Mao Zedong ("The Little Red Book"), considered to be Mao's bible, with the status of a sacred and holy text during the Cultural Revolution, and which was said to be used to manipulate people's minds. This book applies a Western-based theory of governmentality, very differently from control measures of the past, for two reasons. First, propaganda and thought management were history-based terms, but today's relationship between the Chinese government and the social media is more subtle and sophisticated, as befits the times during China's growth as a socialist-market economy, although the terms are still used. Second, both propaganda and thought management focus upon unidirectional and hierarchical communication, which is top-down, without concern or acknowledgement of citizens' freedom of speech. Weibo is not a passive platform on which propaganda can be imposed; instead, it is a two-way communication platform. Governmentality better represents the current play of the government, especially considering the roles of ordinary people who are now technologically equipped to engage in public expression. Therefore, governmentality better epitomizes recent trends in regulatory measures for social media in what is effectively a more open virtual society, thereby embodying the evolution of the Chinese government's attitudes, intentions and strategies for retaining ultimate control over information. This does not suggest that such practices and the institutions carrying them out will be completely replaced. Instead, the combination of the new and old forms makes for a new configuration of regulatory measures.

Context and Argument

This book addresses a research problem based on the regulatory nexus of new controls and new freedoms interacting within the Weibo sphere in contemporary China. Its premise is that Weibo is a governable object where the Chinese government deliberately allows greater freedoms and exercises control to regulate it. In this way, it questions the ways in which the boundaries of a public sphere are being redrawn in a Chinese context, and the implications of these factors. This book considers a more complex exercise based on how the Chinese government adapts to the new era to combine both authoritarian and liberal governing strategies, together with the regulation of social media. It aims, therefore, to make sense of how the government calculation or thinking is reflected specifically in Weibo regulation by navigating both liberal ideas and authoritarian practices.

Since the introduction of the internet in China, the Chinese government has exhibited changes in its practices that reflect the need to recognize but also to manage its opportunities. For instance, the government could not be clearer that each "individual must be granted enough freedom in the cyber world", as "too much control will only kill (the) individual's desire to go online" (Tai 2006, p. 97). Hence the government has had to take a balanced position rather than a strictly authoritarian position, to meet its multiple objectives. Accordingly, its strategies of control have had to be altered to meet these multiple objectives—of contributing to economic growth in an internationally competitive environment and being seen to give internet users the freedom to communicate, while maintaining a high degree of strategic manipulation behind the scenes to ensure ultimate control over internet usage in China.

The appearance of Weibo has indeed significantly changed aspects of Chinese culture with some events having been managed very differently to the past. This development has matched the public expectations of massive citizen participation. Scholars who look at this situation have considered it a sign of expansion of what appears to be a great new freedom of speech online. This study explores the changing methods of government censorship, particularly focusing on the technologies the government uses to realize its ambitions. Instead of taking an "either/or" approach to depict the freedom or control of China's Weibo, this study illustrates the interweaving relations between freedom and control. Weibo has become a dynamic base for a generation, a sharing of public opinion in an unprecedented manner in the Chinese culture: it is therefore of great importance for the authorities to "manage" Weibo.

In recent decades, rapid economic development and social change in China have brought about a series of social problems; however the corresponding solutions have been much slower than the developments, resulting in a widespread public feeling of unfairness and social resentment. It is apparent in the appearance of the internet and in particular, Weibo, through which "online activism" as identified by Yang (2009), has profoundly influenced the direction of certain events and even politics. However, this book aims to go beyond earlier scholarship on the potentially transformative power of Weibo in an authoritarian Chinese political framework, in seeking answers to the following argument.

Though Weibo has been widely used throughout the country and has even exercised liberalizing effects on some internet events, the Chinese government nevertheless deliberately allots Weibo users greater freedom selectively at specific times in order to facilitate overall control in the public sphere. In addition, through carefully adopting both greater relaxation and control strategies in particular cases, this book argues that these practices contribute to the government's achievement of goals to bolster its legitimacy, therefore producing a distinctly Chinese version of the public sphere. Such calculated approaches to information regulation of the Chinese people's sense of cultural and political identity indeed remake the people and the public sphere.

Through these arguments, this book seeks to contribute to a deeper understanding of the use, control and political dynamics of China's contemporary social media landscape. In addition to answering the "what" and "how" questions, mainly concerning specific strategies and techniques, this book particularly seeks to shed light on the "why" question, exploring Chinese statecraft as it encounters outside views of an emerging an "public sphere". Moreover, the book acknowledges that Weibo users are not passive. They are increasingly using their voices as witnesses who want answers. The central question therefore is one of whether the outcome of increased access to Weibo will result in benefits to both users and regulators.

Briefly, the case studies in Chapters Five and Chapter Six will draw upon specific events to illustrate the Chinese government's governance strategies for regulating online practices, revealing more complicated and ambiguous relations between the state and netizens. The major activities of the internet regulatory agencies can be seen as aligning with Foucault's theories of the "procedures of prohibition": that is, the "most familiar and obvious" of the procedures by which the production of discourse is "controlled, selected, organized and distributed" (Foucault 1991, p. 52). Despite the fact that directly repressive measures such as censorship still exist in China's cyberspace, the Chinese government has also adopted certain neo-liberal strategies of governing from a distance, through the development of what can be seen as new technologies of the self, that is, by appearing to offer new freedoms of online communication, while instrumentalizing these new freedoms to achieve the desired regulatory outcomes.

Theoretical Framework and Methodology

This complex picture of the Weibo sphere takes a cross-disciplinary approach and is situated between new media, cultural and political science studies. This holistic approach allows a more contextualized and comprehensive analysis of an interactive framework that captures the interplay between technology, the government and public expression. The book draws on two strands with which to view the government's regulatory measures, from the perspectives of both cultural practice and institutional practice. The ways in which the new and evolving governmental practices may produce new versions of a public sphere are highlighted. The multiple publics on Weibo are not only treated in this book as "empowered" subjects but also as objects of governance. To trace the adaptations and evolutions of the Chinese government's regulatory strategies for Weibo, empirical research has been necessary to identify specific outcomes from the new arts of government regulatory behavior targeting social media, and specifically, Weibo. The political dimensions of this new era for Chinese information and behavior control have rarely been discussed in previous scholarship.

This book draws on two major theories with which to analyze these changes. The first is the idealized concept of the public sphere, as formulated by Jurgen Habermas, to describe the space "where information, ideas and debate can circulate in society, and where political opinion can be formed" (Dahlberg 1995, p. ix), and the second is governmentality, defined succinctly by Michel Foucault as "the conduct of conduct" (Foucault 1991) or "a way of doing things" (Burchell, Gordon & Miller 1991, p. ix), focusing on the ways power operates beyond the state and where multiple organizations, groups and individuals are invited to be involved in the process of governing (Foucault 1991), which can best be used to explain the regulatory process in China since the rise of Weibo communication.

The theory of the public sphere has been widely used by scholars from a broad range of areas. Since online conversations exist primarily in the realm of a social media platform—a virtual space where ideas and information are circulated and exchanged freely by people from all over the world—many scholars have examined the power of social media in China, raising the question of whether Weibo is creating a version of a public sphere (Diamond 2010; Sullivan 2014; Rauchfleisch & Schäfer 2014). Rather than existing as a completely unregulated public sphere, Weibo is subject to both the government's and commercial companies' regulation. The government increasingly assumes a role in the Weibo public sphere, which allows it to negotiate Weibo dialogues and to create a mediated version of what is being expressed. In some cases, more freedom is given which allows users to discuss even taboo topics, while in other cases new forms of greater control are exercised.

The theory of governmentality is therefore used to illustrate this complexity. Studies of governmentality have not only been adopted widely by scholars from a number of disciplines to examine governmental strategies in politically liberal contexts, but additionally, in the non-liberal and non-Western context of China (Jeffrey 2009; Sigley 2006). This book extends earlier examinations of governmentality to the realm of social media in China where many see accompanying expectations of democratization. Therefore, it is particularly meaningful to examine the processes by which the seemingly free mode of Weibo is tactically managed to achieve a strengthening of the state rather than an undermining of Chinese government control.

This book centers on the "interaction" of the public sphere and governmentality. The concept of governmentality is applied to an analysis of the governing and regulation in the Weibo sphere, and further explored in the two case studies of Chapters Five and Six. This calibrated set of interventions or interactions between the public sphere and governmentality encapsulates the argument of this book: that although the Weibo public sphere continuously expands in China, the authorities' management and manipulation of public discourse in China is a complex, interactive, proactive and adaptive process, by which the state selectively tightens and loosens control of public discourse online, in order to facilitate ultimate control. In this way, it re-makes or re-shapes the formation of distinct public spheres on Weibo.

In examining the evolving regulation and instrumentalization of social media by the Chinese government, this research takes illustrative studies of a notorious recent anti-corruption trial broadcast on Weibo for analysis using the themes of the public sphere and governmentality. In addition, the book draws on a second case study, also a Weibo phenomenon. These examples were selected for three reasons. First, both cases are contemporary, taking place in 2013; second, in addition to one sensational case, which may or may not represent a lasting trend in the government's evolving management of Weibo, a more long-standing case was also selected. The third reason was that the balance in the case studies illustrates the increasing sophistication of the government's overall planning against an international political background. This book focuses on one case which takes place in the international media, using management techniques that acknowledge the global rise of China, where the government is eager to demonstrate its soft power rather than simply its economic growth. The other was a politically sensitive case responding to the government's long-standing prioritization of political and social stability.

The interaction between versions of the public sphere and governmentality can be widely seen in online events on Weibo, as will be illustrated in Chapters Five and Six, in which the seemingly free medium of Weibo is used strategically to strengthen rather than to undermine the government's control. Chapter Five examines the impact of Weibo during the trial of Bo Xilai, a high-profile political figure in China, in what was seen as China's trial of the year. In a rare display of openness, the trial of Bo Xilai was broadcast on Weibo, which attracted huge public attention and was considered as marking "historical progress" (Zhang 2013). At the same time, however, it was criticized by the foreign media as "a smoke screen for the benefit of China's President" (Fulda 2013). In this way, the fundamental question of how China has developed its own strategic balance between selectively loosening and tightening control of information on Weibo has provided the main platform for such commentary, as it has changed the perceptions and actions of both Chinese government and individual Weibo users. In Chapter Six, the case of "Ding was here" is studied which focuses on graffiti made by a Chinese junior school boy in an ancient Egyptian temple when travelling in Egypt with his family a few years ago. This case, exposed by an online photograph of the graffiti, generated a great wave of public uproar based on "national embarrassment" and "national patriotism". This public outcry is shown in this study's analysis to be a result of the Chinese government's long-term and ongoing work to subtly shape the public thinking of the Chinese people. One significant outcome of governmentality applied over a long period, is the empowering of subjects to be self-disciplined, based on perceived autonomy and a sense of responsibility (Rose 1999). To fail is a cultural "wrong" that signals that someone has let down the state. The government's timely responsiveness maximized the impact of this story and served its own larger agenda. This case illustrates the intentions and apparatus of governmentality at work, not only at the institutional governance level, but also at the level of everyday practices (Lemke 2007).

Therefore, the case studies in Chapters Five and Six in this book both clearly illustrate the practices and tactics that the contemporary Chinese government employs to govern Weibo through the careful management of its apparent freedom. The case of the Bo Xilai trial has illustrated the extent and effectiveness of the well-crafted implementation of a political agenda by carefully opening up, and above all, regulating the population's response to such politically sensitive issues. The governmentalization of the Bo Xilai trial coincides with China's greater economic presence on the world stage, illustrating a determination to fight corruption, so fulfilling multiple agendas. The case of "Ding was here" illustrates how contemporary Weibo is being used for government intervention in this populist Weibo phenomenon, to build on the state's earlier work in regulating people's hearts and minds to fit its national agenda and construct a politically useful narrative.

On the methodological level, this book exclusively focuses on the reading of given textual sources using the theories of governmentality as an analytical tool. In the existing scholarship, where many scholars treat governmentality as a set of arguments, other scholars view governmentality as a set of analytical tools rather than a theory per se (Walters 2012). In *Governmentality: Critical Encounters*, Walters (2012) examines new territories of power and new techniques of governance from empirical and analytical perspectives. This book takes up Walters' approach to treat governmentality as both a theory and an analytical tool with which to examine contemporary Chinese examples of the aims and apparatus of governmentality at work at the level of everyday practices and institutional practices.

In addition, Dean (1999, p. 20) describes governmentality as "an analytics of government" and provides a useful means to access that role. Such an analytics helps us to understand how people are governed by different regime practices, in particular, emphasizing four dimensions: characteristic forms of visibility; distinctive ways of thinking and questioning; specific techniques and ways of behaving and characteristic ways of forming subjects. In these two case studies, the four dimensions are interchangeably explored to consider how the subjects are governed, and under what authority and circumstances, through investigating relevant policy papers, official publications and legal texts. This study considers how certain phenomena are constructed as problems and how governmental interventions or strategies are provided to address those problems.

This book aims to offer a more nuanced view of current online cultural-political practices. It attempts to do this in two ways: first, by focusing on the analysis of two types of online discourse; and second, by relating these cases to some broader theoretical concerns about the nature of governance in contemporary China.

Methods. The sources and methods in this study have been a combination of qualitative and quantitative methods, though mainly qualitative in nature for Chapter Five, 'The Bo Xilai Trial', and Chapter Six, 'Case Study of Chinese Weibo Community'. It combines text-based analysis of Weibo postings and government documents such as media releases from state-controlled media to address the proposed research argument and research aims of this book. Different approaches are used to evaluate the elements which are considered essential to reflect the simultaneity of both greater freedom of information and greater control, specifically, the enlarging and containing of a public sphere through strategic government interventions, behind the scenes. By examining a selection of Weibo incident cases and related discussions on microblogs, both textual and discourse analysis will be conducted. This approach will help to capture an overview of the complex arrangements between the state and the growing social media environment. Some minor, supporting quantitative research was also undertaken to examine Weibo practice in China in recent years, including both typological observations and statistical analysis.

These methods are fully displayed in case study chapters of Chapters Five and Six when collecting Weibo users' comments and analysis of them. It is notable that all comments posted on Weibo are available to every Weibo user. Throughout the research, a case study method is adopted through a tracing process and a measuring of the trends in relation to the two cases. Case studies allow a particular focus on individual instances, and the aim is to illustrate the general by looking at the particular. Rather than dealing with isolated factors, the purpose of case studies is "to focus on relationships and processes in a natural setting to discover interconnections and interrelationships, and how the various parts are linked" (Jones 2006, p. 315). As to the data collection, some claim that there are six types of data that could be collected in case studies, including documents, archival records, interviews, direct observation, participant observation and artifacts (Williams, Rice & Rogers 1988). The strength of case study research is that it "can describe complex relationships, personal interpretations, and historical narratives of the phenomenon", while being limited to a single setting or background (ibid., p. 38). Moreover, there are four subdivisions of case study, each of which is selected depending on the researchers' objectives: illustrative case studies; exploratory case studies; cumulative case studies; and critical instance case studies, which examine one or more instances, either for examining a situation with or without generalization, or for challenging a more universal assertion (ibid.). This book will apply the latter of these approaches to understand what took place in each event, and the reasons for the outcome.

As this study reveals, there were contradictory public reactions in certain incidents, with public attitudes a crucial factor. Given the large number of posts in each case, this study first collects all the posts submitted on particular days and then uses a random sampling method to extract data to obtain a general sense of public attitude towards the incident. In addition, several qualitative methods are applied to make a detailed analysis of certain typical single posts generated in response to the incidents. This method, on the one hand, avoids the risk of being subjective as the survey results are provided by quantitative indicators, while on the other hand, it shows the vivid picture of how Weibo users' comments are shaped by the Chinese government. To better access the role of the Chinese government, in the case study, particular attention is paid to the timelines of the incidents.

Unlike other Weibo studies that exclude identical posts from the sample in order to count each one only once (Shi & Chen 2014), this study takes the identical posts into consideration to analyze the Chinese government's regulatory techniques, such as those expressed by the Fifty Cents Party, which will be discussed in detail in later chapters. Frequent and repeated post comments tend to favor Party policies that attempt to sway public opinion. Purely emotional posts, which are normally ignored by scholars, are also taken into account in this analysis to detect individual users' attitudes. However, this data set does not contain comments such as those expressed in commercial advertisements. Content analysis is applied in each case in order to address the proposed research questions and research aims.

Organization of the Book

A common dilemma facing all new media studies is that technology is frequently updated and its dynamics and popularity are constantly evolving. Therefore, it can be difficult to argue convincingly in a timely manner about a particular medium. Since Weibo's introduction into China in 2008, for example, the number of Weibo users reached a peak by June of 2013, and then encountered a decline, though at a slower rate, as another social media platform, WeChat (China's homegrown version of WhatsApp) started to gain in popularity. But no matter how frequently technologies update, the larger social and political contexts are always discernible, therefore, the logic behind the book is that Weibo is an important reflector of the temporal shifts occurring in China's social, political and technological sphere. Moreover, the changes observed and noted are in a narrow sense based on the particular platform of Weibo and at a particular time in a particular culture and place.

This book is composed of seven chapters. Chapter One is the introductory chapter, which outlines the research aims of the project. Specifically, it illustrates the research questions, the theoretical framework and methodology of this book. With Weibo's significant challenge to the Chinese state, better control of public opinion is what the authorities hope for. Previously the Chinese government successfully carried out overt censorship of the mass media, even into the early internet era. However, in the Weibo era, with its instantaneous communications drawing on citizen monitoring of events and the potential for subversive exchange of information within 140 Chinese characters, it requires more specific and sophisticated management strategies from the authorities. In this way, the book seeks to answer questions around the themes of the new and changing regulatory strategies that are evolving in the Weibo era. These include the manner in which the Chinese government carefully balances public expression and official control, and its effects. More importantly, it seeks to monitor and check whether the opening up of public expression is actually bringing greater democracy to Chinese society. It also outlines theories which are used to explain this phenomenon and why. Briefly, this chapter shows the starting point for, and the overall map of this book.

Chapter Two provides the theoretical foundations of the book. Theories of the public sphere and governmentality are investigated in this chapter. The interaction of these two theories is helpful for an understanding of how the Chinese government deliberately allows for the liberal leanings of Weibo in some cases, while ensuring the ultimate control remains with the authoritarian state of China. This reading draws on Habermas' theories of the public sphere and the theory of governmentality first discussed by Michel Foucault—and briefly defined as the conduct of conduct—to make sense of the Chinese government's approach towards the governing and regulation of China's social media. This chapter particularly focuses on the specific "arts of governmentality", which employ a variety of strategies and tactics to govern the population instead of merely imposing brute force or restrictive administrative apparatus.

Chapter Three sets up the background to this book, outlining the introduction of the internet and Weibo in China. The first part introduces the arrival of the internet and briefly includes its development and considers common Western assumptions about its political potential. In addition, it also illustrates official controls and regulations used to police the internet and its users. The second part provides the background to the social media site, Weibo, including its unprecedented opportunities for use by ordinary people, for citizen activism and protest. It then undertakes a demographic analysis of Weibo users since its arrival in Chinese society in 2008 to reveal user profiles. Finally, it provides a typological analysis of Weibo users, based on who uses Weibo and for what purposes.

Chapter Four is titled "Weibo regulation: Potentially transformative regulatory measures", and provides a description of the historical evolution of the Chinese government's regulatory measures over the internet. It particularly focuses on Weibo in order to capture the Chinese government's evolving aims, strategies and tactics in regulating Weibo. In addition to the "hard" regulatory measures of censorship, more significantly, this chapter highlights the new channels for active government involvement in the regulation of Weibo, including the establishment of government Weibo accounts through which to interact with the public. This proactive measure for using Weibo has a number of advantages, such as improving the government's transparency and strengthening its legitimacy. To expand official monitoring of Weibo, the government delegates some degree of control to private, external companies such as ISPs (Internet Service Providers), to exercise self-censorship and monitoring of the public information appearing on their sites. This chapter lays the basic foundation of the general trends of government control over Weibo.

Chapter Five examines the controversial Bo Xilai trial and the role of China's governmentality as the first case study in this book, elucidating the tactics the Chinese government adopts to regulate Weibo at the institutional level. By discussing how the Chinese government deliberately opens up public expression in the politically sensitive trial of the prominent political figure, Bo Xilai, this chapter assesses and demonstrates the state's effectiveness and success in opening and yet controlling the public discussion in a deliberate and subtle way. It argues that the apparent freedom of public expression in such a politically sensitive event is in fact based on the Chinese government's sophisticated calculation of how to balance public security and ultimately consolidate final control of public debates. This chapter examines this paradoxical situation in depth, while noting that more traditionally repressive measures also co-existed in this process to help to shore up the CCP's political legitimacy and transparency.

Chapter Six examines the case of "Ding was here", and displays the role the Chinese government plays in regulating Weibo from the cultural practice perspective. Through examining an autonomous sense of national embarrassment and subsequent debates on patriotism, all appearing on Weibo as the result of a Chinese child's graffiti of "Ding was here" in an Egyptian temple, this chapter argues that the empowered "free" space on Weibo is actually constructed and manipulated by the Chinese government to fuel surging patriotic identity, in order to strengthen discipline in the Chinese people. This type of national patriotism drawing on a relatively small incident of failed travel etiquette contributes to the Chinese government's many years of ongoing work in shaping the Chinese people's national identity in the form of patriotism. In addition, this chapter analyses the Chinese government's astute and proactive timing in becoming involved in this incident, in order to serve its long term agenda. Through making commentaries in official newspapers and issuing relevant regulations, the intervention illustrates that, apart from its ongoing efforts to influence public awareness, the Chinese state has also displayed strategic planning in selectively choosing this incident to maximize its impact in reinforcing its political status quo. In addition, the end of this chapter discusses the two case studies and summarizes the key findings that: 1) Weibo is used by the authorities selectively for liberation or repression, displaying unique characteristics based specifically in the Chinese context, 2) both cases show the integration or interaction between the official media and Weibo, and indicate that the Chinese authorities effectively use both official media and Weibo to fulfil their political agendas, therefore, 3) leading to the evaluation of Weibo's role in the current Chinese context, and finally 4) a rethinking of the different typologies of the public sphere on Weibo in terms of government intervention.

Chapter Seven concludes the book by addressing potential limitations and exploring future implications. It asserts that Chinese Weibo space is complex and suggests that it is too early to draw an equation between Weibo and China's potential for democracy. Therefore, it has significant implications for the Chinese public sphere. Far from being fearful of the constantly updated information technology, the Chinese government has evolved as a robust and flexible regime that skillfully adapts to new environmental conditions, both at the institutional level and in ordinary cultural practices. Through the government's allowing a degree of "free" space on Weibo, Chinese Weibo users can find a channel to voice their views as a "safety valve", while also meeting the growing demands for a free exchange of information. However, the construction of this "free" space on Chinese Weibo has been accompanied behind the scenes by the authorities' strategic calculation and management. Therefore, understanding these dynamics is crucial for understanding the CCP's logic of national overall planning in a dramatically changing social, economic and technological environment. Based on the two case studies, this book establishes that the Chinese state's governance strategies for information have evolved considerably, reaching a level of sophistication far beyond the propaganda era. This understanding sheds new light on contemporary Chinese society, and especially the political implications and management of fast evolving new media technologies. Through the emergence of these new media technologies and a responsive government, the Chinese state has been able to show how it can regulate social media through subtle means, resulting in both a strong Weibo and a smart government.

References

Bandurski, D. 2010, 'Listen to the citizens, and control them', China Media Project, 22 June, viewed 20 June 2014, <http://cmp.hku.hk/2010/06/22/6281/>.

Boas, TC. 2006, 'Weaving the authoritarian web: The control of internet use in nondemocratic regimes', in Zysman, J & Newman, A (eds.), How revolutionary was the digital revolution? National responses, market transitions, and global technology, Stanford Business Books, Stanford, CA, pp. 361–378.

Brady, A. 2012, 'State Confucianism, Chineseness, and tradition in CCP propaganda', in Brady, A (ed.), China's thought management, Routledge, New York, pp. 57–75.

Burchell, G, Gordon, C & Miller, P (eds.). 1991, The Foucault effect: Studies in governmentality, Harvester Wheatsheaf, Hertfordshire.

CNNIC. 2018, 'Statistical reports on the internet development in China, the 41st survey report', January, viewed 24 January 2018, <http://www.cnnic.net.cn/hlwfzyj/hlwxzbg/hlwtjbg/201801/P020180131509544165973.pdf>.

Dahlberg, P. 1995, Television and the public sphere: Citizenship, democracy and the media, Sage, Thousand Oaks, CA.

Dean, M. 1999, Governmentality: Power and rule in modern society, Sage, London.

Diamond, L. 2010, 'Liberation technology', Journal of Democracy, vol. 21, no. 3, pp. 69–83.

Foucault, M. 1991, 'Governmentality', in Burchell, G, Gordon, C & Miller, P (eds.), The Foucault effect: Studies in governmental rationality, Harvester Wheatsheaf, Hemel Hempstead, pp. 87–104.

Fu, K-W, Chan, C-H & Chau, M. 2013, 'Assessing censorship on microblogs in China: Discriminatory keyword analysis and the real name registration policy', IEEE Computer Society, vol. 17, no. 3, pp. 42–50.

Fulda, A. 2013, 'Bo Xilai's trial is a smoke screen for the benefit of China's president', The Guardian, 27 August, viewed 24 September 2014, <http://www.theguardian.com/commentisfree/2013/aug/27/bo-xilai-china-trial-smokescreen-president>.

Habermas, J. 1997, 'The public sphere', in Robert, EG & Philip, P (eds.), Contemporary political philosophy: An anthology, Blackwell Publishers, Oxford, pp. 105–108.

Hassid, J. 2012, 'Safety valve or pressure cooker? Blogs in Chinese political life', Journal of Communication, vol. 62, no. 2, pp. 212–230.

Jeffreys, E (ed.). 2009, China's governmentalities: Governing change, changing government, Routledge, Abingdon.

Jiang, Y. 2012, Cyber-nationalism in China, University of Adelaide Press, Adelaide.

Jones, G. 2006, 'Other research methods', in Walter, M (ed.), Social research methods: An Australian perspective, Oxford University Press, Oxford, pp. 307–341.

King, G, Pan, J & Roberts, M. 2013, 'How censorship in China allows government criticism but silences collective expression', American Political Science Review, vol. 107, no. 2, pp. 326–341.

Lagerkvist, J. 2006, The Internet in China: Unlocking and containing the public sphere, Lund University, Lund.

Lemke, T. 2007, 'An indigestible meal? Foucault, governmentality and state theory', Distinktion: Scandinavian Journal of Social Theory, vol. 8, no. 2, pp. 43–64.

MacKinnon, R. 2008, 'Flatter world and thicker walls? Blogs, censorship and civic discourse in China', Public Choice, vol. 134, no. 1–2, pp. 31–46.

MacKinnon, R. 2011, 'China's "networked authoritarianism"', Journal of Democracy, vol. 22, no. 2, pp. 32–46.

McKee, A. 2005, The public sphere: An introduction, Cambridge University Press, UK.

Noesselt, N. 2013, 'Microblogs in China: Bringing the state back in', GIGA Working Papers.

Qian, G & Bandurski, D. 2010, 'China's emerging public sphere: The impact of media commercialization, professionalism, and the internet in an era of transition', in Shirk S (ed.), Changing media, changing China, Oxford University Press, Oxford, pp. 39–76.

Rauchfleisch, A & Schäfer, MS. 2014, 'Multiple public spheres of Weibo: A typology of forms and potentials of online public spheres in China', Information, Communication & Society, no. ahead-of-print, pp. 1–17.

Rose, N. 1999, Governing the soul: The shaping of the private self, Free Association Books, London.

Rosen, S. 2010, 'Is the internet a positive force in the development of civil society, a public sphere and democratization in China?', International Journal of Communication, vol. 4, pp. 509–516.

Shi, J & Chen, L. 2014, 'Social support on Weibo for people living with HIV/AIDS in China: A quantitative content analysis', Chinese Journal of Communication, vol. 7, no. 3, pp. 285–298.

Sigley, G. 2004, 'Liberal despotism: Population planning, subjectivity, and government in contemporary China', Alternatives, vol. 29, no. 5, pp. 557–575.

Sigley, G. 2006, 'Chinese governmentalities: Government, governance and the socialist market economy', Economy and Society, vol. 35, no. 4, pp. 487–508.

Sullivan, J. 2014, 'China's Weibo: Is faster different?', New Media & Society, vol. 16, no. 1, pp. 24–37.

Tai, Z. 2006, The Internet in China: Cyberspace and civil society, Routledge, New York.

Tong, Y & Lei, S. 2013, 'War of position and microblogging in China', Journal of Contemporary China, vol. 22, no. 80, pp. 292–311.

Walters, W. 2012, Governmentality: Critical encounters, Routledge, Abingdon.

Williams, F, Rice, R & Rogers, E. 1988, Research methods and the new media, The Free Press, New York.

Xiao, Q. 2011, 'The battle for the Chinese internet', Journal of Democracy, vol. 22, no. 2, pp. 47–61.

Yang, G. 2009, The Power of the internet in China: Citizen activism online, Columbia University Press, New York.

Yeo, G & Li, E. 2012, 'Governance and social media', The World Post, 20 January, viewed 12 February 2014, <http://www.huffingtonpost.com/eric-x-li/china-internet_b_1217436.html>.

Zhang, Q. 2013, 'Microblogging the Bo Xilai trial: Transparency or theatre?', BBC News, 23 August, viewed 25 August 2013, <http://www.bbc.com/news/world-asia-china-23806657>.

Zheng, Y. 2008, Technological empowerment: The Internet, state, and society in China, Stanford University Press, Stanford.

· 2 ·

THEORETICAL FOUNDATIONS: PUBLIC SPHERE AND GOVERNMENTALITY

Introduction

This chapter provides the theoretical foundations for the book by exploring the changing notions of the public sphere in contemporary China and the ways in which the concept of governmentality, as developed by Foucault, can be applied to it. In other words, it will outline the changing status of freedom and control in China, based on theories of the public sphere and governmentality. In recent decades, an important new dimension for the public sphere in China has been the fast evolving online world, and in particular, the social media platform of Weibo. Many scholars have looked to Weibo in China as offering the potential for transformation from great control to great freedom. Through this social media platform in contemporary China, one could begin to see a liberalization of freedom of speech in a reportedly illiberal society; Weibo has developed into a vital public communications arena for a lively and dynamic exchange of information, contentions, accusations and scandalous revelations. The emergence of Weibo has heightened people's expectations of technologies in promoting democracy, and has often been considered as a "micro revolution" (Hu 2010) in offering a seemingly freer channel for individual-to-individual communications. In this way, a version of what has been historically known as 'the public sphere' is opening up in China.

The concept of the public sphere has been defined by Habermas as the provision of social arena/s for public communication in which publicly relevant concerns can be discussed critically and rationally by different actors free of social and state power (1992, p. 27). The public sphere, offers an opportunity for personal and communal self-expression, and the introduction of the internet and Weibo in China have been viewed by many as unlocking such a public sphere (Lagerkvist 2006). However, changes in public communications in China since the arrival of the internet, particularly Weibo, are always matched by new measures and systems of control. In other words, the free space has been carefully managed at every step by counterbalancing measures from the Chinese government, creating an always evolving dynamic between free space and regulation. While it offers a new cultural space which is to be celebrated, at the same time, it is strictly regulated within political limits.

To fully understand this dynamic of "point/counterpoint", it is therefore essential to conduct a detailed examination of the new social media based on freedom of information arriving in contemporary China as it is matched with new mechanisms of control. This chapter will therefore establish the theoretical framework within which a potentially emergent public sphere in China presents new freedoms and the applied theory of governmentality illuminates new and evolving mechanisms for control of information in China. This chapter provides a systematic framework to support the case studies in later chapters in illustrating how regime structures have allowed freer public sphere discourses in China to some extent, while ultimately shaping public discourses to facilitate and ensure its control.

Before moving to Foucault's governmentality, this chapter will begin by historically tracing the concept of the public sphere. Three aspects will then be explored to illustrate the application of this theory: 1) The historical evolution of the public sphere and its current evaluation; 2) The rise of online versions of the public sphere; and 3) The application of the concept of the public sphere in the Chinese context, especially in the field of social media. This study also draws on Foucault's concept of governmentality to be further discussed later in this chapter. When examined through the lens of governmentality theory, it becomes apparent that the surface freedoms which audiences enjoy on social media are in fact, subject to carefully constructed government controls.

Studies of governmentality have been used widely in the past in liberal contexts. However, studies of government techniques and mindsets in non-Western and non-liberal contexts have been for the most part neglected in the past (Sigley 2006). Recently, a number of scholars have used a governmentality framework to illuminate the art of governing the Chinese state (Jeffreys 2009; Jiang 2012), but this scholarship is limited and has not focused on China's social media platforms. This study specifically considers the Chinese government's techniques and mindsets as used to strengthen its control of Weibo, while appearing to liberate and encourage it, suggesting that the Chinese government astutely employs Foucault's 'technologies of the self', to both endow Weibo users with greater freedom while actually maintaining censorship and internet regulation. The theoretical foundations of this book will therefore be based on two key sets of theoretical principles, the first related to freedom in the public sphere, and the second to control, through governmentality. Based on these two theories, the following chapters will then outline specific strategies through which the government achieves its complementary goals.

Theory of the Public Sphere

The Historical Evolution of the Public Sphere.

> By "the public sphere" we mean first of all a domain of our social life in which such a thing as public opinion can be formed. Access to the public sphere is open in principle to all citizens. A portion of the public sphere is constituted in every conversation in which private persons come together to form a public...Citizens act as a public when they deal with matters of general interest without being subject to coercion; thus with the guarantee that they may assemble and unite freely, and express and publicize their opinions freely. (Habermas 1991, p. 399)

The public sphere is a much-examined concept for which many scholars have put forward different conceptualizations based on different normative and empirical situations (Habermas 1991; Calhoun 1992). It is, however, an evolving historical and philosophical concept adapting to different circumstances; therefore, there is no one widely shared concept, though different conceptualizations share a number of fundamental assumptions. However, even these shared criteria are realized to different degrees in different countries with different scopes (Gerhards & Schäfer 2010; Rauchfleisch & Schäfer

2014). This study takes the public sphere as an evolving and ever-changing concept.

The American political philosopher, John Dewey, was among the first to develop the concept of the public sphere when he considered it as an essential component of democracy. However, the theory of the public sphere was later expanded and most fully illustrated by German philosopher, Jürgen Habermas, in his classic work *The Structural Transformation of the Public Sphere: An inquiry into a category of bourgeois society* (first English version published in 1989), which has inspired many scholars who are concerned with communicative power and civil society. Habermas traces the emergence of a bourgeois public sphere in Europe in the seventeenth and eighteenth centuries, founded on the circumscription of both religion and aristocratic protocol, and primarily focused on individual people gathering together in a forum and engaging in critical and rational discussion over key issues and publicly relevant matters such as governing, commodity exchange and social labor. The public sphere has a double existence. Different from a physical space, public sphere is metaphor that is used to describe the virtual space where people interact in large societies to reach a consensus on certain issues (Hartley 1992, p. 1). As the head of the second generation of the Frankfurt School and arguably one of his generation's most influential philosophers, Habermas' works have exerted significant influence upon Chinese academic scholars for the last three decades. Rather than focusing on the forces of state or market, Habermas probes a middle space "between civil society and the state, in which critical public discussion of matters of general interest was institutionally guaranteed" (Habermas 1989, p.xi); therefore, public opinion could be formed out of rational public debate. These discussions can be seen as generally distinct from, and critical of, the state. The conceptual meanings formed are distinct from other traditionally accepted spheres including the patriarchal family, state and market. In contemporary times, this new sense of the public sphere relies heavily on the mass media, and as Habermas notes:

> The mass media obviously plays a central role in the public sphere, as it is only in the mass media that vast populations of people can come together and exchange ideas. When the public is large this kind of communication requires certain means of dissemination and influence: today, newspapers and periodicals, radio and television are the media of the public sphere. (Habermas 1997, p. 105)

In his work, Habermas describes the ups and downs of the bourgeois public sphere. It is the changing structural conditions within a society that play a pivotal role in the forming of the public sphere. While the Habermasian ideal type of a bourgeois public sphere delineates a social space where public opinion can be formed by private individuals through an open and rational debate free of state power, a structural transformation took place in the nineteenth century due to what Habermas called "welfare state capitalism and mass society", in which the intervention of state and society eroded the distinction between public and private realms (Habermas 1989). In this regard, Habermas is highly critical of the role of mass media in the twentieth century, whose function has degenerated from facilitating rational debates in the bourgeois public sphere, and as the result, is unable to promote free and plural communication. For Habermas, issues such as media ownership or commodification render the public sphere on the verge of extinction. The newspaper industry, which takes its base as the critical-rational tradition, is said to have dispensed with its original ideological function and paved the way for commercialism and entertainment. Consequently, public opinion has been invaded by the attractiveness of advertising and the practitioners of public relations have emerged as dominant. Habermas claims that in this new era:

> Editorial opinions recede behind information from press agencies and reports from correspondents; critical debate disappears behind the veil of internal decisions concerning the selection and presentation of the material. (Habermas 1991, p. 169)

Therefore, Habermas argues that it is necessary to re-politicize the public sphere by providing citizens with opportunities to engage in what he calls "communicative interaction" in order to overcome the resulting legitimacy crisis. In fact, the public consequences of mass media are not necessarily "uniformly negative" because "there may be more room than Habermas realized for alternative democratic media strategies". Even Habermas himself "has now rejected the tradition of ideology critique out of which his approach to historical reconstruction came" (Calhoun 1992, pp. 33–40). As a public sphere which meets these requirements has never been fully established, it may be meaningless to discuss the decline of the public sphere, but rather, "we first need to actualize the concept of the 'public sphere' in accordance with our modern social context" (Verstraeten 1996, p. 349). Although the concept of the public sphere was framed as a historical account, much of the scholarly work considers it as a normative concept which is an ideal type of communication. Many scholars have formulated normative theories to describe how the public sphere should be structured ideally to fulfill its role.

Carey (1995) also emphasizes the importance of the social system within which a public sphere could arise. He contends that a mass commercial culture has eroded the public sphere and calls for the revival of a public life that would maintain the independence of cultural and social life. The debate surrounding the Habermasian public sphere is based on an ideal model of mediated communication and, as Lewis (2013) contends, much of the resulting criticism relates to the political influence, commercial interests as well as the social biases of contemporary cultures, including China's. Ideally then, some suggest that the public sphere plays an essential role in the society because it offers a free space where people can gather together to articulate their autonomous and critical views, with the aim of influencing the political institutions of society (Castells 2008, p. 78). However, this concept of the public sphere has been much criticized. A number of scholars have expressed doubts about Habermas' single, unified and idealized public sphere model and have proposed alternative multiple public spheres, to better understand the public sphere today.

From a feminist perspective, for example, Fraser (1992) points out that Habermas' conceptualization of the bourgeois public sphere is flawed by its gender exclusion, restricted in scope to white males who practice their managing skills, whereas it excludes women and lower class people. In this regard, she proposes that a number of non-bourgeois publics such as "counter-publics" or "subaltern publics" should be taken into account to coexist with the bourgeois public sphere. Similarly, Schudson (1992) also stresses the extent of participation, which he considers as a key measure for a functioning public sphere. He also doubts whether the early public sphere could produce more rational and critical debate. Although Garnham (1992, pp. 359–376) is more positive towards the Habermasian concept of a public sphere, he is not altogether uncritical. He notes, for example, that Habermas neglects the importance of the contemporaneous development of a plebeian public sphere alongside the bourgeois public sphere; he idealizes the bourgeois public sphere, excluding the household and the economy from the public sphere. For Calhoun (1992), the central weakness of *The Structural Transformation of the Public Sphere: An inquiry into a category of bourgeois society* approach, is that Habermas does not treat the early bourgeois public sphere and the later public sphere equally, drawing comparisons, for example, between Kant in the eighteenth century and the suburban television viewers of the twentieth century. Roberts and Crossley (2004, pp. 10–17) also draw out comprehensive critiques of Habermas' position from two areas: practical criticisms and theoretical criticisms.

The first focuses on three aspects: idealizing rational discussion, underestimating the role of the masses in the utilization and construction of mass media, and neglecting to see the other public spheres. The second probes the theoretical perspective, mainly illustrating three main schools of thought that could form other public spheres. Fraser (2007) divides the critiques of the public sphere into two types: legitimacy critiques and efficacy critiques. Legitimacy critiques generally refer to the shortcomings of the public sphere, historically, a lack of power. Efficacy critiques identify the lack of a communicative bridge linking the public and the institutions.

In spite of these critics, however, whether a public sphere is sufficient for a democratic polity depends on "both quality of discourse and quantity of participation", that is, a form of rational-critical discourse and openness to popular participation (Calhoun 1992, pp. 2–4). In addition, while different conceptualizations have not converged into a widely shared concept, there are three agreed descriptions for the public sphere: openness: the degree to which a public sphere is open according to its content; longevity, that is, how long a debate can last and its quality, and the degree to which participants are allowed to participate (Ferree et al. 2002). Verstraeten (1996) also proposes three predominant components that comprise Habermas' concept: a "forum" that is accessible to as many people as possible to express social experiences; the various arguments and views being confronted through rational discussion; and systematically and critically checking on government policies.

Though the quality of discourse and quantity of participation may not be fulfilled in an ideal way (one might question whether they have ever been fulfilled in history), they differ in different contexts and to different degrees (Verstraeten 1996). In fact, there are two aspects inherent in the notion of the bourgeois public sphere—empirical and normative aspects, with one stressing the historical category that "cannot be transferred, an ideal typically generalized" to any other historical situations (Habermas 1989, p. xvii). The other emphasizes the "generalized phenomenon" of an increasingly growing public realm of life with various forms of which "'the bourgeois' is but one variety" (Huang 1993, p. 217).

From the empirical perspective, there are different types of public spheres, which locate within different historical contexts. All modern societies obtain certain forms of public sphere to different degrees and with different scopes (Rauchfleisch & Schäfer 2014; Gerhards & Schäfer 2010). Castells (2008) also argues that the concept of public sphere is a changing process that varies in terms of context, history and technology. He illustrates its different connotations within constantly changing contexts, from physical space as formulated by Habermas, to the networked society where media has become the major component of the public sphere, and then to the digital era, which includes mass media and the internet. The most significant meaning of the Habermasian public sphere, as *A Theory of Justice* (1999) notes, offers "an ideal model of the public sphere as a reference point with which theorists can gauge how far a particular system deviates from truly legitimate representative government" (see Lewis 2013). The idea of "the public" is the sphere of activity distinct from "the private" domain, the latter of which is drawn as a result of the modernization of welfare states, in which governments reduce their role in directly providing services, instead, expanding their regulating and coordinating activities (Newman 2005, p. 3). However, on many occasions, the boundaries between public and private are fluid and contested.

Online Public Spheres. Rooted in a liberal Western context, the Habermasian concept of the public sphere discusses the interaction of publics, media and government. The role of media in a dynamic public sphere was well explained by Habermas, who saw it playing an essential role as it can provide an independent place for public discussion and the dissemination of important information to the public (Habermas 1989). Public sphere scholarship has long focused on the role of traditional media, including print media and television, in creating a public sphere under different and evolving historical circumstances (Postman 1985). Recent changes in the fast moving media landscape, however, have certainly provided new dimensions for examining the public sphere in today's society.

The advent of the internet, with its interactive and decentralized nature, has triggered scholarly debates about its role, in particular in the public sphere (Dahlberg 2001; Papacharissi 2002). While some scholarly works hold the position that the advent of the internet has indeed provided people with opportunities to express themselves and to engage in public debates (Dahlberg 2001; Dahlgren 2005), others hold critical views noting that it leads to fragmented debates and fails to meet normative criteria of the public sphere to foster more civil and rational debate (Papacharissi 2002). Papacharissi (2002) critically reviews the internet as a new arena for the public sphere from three broad perspectives: information access inequalities, the ability of the internet to bring people together, and its possible compromises with global capitalism. She further argues that there is a need for a clarification between the concepts of public space and public sphere: whereas public space offers another forum for public discussion, the public sphere promotes and facilitates public discussion and enhances democracy. Therefore, a public space does not necessarily equal a democratic public sphere (ibid.). In this way, she concludes that the view of the internet as a public sphere remains "a vision, but not yet a reality. As a vision, it inspires, but has not yet managed to transform political and social structures" (ibid., p. 23).

In addition to the studies of the public sphere that have focused on democratic countries, it is particularly interesting to examine the online public sphere in authoritarian countries such as China, where the Chinese government has long enjoyed absolute control of information through the conventional media so as to limit and steer public debate. Therefore the liberating nature of the internet has facilitated new platforms for information production and dissemination to and between the Chinese people. In the existing scholarship on the concept of the public sphere to describe an increasingly networked Chinese society, Lewis (2013) explores the democratic implications of new media in China based on three criteria from theories of deliberative democracy: information access, rational-critical discussion and mechanisms of vertical accountability that allow publics to exert influence over policy. In earlier work, Yang (2003, 2009) applies the definition of the public sphere and focuses on "free spaces" where citizen public expression facilitates civic association, collective identity building and popular protest. McCormick and Liu (2003, p. 139) use the concept of public sphere as "the stock of ideas and information accessible to broad sectors of society", while Goldberg (2010, p. 741) succinctly defines the networked public sphere as "a site of social activity comprised of rational discourse which occasions the informal constitutions of the public will". He argues that a networked public sphere is "framed as a migration or extension of an already existing public sphere to an online platform, a resuscitation of an ailing public sphere, and/or a first-time venture whose success has been made possible by the advent of digital network technologies" (p. 741).

In all of these previous works, the internet is considered as a means to facilitate user-generated content, expanding the space for freedom of speech and providing a platform for public discussion. With the advent of social media, in particular with the emergence of Weibo, we have seen an explosion of debate; therefore, it is important to examine the role of Weibo in creating a public sphere. One view sees Weibo as ideal alternative platform for public expression, by providing an opportunity for netizens to skillfully make sophisticated critiques of the regime without harsh repression (Esarey & Xiao 2008). Indeed, Twitter, which closely resembles Weibo, has been successfully used elsewhere for social mobilization, such as in the Arab Spring uprisings of 2010–2011. As these examples confirm, the concept of the public sphere is not fixed but changing, conceptual and virtual. It is not the physical milieu such as a coffeehouse or a newspaper; instead, it is "an abstract forum for dialogue and ideology—free public opinion, a lively debate on multiple levels within society" (Boeder 2005, p. 3).

Applying the Concept of the Public Sphere in the Chinese Context. The concept of the public sphere has been controversial when applied to China's settings, as Habermas' study of the public sphere was originally based on historical events mainly centered in the Europe of the eighteenth century. In work originating in 1991, Wakeman argues that it is inappropriate to apply the concept of the public sphere to China because of the prevailing and prominent role of the state, under which "Chinese citizens appear to conceive of social existence mainly in terms of obligation and interdependence rather than rights and responsibility" (Wakeman 1993, p. 134). Moreover, if civil society, on which the public sphere is built, is defined as "an arena of independent associational activity, free from state interference" (Perry & Fuller 1991, p. 663) or as the "intermediate public realm between the state and the private sphere" (Yang 2003, p. 406), whether civil society actually exists in China, becomes a debatable question.

Nevertheless, with China's great economic reforms of three decades ago, some scholars argue for accompanying signs of the revival of civil society. With such a re-invented economic sphere, civil society could begin to detach itself from the state and "an obvious pre-modern civil society could be seen (to emerge) in corporate groups and voluntary associations" (Yang 1989, pp. 35–59). Based on the dichotomy between the state and society as formulated by Habermas, Huang (1991) offers an alternative illustration of the concept of the public sphere, by proposing 'the third realm', based on state, public sphere and society. Furthermore, he proposed a public sphere that "was not merely the expansion of the public realm of life that was crucial, but rather its expansion in the context of the assertion of civil power against state power" (Huang 1991, p. 321). Liu and McCormick (2011, p. 116) define the public sphere as "a configuration of power relations among various discourses, depending on the context of time and place", and they further note that "China does have a public sphere, and this public sphere is critical to understanding politics and political change in China".

This book builds on the work of other scholars who have utilized the concept of the public sphere to describe Chinese society. Indeed, there has been a range of scholarly reflections on the public sphere in the Chinese context from various perspectives. For example, Zhan (2002) systematically and comprehensively reviews the Habermasian concept of the public sphere, suggesting that it should be taken into consideration in Chinese media studies. Xu (2003) discusses the public sphere in modern China and takes Shanghai as a case, in which he explores the context for its development of the public sphere. These are primarily discussions of the public sphere theory per se at a relatively early stage in its evolution. In China, the public sphere has been widely reviewed in media studies, with two sets of views emerging. Some scholars contend that new media provides a public sphere for collective actions of various sorts (Sima 2011; Segerberg & Bennett 2011). For example, Yang and Calhoun (2007) examine how public controversies prompted the Chinese government to halt a proposed hydropower project. Mass media and the internet are the main channels in producing this critical discourse, and Wu (2011) maps out the structures of representation surrounding a popular TV talent show, Super Girl, from Hunan TV in China in 2004, contending that cultural critics have helped nurture the public sphere through entertainment programs.

Other scholars take a different view and insist that the empowering and democratizing impact of the internet and the social media is exaggerated (Iosifidis 2011). As Lunt and Livingstone (2013) contend, most published critiques either refer to Habermas' early book, The Structural Transformation of the Public Sphere, or to his synoptic written articles published in English. However, in his subsequent work, Habermas went on to shift his position and to significantly advance his thinking about participation and the public sphere, as it is beginning to be recognized in media studies (ibid., p. 88). Habermas admits the power of mass media, particularly television, in the age of transformation as the technology has indeed served a very powerful role in the age of the internet, but its counteracting side effects cannot be neglected.

The public sphere in the Chinese context follows a different trajectory compared with its Habermasian views, as it characterizes less individual participation. The Chinese government has played an important role in shaping the public sphere, despite the fact that the emergence of the internet has catalyzed a re-evaluation of the role of communications in the public sphere, and Weibo seems to provide opportunities for multiple public spheres (Rauchfleisch & Schäfer 2014). This book therefore employs another theory of governmentality as an appropriate foundation to measure the political impact of Weibo in later chapters. In doing so, this study contributes to an already extensive literature on Weibo versions of the public sphere, with recent changes to both freedom and control of communication in the media landscape adding a new dimension.

Theory of Governmentality

Effecting Foucault's Governmentality. The works of the influential twentieth century French philosopher Michel Foucault cover a wide range of issues including political science, economics, history, and language and have exerted great influence on many disciplines. The term governmentality was introduced by Foucault in the 1970s in the course of his investigations into political power at the College de France, though the concept expanded with a series of publications into various forms of and as a context for, governmentality. By the early 1990s, a number of Foucault's lectures were published and studies of governmentalities, inspired by Foucault's lectures and writings, have been employed by a number of scholars (Dean 1999; Miller & Rose 2008; Rose 1999). In addition, there are new areas for the application of governmentality in contemporary societies across the world, such as climate change and body and health (Binkley & Capetillo 2009; Walters 2012). Some scholars propose that governmentality should also be viewed as a number of analytic tools rather than as a singular theory (Walters 2012). In this way, a number of empirical examinations are required to analyze the rationalities and techniques, in both everyday practices and the institutions of governance (Lemke 2007).

The succinct definition of governmentality as 'the conduct of conduct' has stressed the study of rule in liberal democracies, dealing with how we govern and how we are governed (Dean 1999, p. 2), although there have been some investigations of specific institutional contexts, such as in Foucault's three volumes on *The History of Sexuality* (1976, 1984, 1992); *Discipline and Punish: The Birth of the Prison* (1977) and *The Birth of the Clinic: An Archaeology of Medical Perception* (1973).

Foucault's specific writings on the subject of governmentality have been interpreted based on his texts and other studies inspired by his work, for example, *The Foucault Effect: Studies in Governmentality* (Burchell, Gordon & Miller 1991), which specifically deals with what Rose and Miller (1992, p. 181) term "programs of government", in which the activities of government are to provide an appropriate response to 'considered problems', in other words, to rectify failings. Mitchell Dean's *Governmentality: Power and Rule in Modern Society* (1999) clarifies key studies of governmentality and offers a framework for their use. For Dean, the analysis of government deals with "any more or less calculated and rational activity", concerning how techniques or knowledge are employed by different agencies for a variety of ends (1999, p. 11). In other words, here government involves some sort of deliberate attempt, calculation or "problematizing activity" by government (Rose & Miller 1992, p. 181).

The way we are governed and govern is ubiquitously seen through public administration or the political power of the nation-state. In authoritarian states, this is shaped by coercion or force. Foucault's work on governmentality offers a new perspective on power, based on—"an art of government"—by much more subtle means, which deals with different "mentalities" of governing agencies and authorities, and considers how government takes different measures or strategies in the exercise of power in certain societies (Burchell, Gordon & Miller 1991, p. ix). Foucault (1991, p. 95) states that "with government it is a question not of imposing law on men, but of disposing (of) things; that is to say, of employing tactics rather than laws, and even of using laws themselves as tactics—to arrange things in such a way that, through a certain number of means, such and such ends may be achieved". Governments, therefore, may use distinctive means and may set particular conditions to maintain their interests while allowing people a certain freedom (Scott 1995). In addition, Dean concludes that liberal ways of governing often conceive the freedom of the governed as a technical means of securing the ends of government (1999, p. 15).

In this regard, government could be seen as "an inventive, strategic, technical and artful set of 'assemblages' fashioned from diverse elements, put together in novel and specific ways, and rationalized in relation to governmental objectives and goals" (Dean & Hindess 1998, p. 8). In addition, the assemblages include a number of mundane and specific practices and techniques (ibid.). As O'Malley (1998, p. 156) notes, studies of governmentality do not only consider the government through a "reflection on the art of rule", but also understand it as a practical exercise. Within this framework, authorities have asked themselves practical questions which follow this sociological form:

> what is the condition of the people, the economy, the family; what accounts for the problems and what would lead to their improvement; what effects have our strategies produced in the past; what can and should be done and by whom, in order to do things better? (Rose 1993, p. 288)

Foucault bases the term governmentality on government, as the state with instrumental purpose, claiming an independent territorial monopoly (Dean 1999, p. 9). However, governmentality, from Foucault's perspective extends far beyond the nation-state; it is interpreted as a thinking approach associated with government, taking multiple strategies or procedures such as practical knowledge, calculation, authority, and architectural forms, to render programs operable (Rose & Miller 1992, p. 193; Rose 1999, p. 52). In other words, it deals with the current thinking or calculations of government, or the thinking behind government as we often take a set of accustomed and received ways of thinking for granted. Aspects of behaviors or actions associated with governmentality attempt to lead or shape the human conduct of individuals or groups by calculated means (Gordon 1991, p. 2), therefore Foucault's conception of governmentality refers to the emergence of political calculation, or thinking of rule, where rule becomes a matter of the calculated management of affairs to achieve certain desirable objectivities (Foucault 1991). As a calculated set of activities undertaken by multiple authorities and agencies, using a variety of techniques, governmentality, according to Foucault, seeks to shape conduct based on desires, aspirations and beliefs.

> Government is any more or less calculated and rational activity, undertaken by a multiplicity of authorities and agencies, employing a variety of techniques and forms of knowledge, that seeks to shape conduct by working through our desires, aspirations, interests and beliefs, for definite but shifting ends and with a diverse set of relatively unpredictable consequences, effects and outcomes. (Dean 1999, p. 11)

The notion of governmentality has brought a new approach toward thinking about power. Government comes to be viewed as "a kind of intermediate region which is not purely one of either freedom or domination, either consent or coercion" (Dean 1999, p. 46). To realize the governmental goal of getting populations to behave and conduct themselves in terms of its own ambitions and desires, various tactics are employed. One distinctive approach is liberalism. Rather than being viewed from a philosophical perspective, the notion of liberalism is considered as a way of solving problems. As Dean argues above, it employs tactics to regulate conduct by working through "our desires, aspirations, interests and beliefs." Gordon (1991, p. 14) stresses that: "what is distinctive, albeit not unique, about Foucault's perspective here is his concern to understand liberalism not simply as a doctrine, or set of doctrines, of political and economic theory, but as a style of thinking quintessentially concerned with the art of governing."

Foucault uses the concept of governmentality principally within a liberal, Western context, as the substantial problems he addresses are largely based in liberal democracies. Therefore, the majority of governmentality studies have been primarily focused on liberal-democratic states (Jeffreys & Sigley 2009, p. 5), with freedom and liberalism as foundations. However, signs of illiberality and apparent authoritarianism may appear within liberal forms of government, as observed by Dean (1999, pp. 131–148). Scandinavia, including Finland, Norway and Denmark, for instance, has experienced forced sterilization of their people in the name of eugenic utopia. Dean goes on to argue that non-liberal forms of thought and practice are a component of liberal rationalities, which could gain a certain legitimacy in liberal democracies (ibid., p. 134). Hindess (2001) notes the practice of authoritarian measures inherent in liberal and rational political cultures, proposing the practice of "the liberal government of unfreedom." In this way, previous forms of rule, sovereignty and discipline play a constitutive part and not simply a substitutive role in liberal forms of government (Jiang 2012, p. 50). As Gordon (1991, p. 7) argues, "rather than displacing discipline or sovereignty, the modern art of government recasts them within this concern for the population and its optimization (in terms of wealth, health, happiness, prosperity, efficiency), and the forms of knowledge and technical means appropriate to it." In this sense, liberty and domination, or freedom and 'unfreedom' are like two sides of a single coin (Hindess 2001).

Just as liberal governments can be seen to exercise 'unfreedom' on their subjects when examined through the lens of governmentality, authoritarian states could accurately be described as governments based on unfreedom. However, there is an apparent distinction between liberal forms of government and non-liberal forms of rule, as the latter "do not accept a conception of limited government characterized by the rule of law that would secure the rights of individual citizens" (Dean 1999, p. 147). A further distinction can be drawn specifically between non-liberal technologies within liberal rationalities and non-liberal rationalities. The former uses governing tactics through freedom but the latter sets the objective of improving the target subject (Sigley 2006, p. 493). This distinction is much more problematized in contemporary China, with one-Party rule still dominant, so that the realization of governing has recourse to a rule of law or through governmental interventions (Jeffreys & Sigley 2009, p. 6). In other words, with regard to knowing the limits of the objects to be governed, the methods that China takes are largely based on deliberation or premeditation for the good of the state. It is therefore misleading to declare that Western concepts or terms equate to their Chinese counterparts (Sigley 2006), as the understanding of 'imported' terms should take into account the complex social and historical context of China.

When examining the appropriateness of applying Foucault's concept of governmentality to a non-Western and non-liberal context such as China, it may be seen as problematic given its original focus on liberal democracies. However, it should be clarified that rather than seeing power as a thing intrinsic to the bureaucratic apparatus which exercises its power from the top to the down, the analytic of governmentality asks how different locales exercise authority and power, how certain powers are attributed to certain agents, and how particular domains are constituted as governable and administrable (Dean 1999, p. 29). In addition, in cases of "authoritarian governmentality" (Dean 1999), liberal and non-liberal forms of government share certain similarities, with "both comprised of elements assembled from bio-politics, pastoral power and sovereignty, and both can also be located on the trajectory of the governmentalization of the State" (Dean 1999 cited in Sigley 2006, p. 492).

In the last decade, changes in China's mass communications, media and cultural economy have been much discussed in Western academic circles. One of the common assumptions is that the implementation of market reforms and the rise of new technology are likely to undermine Party controls. Since the emergence of the internet in China, the Chinese government has shown ambivalence towards it, using it to push its economic development on the one hand while limiting its risks to social order on the other (Tai 2006; Lagerkvist 2006; Xiao 2011). The emergence of Weibo in particular, was expected to erode the CCP's monopoly over the public agenda and to further open a limited public sphere (Qian & Bandurski 2011). Thus, the tension between governmental control and new media freedoms prompted the authorities to adopt new regulatory tactics to maintain stability. The Chinese authorities have chosen to give up some degree of control over the internet for their own benefit: being seen to improve the government's performance and strengthening their popular support with the ultimate aim of facilitating control (Qian & Bandurski 2011; Xiao 2011).

In this case, we find a form of government that integrates public demands and the governmental interventions to regulate China's social media, in order to govern the whole population in both liberal and authoritarian manners. While the government offers a degree of freedom of speech, at the same time it takes a number of non-liberal approaches to limit speech. For example, the government requires that internet content providers play a role in checking each post for appropriateness, for their own "safety", or it will arrest the offenders when necessary. Foucault's formulation of the concept of governmentality is relevant here as it specifically analyses a range of comparable changes in the modern state as reflected in the practices of government (Gordon 1991, p. 4).

Specific aspects of government have particular relevance in the Chinese context. First, government is a "problematizing activity", which poses the obligations or problems for the government to address with deliberate attempt or calculation (Rose & Miller 1992, p. 181). Therefore, the ideal government is supposed to handle the failings or ills, to rectify them.

Second, government or governance in China may extend far beyond the nation-state. In most cases, the question of government is identified with the state, which is a sovereign body that claims a monopoly on territories. While the state has a significant contribution to make in constituting regulatory order, non-state actors can also play an essential role in the exercise of political power that extends beyond the state (Rose & Miller 1992).

The third essential feature of the governmentality approach is that it stresses the active engagement or action of the subject in the course of government rather than simply exercising power. However, in most cases, the question of government is identified with the state, which is a sovereign body that claims a monopoly on territories (Dean 1999, p. 9), as it has a significant contribution to make in constituting regulatory order. However, as exemplified by the compulsory role of internet content providers, non-state actors also play an essential role in the exercise of "political power beyond the state" (Rose & Miller 1992). Hence, the concept of governmentality can still usefully be applied in the Chinese context, as the rule of China is marked by a combination of both socialist authoritarianism and liberal rules; additionally, China's 'socialist arts of government' obviously share a close genealogy with 'liberal' notions in the West (cited in Jeffreys & Sigley 2009, pp. 6–7).

Though the Party remains authoritarian in China, the transition to a market economy has brought important changes in the state's governance. However, rather than adopting an absolutely authoritarian political and technocratic way of thinking, or moving significantly towards greater liberalism, in analyzing the two types of political tradition, a hybrid socialist-neoliberal model has been proposed to describe the shifts in how the practice and objects of government are understood and calculated in the process of China's transition from 'plan' to 'market' (Sigley 2006, p. 489). Hindess for example, concludes that rather than debating the level of liberty in a liberal society or the level of authoritarianism in an illiberal society, the common grounds of the two competing rationalities have a more significant meaning than those of the differences (Hindess 1996, p. 77). This could be aptly described by a Chinese saying, *qiutongcunyi*, which means 'to seek common ground while reserving differences'. Thus, liberal governmentality can be seen to have been successfully grafted onto the Chinese context, an idea supported by a range of scholars. This Chinese version of governmentality was characterized as a blended form by Sigley (2006), where it combines the traditional Chinese socialist technologies of government and the recent seemingly neoliberal strategies to govern through individuals' desires. This form covers a variety of demographics, including consumers, property-owners, job-seekers and ordinary citizens.

Chinese examples of governmentality at work cover various subjects, including prostitution control and tobacco control (Jeffreys 2004; Kohrman 2004). In addition, China's Nationalist Party (often referred to as the KMT in China), uses military training, as well as schooling, to promote cultural citizenship (Culp 2006), and a number of scholars have focused on different aspects of governmentality in China. In *China's Governmentalities: Governing Change, Changing Government* by Jeffreys and Sigley (2009), the Chinese government's shifts in practice are noted, accompanying its post-1978 transition from 'socialist plan' to 'market socialism', including in the fields of education, environment, religion, and sexual public health. These are areas in which the liberal and illiberal are both in play in a very controlled way. Woronov (2009) analyses different aspects of contemporary Chinese society and politics where governmentality is at work, such as the educational practice of "Education for Quality". Yang (2011) examines the dang'an (personal dossiers) system as well as its post-Mao transformation in China in order to explore China's neoliberal technologies.

This chapter therefore sets up the theoretical foundation of this book, considering how the concept of governmentality is extended and employed in China, a non-Western and non-liberal state. It focuses on the Chinese government's specific approaches to regulating Weibo in order to govern the Chinese people using techniques and strategies that achieve certain identified outcomes. The direct application of the concept of governmentality in a non-liberal society would appear to be problematic and inappropriate. Nevertheless, some scholars argue that the notion and exercise of governmentality as the "conduct of conduct" can be applied within any liberal or illiberal context (Colebatch 2002), rather than through the more familiar tactics of 'freedom and liberty', the Chinese paradigm for governmentality takes the form of 'distinct planning and administrative' rationality (Jeffreys & Sigley 2009, p. 5). In the process, there are a number of specific governmental strategies or programs which are used for individuals to self-regulate, which Foucault refers to as the government of oneself (1991, p. 87). This will be discussed in the next section.

Technologies of Self-Government. To render policies and programs operable, government authorities need to use multiple strategies and techniques to ensure appropriate connections between their intentions and the activities of individuals. Scholars have referred to the variety of such mechanisms as 'technologies of government' (Miller & Rose 1990). According to Foucault (1988a, 1988b), there are four types of such "technologies": "technologies of production", which allow the production, transformation or manipulation of material objects; "technologies of sign systems", which permit the use of signs, meanings, symbols or signification; "technologies of power", which determine the conduct of individuals and submit them to certain ends or domination, and "technologies of the self", which permit individuals to effect change by their own means or autonomy, or with the help of others. As other scholars have noted, the art of governing can take a variety of positions in relation to the freedoms involved in such transactions. It can be presupposed, reduced, shaped, and treated as an "artifact of…governmental arrangements", and it can use freedom as a technical means for achieving its ends (Dean 2002, p. 37).

Thus, in addition to the overt exercise of authority over others as a means of guiding, shaping or solving social problems, the concept of governmentality can also relate to how we govern ourselves, in other words, "to control one's own instincts, to govern oneself" (Rose 1999, p. 3). The practice of self-governing or the 'technology of the self' which is produced through governmentality, is an important theme of Foucault's technologies. For instance, Foucault uses the concept of the *panopticon* to explain how prisoners are manipulated to regulate their own behavior (see Foucault 1977). If there is a central point in a prison from which all prisoners can be seen, anyone has the potential to be punished at any time. Therefore in the expectation that they may be being watched, prisoners regulate their own behavior rather than risk being punished. This strategic control of others therefore becomes defined as a technology of the self consisting of:

> intentional and voluntary actions by which men not only set themselves rules of conduct, but also seek to transform themselves, to change themselves in their singular being, to make their life as a collective oeuvre that carries certain aesthetic values and meets certain stylistic criteria. (Foucault 1979, pp. 10–11)

Technologies of the self permit "individuals to effect by their own means, a certain number of operations on their own bodies, [...] on their own conduct, and in this manner to transform themselves, modify themselves, and to attain a certain state of perfection, of happiness, of purity, of supernatural power, and so on" (Foucault 1993, p. 203). Generally such technologies refer to the adoption of certain practices to make ourselves accountable for our own actions or comportment. To these ends, the techniques or knowledge employed are various, but generally, by internalizing the codes or ethics of conduct, control of the minds of individuals or the collective is achieved.

In a key difference from the past administration mode, power not only imposes constraints or regulations upon populations, but enables the people to keep a certain kind of "regulated freedom" in mind (Rose & Miller 2010, p. 272). For the present, as Foucault affirms, what is really essential is "not so much the State-domination of society, but the 'governmentalization' of the state" (Foucault 1979, p. 20). Therefore, in light of updated new media ecology, the omnipotent and direct internet censorship which played such an important role in the past may not be entirely feasible in the contemporary era. It is therefore essential for the government to utilize technologies such as the issuing of documents, strategies and other measures to maximize its purposes or goals. These include optimizing economic development while at the same time regulating the social order. In this process the application of principles and strategies of governmentality, and the strategic monitoring of technologies of the self, have been valuable.

Such technology of self-government has been described as 'action at a distance', that is to do things in the center that sometimes makes it possible to dominate at the periphery, spatially as well as chronologically (Latour 1987, p. 232). Rose and Miller (1992) extend Latour's explanation, and interpret it as "governing at a distance". Apart from the literal meaning of "action at a distance" in a geographical sense, it has another meaning derived from a constitutional sense, referring to the government's indirect control through "the activities and calculations of a proliferation of independent agents including philanthropists, doctors, hygienists, managers, planners, parents and social workers" (ibid., p. 180). These are all potential channels for self-regulation of any new medium that enters the public sphere.

The media may also play an important role in enforcing ethical behaviors (Jeffreys 2009; Sigley 2006), through for example, the governmental practice of public service broadcasting to promote citizenship (Nolan 2006); and the relationship of news and governmentality in indigenous societies (Mickler

1998). Ouellette and Hay (2008) explore the government's uses of television to inform viewers. Few scholars have examined the control of the internet to this end. Qiu (2007) contends that the entertainment-and-consumption pattern of internet use at the micro level is often closely related to a control model at the macro level. Jiang (2012) also explores notions of "liberation" and "political democratization" in Chinese cyberspace, revealing that the online population is increasingly being shaped in the name of nationalism, but the most profound level of control is through consumerism. Therefore, from these points of view, the internet could be considered a means, or at least a tool, of control.

Conclusion

This chapter provides the theoretical foundation to the book by outlining the Habermasian theory of public sphere and Foucault's concept of governmentality in advance of this study's examination of the coexistence of freedom and control in social media in contemporary China. In this chapter, the public sphere has been defined as a domain of social life where critical and rational debate can be formed without any intervention from the state or society, and the concept of the public sphere in Habermas' sense describes the complex interactions that take place among publics, media and the government. Foucault's notion of governmentality has been defined as "the conduct of conduct" (Dean 1999, p. 2), the government's practices for governing. As this book will show, these are both crucial elements in making sense of China's specific attitude towards Weibo regulation.

A typology of different kinds of public spheres has been developed as applicable in contemporary China, in which critical and open debates take place under specific circumstances, including thematic public spheres, short-term public spheres, encoded public spheres, local public spheres, non-domestic political public spheres, mobile public spheres and meta public spheres (Rauchfleisch & Schäfer 2014). However, the following chapters will focus on a new typology of public sphere that centers on the interaction of freedom and control.

The following chapter examines the great expansion in China of the frequency of examples of public sphere behavior through the internet, with greater information access and broader public debates than ever before (Qian & Bandurski 2011). While previous scholars have focused on what they conclude is an ambivalent attitude by the Chinese government to social media, and to Weibo in particular, this book interprets such behavior through the lens of governmentality, where the government's strategic thinking includes more sophisticated information management and more strategic censorship behind the seemingly greater freedoms and openness in selected instances.

References

Binkley, S & Capetillo, J (eds.). 2009, A Foucault for the 21st century: Governmentality, biopolitics and discipline in the new millennium, Cambridge Scholars Press, Newcastle.

Boeder, P. 2005, 'Habermas' heritage: The future of the public sphere in the network society', First Monday, vol. 10, no. 9, <http://firstmonday.org/ojs/index.php/fm/article/viewArticle/1280>.

Burchell, G, Gordon, C & Miller, P (eds.). 1991, The Foucault effect: Studies in governmentality, Harvester Wheatsheaf, Hertfordshire.

Calhoun, C. 1992, 'Introduction', in Calhoun, C (ed.), Habermas and the public sphere, MIT, Cambridge, pp. 1–48.

Carey, J. 1995, 'The press, public opinion, and public discourse', in Glasser, T & Salmon, C (eds.), Public opinion and the communication of consent, Guilford, New York, pp. 373–402.

Castells, M. 2008, 'The new public sphere: Global civil society, communication networks, and global governance', The Annals of the American Academy of Political and Social Science, vol. 616, no. 1, pp. 78–93.

Colebatch, HK. 2002, 'Government and governmentality: Using multiple approaches to the analysis of government', Australian Journal of Political Science, vol. 37, no. 3, pp. 417–435.

Culp, R. 2006, 'Rethinking governmentality: Training, cultivation, and cultural citizenship in nationalist China', Journal of Asian Studies, vol. 65, no. 3, p. 529.

Dahlberg, L. 2001, 'The internet and democratic discourse: Exploring the prospects of online deliberative forums extending the public sphere', Information, Communication & Society, vol. 4, no. 4, pp. 615–633.

Dahlgren, P. 2005, 'The Internet, public spheres, and political communication: Dispersion and deliberation', Political Communication, vol. 22, no. 2, pp. 147–162.

Dean, M. 1999, Governmentality: Power and rule in modern society, Sage, London.

Dean, M. 2002, 'Liberal government and authoritarianism', Economy and Society, vol. 31, no. 1, pp. 37–61.

Dean, M & Hindess B. 1998, 'Introduction: Government, liberalism, society', in Dean, M & Hindess, B (eds.), Governing Australia: Studies in contemporary rationalities of government, Cambridge University Press, Cambridge, pp. 1–19.

Esarey, A & Xiao, Q. 2008, 'Political expression in the Chinese blogosphere: Below the radar', Asian Survey, vol. 48, no. 5, pp. 752–772.

Ferree, MM, Gamson, WA, Gerhards, J & Rucht, D. 2002, 'Four models of the public sphere in modern democracies', Theory and Society, vol. 31, no. 3, pp. 289–324.

Foucault, M. 1973, The birth of the clinic: An archaeology of medical perception, Pantheon, New York.

Foucault, M. 1976, The history of sexuality vol. 1: The will to knowledge, Penguin, London.

Foucault, M. 1977, Discipline and punish: The birth of the prison, Pantheon Books, New York.

Foucault, M. 1979, 'On governmentality', in Burchell, G, Gordon, C & Miller, P (eds.), The Foucault effect: Studies in governmental rationality, Harvester Wheatsheaf, Hemel Hempstead, pp. 5–21.

Foucault, M. 1984, The history of sexuality vol. 3: The care of self, Penguin, London.

Foucault, M. 1988a, 'Technologies of the self', in Martin, LH, Gutman, H & Hutton, P (eds.), Technologies of the self: A seminar with Michel Foucault, The University of Massachusetts Press, Amherst, pp. 16–49.

Foucault, M. 1988b, 'The political technology of individuals', in Martin, LH, Gutman, H & Hutton, P (eds.), Technologies of the self: A seminar with Michel Foucault, The University of Massachusetts Press, Amherst, pp. 145–162.

Foucault, M. 1991, 'Governmentality', in Burchell, G, Gordon, C & Miller, P (eds.), The Foucault effect: Studies in governmental rationality, Harvester Wheatsheaf, Hemel Hempstead, pp. 87–104.

Foucault, M. 1992, The history of sexuality vol. 2: The use of pleasure, Penguin, London.

Foucault, M. 1993, 'About the beginning of the hermeneutics of the self: Two lectures at Dartmouth', Political Theory, vol. 21, no. 2, pp. 198–227.

Fraser, N. 1992, 'Rethinking the public sphere: A contribution to the critique of actually existing democracy', in Calhoun, C (ed.), Habermas and the public sphere, MIT, Cambridge, pp. 109–142.

Fraser, N. 2007, 'Transnationalizing the public sphere: On the legitimacy and efficacy of public opinion in a post-Westphalian world', Theory, Culture & Society, vol. 24, no. 4, pp. 7–30.

Garnham, N. 1992, 'The media and the public sphere', in Calhoun, C (ed.), Habermas and the public sphere, MIT, Cambridge, pp. 359–376.

Gerhards, J & Schäfer, MS. 2010, 'Is the internet a better public sphere? Comparing old and new media in the USA and Germany', New Media & Society, vol. 12, no. 1, pp. 143–160.

Goldberg, G. 2010, 'Rethinking the public/virtual sphere: The problem with participation', New Media & Society, vol. 13, no. 5, pp. 739–754.

Gordon, C. 1991, 'Governmentality', in Burchell, G, Gordon, C & Miller, P (eds.), The Foucault effect: Studies in governmentality, Harvester/Wheatsheaf, London, pp. 87–104.

Habermas, J. 1989 [1962], The structural transformation of the public sphere: An inquiry into a category of bourgeois society, MIT Press, Cambridge.

Habermas, J. 1991, 'The public sphere', in Mukerji, C & Schudson, M (eds.), Rethinking popular culture: Contemporary perspectives in cultural studies, University of California Press, Berkeley, p. 399.

Habermas, J. 1992, 'Further reflections on the public sphere', in Calhoun, C (ed.), Habermas and the public sphere, The MIT Press, Cambridge, pp. 1–31.

Habermas, J. 1997, 'The public sphere', in Robert, EG & Philip, P (eds.), Contemporary political philosophy: An anthology, Blackwell Publishers, Oxford, pp. 105–108.

Hartley, J. 1992, The politics of pictures: The creation of public in the age of popular media, Routledge, London and New York.

Hindess, B. 1996, 'Liberalism, socialism and democracy: Variations on a governmental theme', in Barry, A, Osborne, T & Rose, N (eds.), Foucault and political reason: Liberalism, neo-liberalism and rationalities of government, University of Chicago Press, Chicago, pp. 65–80.

Hindess, B. 2001, 'The liberal government of unfreedom', Alternatives: Global, Local, Political, vol. 26, no. 2, pp. 93–111.

Hu, Y. 2010, 'Micro-revolution: From Twitter to Sina Weibo', New Weekly, p. 315.

Huang, PC. 1991, 'The paradigmatic crisis in Chinese studies: Paradoxes in social and economic history', Modern China, vol. 17, no. 3, pp. 299–341.

Huang, PC. 1993, '"Public sphere"/"civil society" in China?: The third realm between state and society', Modern China, vol. 19, no. 2, pp. 216–240.

Iosifidis, P. 2011, 'The public sphere, social networks and public service media', Information, Communication & Society, vol. 14, no. 5, pp. 619–637.

Jeffreys, E. 2004, China, sex and prostitution, Routledge Curzon, London, New York.

Jeffreys, E (ed.). 2009, China's governmentalities: Governing change, changing government, Routledge, Abingdon.

Jeffreys, E & Sigley, G. 2009, 'Governmentality, governance and China', in Jeffreys, E (ed.), China's governmentalities: Governing change, changing government, Routledge, London, pp. 1–23.

Jiang, Y. 2012, Cyber-nationalism in China, University of Adelaide Press, Adelaide.

Kohrman, M. 2004, 'Should I quit? Tobacco, fraught identity, and the risks of governmentality in urban China', Urban Anthropology and Studies of Cultural Systems and World Economic Development, pp. 211–245.

Lagerkvist, J. 2006, The Internet in China: Unlocking and containing the public sphere, Lund University, Lund.

Latour, B. 1987, Science in action, Open University Press, Milton Keynes.

Lemke, T. 2007, 'An indigestible meal? Foucault, governmentality and state theory', Distinktion: Scandinavian Journal of Social Theory, vol. 8, no. 2, pp. 43–64.

Lewis, OA. 2013, 'Net inclusion: New media's impact on deliberative politics in China', Journal of Contemporary Asia, vol. 43, no. 4, pp. 678–708.

Liu, Q & McCormick, B. 2011, 'The media and the public sphere in contemporary China', Boundary 2, vol. 38, no. 1, pp. 101–134.

Lunt, P & Livingstone, S. 2013, 'Media studies' fascination with the concept of the public sphere: Critical reflections and emerging debates', Media, Culture & Society, vol. 35, no. 1, pp. 87–96.

McCormick, BL & Liu, Q. 2003, 'Technologies, content, commerce and the prospects for the public sphere', in Lee, CC (ed.), Chinese media, global contexts, Routledge, London and New York, pp. 139–158.

Mickler, S. 1998, 'News, governmentality and aboriginality: Beyond pathologies of othering in media studies', Critical Arts: A South-North Journal of Cultural & Media Studies, vol. 12, no. ½, pp. 45–77.

Miller, P & Rose, N. 1990, 'Political rationalities and technologies of government', in Hanninen, S & Palonen, K (eds.), Texts, contexts, concepts: Studies in politics and power in language, Finnish political Science Association, Helsinki, pp. 171–183.

Miller, P & Rose, N. 2008, Governing the present: Administering economics, social and personal life, Polity Press, Cambridge.

Newman, J. 2005, 'Introduction', in Newman, J (ed.), Remaking governance: Peoples, politics and the public sphere, The Policy Press, Bristol, pp. 1–15.

Nolan, D. 2006, 'Media, citizenship and governmentality: Defining "The public" of public service broadcasting', Social Semiotics, vol. 16, no. 2, pp. 225–242.

O'Malley, P. 1998, 'Indigenous governance', in Dean, M & Hindess, B (eds.), Governing Australia: Studies in contemporary rationalities of government, Cambridge University Press, Cambridge, pp. 156–172.

Ouellette, L & Hay, J. 2008, 'Makeover television, governmentality and the good citizen', Continuum: Journal of Media & Cultural Studies, vol. 22, no. 4, pp. 471–484.

Papacharissi, Z. 2002, 'The virtual sphere: The internet as a public sphere', New Media & Society, vol. 4, no. 1, pp. 9–27.

Perry, EJ & Fuller, EV. 1991, 'China's long march to democracy', World Policy Journal, vol. 8, no. 4, pp. 663–685.

Postman, N. 1985, Amusing ourselves to death: Public discourse in the age of show business, Viking, New York.

Qian, G & Bandurski, D. 2011, 'China's emerging public sphere: The impact of media commercialization, professionalism, and the internet in an era of transition', in Shirk S (ed.), Changing media, changing China, Oxford University Press, Oxford, pp. 39–76.

Qiu, JL. 2007, 'The wireless leash: Mobile messaging service as a means of control', International Journal of Communication, no. 1, pp. 74–91.

Rauchfleisch, A & Schäfer, MS. 2014, 'Multiple public spheres of Weibo: A typology of forms and potentials of online public spheres in China', Information, Communication & Society, no. ahead-of-print, pp. 1–17.

Roberts, JM & Crossley, N. 2004, 'Introduction', in Crossley, N & Roberts, JM (eds.), After Habermas: New perspectives on the public sphere, Blackwell Publishing, Oxford, pp. 1–27.

Rose, N. 1993, 'Government, authority and expertise in advanced liberalism', Economy and Society, vol. 22, no. 3, pp. 283–299.

Rose, N. 1999, Power of freedom: Reframing political thought, Cambridge University Press, Cambridge.

Rose, N & Miller, P. 1992, 'Political power beyond the state: Problematics of government', British Journal of Sociology, vol. 43, no. 2, pp. 173–205.

Rose, N & Miller, P. 2010, 'Political power beyond the State: Problematics of government', The British Journal of Sociology, vol. 61, no. s1, pp. 271–303.

Schudson, M. 1992, 'Was there ever a public sphere? If so, When? reflections on the Amercian case', in Calhoun, C (ed.), Habermas and the public sphere, Massachusetts Institute of Technology, Cambridge, pp. 143–163.

Scott, D. 1995, 'Colonial governmentality', Social Text, no. 43, pp. 191–220.

Segerberg, A & Bennett, WL. 2011, 'Social media and the organization of collective action: Using Twitter to explore the ecologies of two climate change protests', The Communication Review, vol. 14, no. 3, pp. 197–215.

Sigley, G. 2006, 'Chinese governmentalities: Government, governance and the socialist market economy', Economy and Society, vol. 35, no. 4, pp. 487–508.

Sima, Y. 2011, 'Grassroots environmental activism and the internet: Constructing a green public sphere in China', Asian Studies Review, vol. 35, no. 4, pp. 477–497.

Tai, Z. 2006, The Internet in China: Cyberspace and civil society, Routledge, New York.

Verstraeten, H. 1996, 'The media and the transformation of the public sphere: A contribution for a critical political economy of the public sphere', European Journal of Communication, vol. 11, no. 3, pp. 347–370.

Wakeman, F. 1993, 'The civil society and public sphere debate: Western reflections on Chinese political culture', Modern China, vol. 19, no. 2, pp. 108–138.

Walters, W. 2012, Governmentality: Critical encounters, Routledge, Abingdon.

Woronov, T. 2009, 'Governing China's children: Governmentality and "education for quality"', Positions, vol. 17, no. 3, pp. 567–589.

Wu, J. 2011, 'Enlightenment or entertainment: The nurturance of an aesthetic public sphere through a popular talent show in China', The Communication Review, vol. 14, no. 1, pp. 46–67.

Xiao, Q. 2011, 'The battle for the Chinese internet', Journal of Democracy, vol. 22, no. 2, pp. 47–61.

Xu, J. 2003, 'The public sphere in modern China: Shanghai as a case', History, vol. 2, pp. 77–89.

Yang, G. 2003, 'The co-evolution of the Internet and civil society in China', Asian Survey, vol. 43, no. 3, pp. 405–422.

Yang, G. 2009, The Power of the internet in China: Citizen activism online, Columbia University Press, New York.

Yang, G & Calhoun, C. 2007, 'Media, civil society, and the rise of a green public sphere in China', China Information, vol. 21, no. 2, pp. 211–236.

Yang, J. 2011, 'The politics of the dang'an: Spectralization, spatialization, and neoliberal governmentality in China', Anthropological Quarterly, vol. 84, no. 2, pp. 507–533.

Yang, M. 1989, 'Between state and society: The construction of corporateness in a Chinese socialist factory', Australian Journal of Chinese Affairs, vol. 22, pp. 31–60.

Zhan, J. 2002, 'Habermasian "public sphere" theory and media', Journal of China Youth University for Political Sciences, vol. 2, pp. 123–128.

· 3 ·

BACKGROUND OF CHINA'S INTERNET AND SOCIAL MEDIA

Introduction

This chapter describes the background and context for China's internet and social media, notably the social media platform, Weibo. This background includes essential information on the development of the internet, the common assumptions about the internet's potential and the degree to which it is controlled. It also examines the specific development of Weibo in contemporary China, and the nature of Weibo's power, providing detailed demographic and typological observations of Weibo users.

Since its advent in the early 1990s, the internet has contributed to enormous economic development in China. According to the 2005 Five Year Plan, it has been considered a cornerstone of the drive for economic development. Former Chinese president Jiang Zemin delivered a message to a computer conference in China in 2000, stressing that "we should deeply recognize the tremendous power of information technology and vigorously promote its development" (Tai 2006, p. 120). The development of the internet has indeed added significantly to China's GDP growth. It is said that online advertising is growing quickly in the Chinese markets and is expected to grow at a rate of 48 percent per annum by 2015, driven through rapidly expanding levels of internet penetration (M2 Presswire 2011). However, the emergence of the internet as a public and interactive platform has created a dilemma for Chinese authorities. On the one hand, the authorities wish to embrace new media technologies in a variety of ways for economic development; on the other hand, officials channel great energy into censoring what is deemed to be 'unwarranted' public information and in regulating new media in order to protect the state's political integrity and to maintain a harmonious society. To achieve these ends requires the government to "control the flow of information, including news and public opinion, and especially citizen dissent" (Weber & Jia 2007, p. 772). In China this is certainly possible as the Chinese government has established one of the world's most technologically sophisticated internet monitoring systems, often referred to as "the great Chinese firewall", in what has been described as 'networked authoritarianism' (MacKinnon 2011). The Chinese authorities have become highly skilled at internet filtering, using second- and third-generation controls.

With rapid technological development, social media has updated every few years. For example, Weibo, has attracted great attention in recent years, and it has been extolled by Western media as a "free speech platform" (Richburg 2011). But at the same time, widespread censorship of Weibo constantly takes place (Zhai 2012), reflecting the fact that the art and strategy of the Chinese government's censorship techniques are also evolving to keep pace.

Despite the striking potential of the internet and other technologies to empower individuals, to expose wrongdoing, to facilitate mobilization and to scrutinize government, authoritarian states including China, as noted, have acquired technical abilities to control these internet behaviors. However, it is not only the technology itself, but also the political organization and strategy and the "deep-rooted normative, social, and economic forces" within it that determines who "wins" the race (Diamond 2010, p. 70). As this study focuses on who 'wins' and on the evolving strategies that the Chinese state has taken to exercise control, it explores how in contrast to previously direct censorship, the current Chinese state has adopted a range of subtle methods to construct a space which both offers greater freedom and consolidated control. The next section therefore describes the development of the internet as well as the corresponding forms of internet censorship in China. In addition, it will examine the nature of Weibo as well as the demographics of its users.

The Development of the Internet in China

Internet Growth in China. The development of the internet in the late 1980s has created a variety of opportunities and provided unprecedented challenges all over the world. Many countries, including the United States and Singapore have demonstrated different strategies to advance this development (Wong 1997; Kahin 1997). Despite the relatively recent history of the internet in China, the scale of its spreading use and influence is nonetheless breathtaking. Since its arrival in China in the early 1990s, it has also made crucial contributions to social development. Chinese leaders believed from the beginning that the emergence of the internet would provide a unique opportunity for China's future development. After decades of perceived humiliation by foreign powers in China's late modern history, Chinese leaders have made great efforts to boost China's pride. After Mao Zedong's revolutionary era following the CCP takeover in 1949, Deng Xiaoping came to power and shifted his focus to economic reform and openness, with later leaders continuing on this path to develop the economy and to build up national strength. Former Chinese president, Jiang Zemin (who assumed the Chinese presidency in 1993), strongly supported the development of new technology. Jiang's successor, Hu Jintao (who took over the presidency in 2003) continued on this path, stressing the importance of a knowledge-based economy. Current president Xi Jinping has also expressed his ambition that China should become a "cyber power" (Wan 2014). The role of the internet as a communication tool is particularly meaningful in China where "citizens previously had little to no opportunity for unconstrained public self-expression or access to free and uncensored information" (Xiao 2011).

China's ongoing internet development has gained wide support from the government, which sees it as a golden opportunity for another platform for economic takeoff using such tools as email and e-commerce (Tai 2006, p. 120). China's internet development can be divided into several phases primarily based on the stages of technological progress. The shift from e-mail use to full-scale internet services reaching a large population in 1993 is seen by Lu and colleagues (2002) as marking the end of the first stage of internet development. The change from email use before 1994 to other applications, is seen by Qi (2000) as marking the beginning of a third phase; between 1994 and 1995, education networks were developed; from 1995 to the present, a wide range of commercial uses have appeared. However, these technological phases could be seen to overlook other evolving aspects in China's government, economy and society, which are also reflected in the internet's development (Tai 2006, pp. 121–122). Taking both technological development and the government's perception of the internet into account, Tai (2006) divides the internet growth into four stages: 1) from 1986 to 1992 when online application was limited to the use of email and was largely neglected by the government; 2) from 1992 to 1995 when the government made clear its determination to advance a national information network infrastructure that would accelerate China's economic expansion; 3) from 1995 to 1997 when the government started to implement technological and policy mechanisms to strengthen its tight control over rapid development of the internet; 4) from 1998 to the present when the internet has quickly reached a mass audience that is inevitably integrated into Chinese society. Correspondingly, the government began to adopt more stringent control measures through each of these stages.

Over the past two decades, China has been home to one of the largest, fastest-growing and most active groups of internet users in the world. The figures for these internet users are compiled by the China Internet Network Information Centre (CNNIC), which is the state network information center of China and approved by the national authorities to publish official government information in June 1997. In terms of CNNIC's survey report (41st), the number of Chinese "netizens" (internet citizens) surged to 772 million by the end of December 2017, and it forms the world's largest cyber-community where netizens account for 55.8 percent of the whole Chinese population (CNNIC 2018). Therefore the internet has become an integral part of Chinese daily life. These statistics help to explain why the internet has become the front-line battle ground in China's new "informational politics" (Yang 2006). As noted, the number of internet users increased very rapidly in the first years after its arrival and rose steadily in recent years.

This increase can be attributed to two significant factors: firstly, the increasing internet penetration rate, and secondly, the rise of blogging, instant messaging and social networking services (SNS) which have increasingly attracted more users to participate and communicate.

Assumptions About the Political Potential of the Internet. Since its arrival, the internet has been envisioned by scholars and politicians as a potentially liberating and democratizing force in the society. The rapid development of the internet in the 1990s boosted a rise in technological innovation to promote democracy in authoritarian states. China has embraced the internet for more than two decades, attracting an increasing number of users and it has brought greater freedom of speech than ever before. Pan's 2006 article 'The click that broke a government's grip' in the *Washington Post* illustrated the profound impact of the internet serving as a catalyst for political change in China, and challenging the Party's ability to control news and public opinion. Other scholars have contended that the advancement of technology will promote social forces independent of the state and enable political and social issues to be discussed in the public domain (Diamond 2010; Hu 2010; Yang 2009; Zheng 2008). This optimistic attitude has been reinforced by a series of internet incidents in recent years, which have prompted the Chinese government to take action to address issues of concern to Chinese citizens, as expressed on the internet on a number of occasions. For example, the case of Sun Zhigang, has been repeatedly cited as demonstrating the success of internet public opinion influencing government policies, in this case relating to the repeal of custody and repatriation regulations (see Yu 2009; Diamond 2010). Sun Zhigang, a 27-year old migrant worker from Wuhan, the capital city of Central China's Hubei province, worked as a fashion designer in Guangzhou. He was brutally beaten to death in Guangzhou for not carrying the temporary residence permit required by law for those who change cities. The national outrage expressed online at his treatment sparked Chinese legal reform (China Daily 2003).

Although many researchers focus on individual political participation, some others investigate how internet use mobilizes collective action. The most well-known example is that of the recent large-scale mass protests that took place in some Middle-Eastern countries, known collectively as the Arab Spring of 2011, as noted earlier. The internet and cyberspace mean borderless communication opportunities for dissidents, effective mobilization of domestic opposition, and increased opportunities for collecting information about alternative political systems (Lagerkvist 2006, p. 16). Meanwhile, the internet may promote social interaction and civic engagement because it allows users to strengthen social bonds and coordinate their actions to address joint concerns (ibid.).

The exponential development of the internet and the parallel amount internet research, has directed scholars' attention to the interactive relations among state, society and technology (Diamond 2010; Ferdinand 2000; Zheng 2008). Although the positive potential of the internet for societal change has been acknowledged, there is still debate on the levels and range of democratic discourse in the public space which could facilitate the possibilities of political participation and the formation of a public sphere (Abbott 2001; Papacharissi

2002; Shane 2004). Moreover, scholars may use a state/society framework to argue the interaction of regulatory relations between the state and society in understanding the political impact of the internet (Zheng 2008).

This debate on the potential of the internet is also true of other countries. In November 1999, two independent journalists, Steven Gan and Premesh Chandran, launched an online newspaper, Malaysiakini, in Malaysia. This soon gained fame by digitally cropping an image of jailed opposition leader (and former deputy prime minister) Anwar Ibrahim, from a group photo of ruling-party politicians. Later the newspaper won a loyal and growing readership by providing reports on long-forbidden subjects such as corruption, human-rights abuses, ethnic discrimination and police brutality, to widen the public sphere through the use of the internet (Diamond 2010).

The internet would allow individuals to publish and disseminate their political opinions more freely to a large audience, and the pervasive use of the internet brings political and social risks to any regime. In response to the potential of the internet to engage citizens in unprecedented ways, China has implemented a range of regulatory measures striking both in scope and sophistication.

Internet Regulation in China

Almost all countries, from the United States to the Middle East to Asia, have implemented various strategies to control the internet to different degrees, for security reasons. China is no exception and often these measures are severe. Since the foundation of the People's Republic of China in 1949, information control has been an important part of the Chinese government's governing strategy. From newspapers and magazines to radio and television, the CCP has maintained monopoly control over the mass media. The media in China has been considered metaphorically as the "throat and tongue" of the Party, that is, its official voice. This perception of media control as essential to political stability was further intensified after June 4, 1989, in the crackdown on the Tiananmen Square student demonstrations in Beijing. Contrary to the strict restrictions on reportage in China, this incident was reported by foreign journalists and shown on foreign televisions. People around the world were shocked by this behavior, and the former Australian Prime Minister Bob Hawke cried for the victims of the Tiananmen Square massacre and issued up to 10,000 visa applications for resident Chinese students (Callaghan 2009).

Therefore, the fear of losing control of media content and images saw the Chinese government intensify control over the entire media and particularly of the large scale adoption of the internet when it arrived in China in the mid-1990s.

This commitment to media control to ensure political stability was maintained during the 1990s, when commercialization and self-funding of the media were allowed to mitigate the state's financial burden and to better compete in the internet marketplace. The so-called "propaganda discipline" was still enforced by the Central Propaganda Department and local censorship organs (Bandurski 2014).

Since the internet was largely adopted in the mid-1990s in China, the Party considered that it could become an essential part of the country's economic advancement and actively develop what would come to be known as e-commerce and e-government projects; on the other hand, recognizing its potential to threaten political stability, the authorities enforced multiple regulatory measures to control online content and to monitor online activities, with "a combination of technical and policy initiatives" (Tai 2006, p. 81). These technical strategies include surveillance, imprisonment, propaganda, and direct blockage, known collectively, as previously noted, as the Great Firewall. Hachigian (2001, p. 118) argues that the Chinese government has since adopted a three-part internet strategy, ensuring economic growth and certain personal freedoms, while controlling the internet's risks, and harnessing its potential.

To fully understand the determination of the government to solidify its control over the internet, it is necessary to examine the relevant bureaucratic regulatory apparatus. There are several political bodies in charge of internet content, including the Central Propaganda Department, which is responsible for the content conforming to the Party line, and the State Council Information Office, which oversees all Web sites. There are also a number of methods that the government employs to control online content, including the filtering of 'sensitive' keywords and the employment of human monitors.

China has always possessed a strict attitude to the control of information and has issued corresponding policies to control the internet which have appeared widely in official policy papers. One such paper was issued by the State Council on February 18, 1994 with the title, "Regulations for the Protection of Computer Information Systems Safety in the People's Republic of China". This focuses more on the "physical entity" of the computer in China, with "no specific mention of the type of content." Later, on February 1, 1996, a more comprehensive paper titled "Temporary Decree on the Management of Computer Information Network International Connectivity in the People's Republic of China" was issued, and revised on May 20, 1997. It was followed on December 8, 1997 by the detailed "Implementation Measures for Enforcing the Temporary Decree on the Management of Computer Information Network International Connectivity in the People's Republic of China". This focuses more on forbidding harmful content. Then in January 2000, another paper appeared, "State Secrets Protection Regulations for Computer Information Systems on the Internet", which forbids sending or discussing state secrets on internet sites such as internet chat rooms or bulletin boards. More importantly, it stated that internet service and content providers should undergo "security certification" to ensure state security. In addition, on August 4, 2000, the first "internet police" were established in Anhui province aiming to "administer and maintain order on computer networks", a measure that was soon followed in more than 20 other provinces (see Tai 2006, pp. 98–99). Subsequently, an internet law, "Decree on the Management of Internet News/Information services" was implemented on September 25, 2005. It primarily stipulated that news sites must receive approval to publish information other than that from their own sources.

With its increasing global importance, the Chinese government has made parallel efforts to control the internet. It was said that the 2010 budget for its internal police force to monitor online activities exceeded that of its defense budget (Forsythe 2011). The Chinese government has always displayed a highly cautious attitude towards 'dangerous' information, therefore both the physical network and the web content are under continuous state scrutiny (Harwit & Clark 2001). The primary purpose of internet censorship is to suppress social unrest that could potentially lead to collective action (Orcutt 2012). In order to control potential social unrest, three major regulatory strategies that are applied to internet control have been identified (Yang 2006). The first is social and political control; examples include arresting cyber dissidents or directly censoring posts. The second is technological control, such as the filtering of keywords or blocking of websites. Internet filtering is the process by which users accessing the internet from a particular network are blocked from visiting certain Web sites. Filtering can be done at many levels, from the household level to the national level (Villeneuve 2006). Filtering is usually achieved by plugging "blacklisted" Web site addresses and keywords into the routers and software systems; therefore leading to China's Great Firewall—the phrase coined informally by internet users (MacKinnon 2009). The third strategy is psychological control, by accustoming citizens to the idea that they are always being watched, inducing in individuals self-disciplined and conformist behavior.

China continues to evolve legal processes of increasing control over the internet and its content, as well as citizen behavior on the internet. Self-censorship is an essential measure for internet regulation, which is often indirect. The Chinese authorities have pushed the internet content and service providers to be responsible for their content, otherwise face fines or closure. In other words, the Chinese government has outsourced some aspects of the censorship to the private sector. This takes the form of the government requiring signed self-regulation agreements for their online content, from Sina, Yahoo and other service and content providing companies (Kahn 2002). Thus, internet service or content providers must set up monitors to filter out content that may be offensive to the authorities, which is said to "walk a fine line" between publishing information for commercial success and filtering out information to be politically safe (Tai 2006, p. 101). In this sense, the Chinese government has adopted a regulatory strategy of implementing control at three levels: the state level, the middle level of the internet content and service providers and finally, at the individual level through the coercive power of the state (ibid., p. 103).

The strategies mentioned above are all based on technical and legal perspectives; however internet regulation is so sophisticated that the regulation of political, linguistic and cultural differences between nations should also be taken into consideration. The following section will discuss the development of the historically powerful and politically challenging internet platform, Weibo.

The Development of Weibo in China

The Nature of Weibo. The social media platform, Weibo has become the fastest source of news in China today. It is gradually dominating the way information spreads. Meanwhile, the agenda-setting on Weibo and the public sentiments expressed on it have played an increasingly influential role. Chinese netizens strongly embrace its potential role in exposing graft, officials' abuse of power, violations of the law and other ethical issues that can now easily become headlines in the traditional media thanks to netizens' efforts (Tong & Lei 2013).

On the 1st of February of 2011, a book titled *Microblog Changes Everything* written by Lee Kai-fu, the ex-head of Google, was released in China. It describes the powerful influence of microblogging. As noted, a microblog that permits instantaneous communication between individuals—called Weibo in Chinese, was launched in China in 2009 by one of the country's biggest web portals—Sina, a year after the 2008 Beijing Olympics. While Facebook and Twitter are not available in China due to its strict internet regulations for foreign-owned or foreign-controlled media, Weibo has provided a unique landscape for the Chinese people to express themselves.

Weibo has a handful of useful and immediate functions. While users are able to post pictures, videos and links just as on Facebook, its features of immediacy and high speed resemble Twitter. Launched in 2009, it has developed rapidly as an information exchange platform following the creation of blogs, and has become an important forum for public opinion in China. Weibo has been the subject of much scholarly attention, comparing its power and agility with the previous media technologies likened to "digital throwbacks to the analogue succinctness of telegrams" (Murthy 2012, p. 780). According to Lee Kai-fu (2011), Weibo's function is more informative and hence, more powerful than its Twitter counterpart. While a limit of 140 English letters allows only one or two sentences, 140 Chinese characters can deliver more and richer information. Compared with Twitter, Weibo has many other advantages. Its functions enable its interaction and community building between its users, a significant reason for the rapid growth of users (ibid.). One of the great advantages of Weibo is its reposting function. If one likes a post, one may click the repost button and send it to one's followers. Therefore, Weibo influence can be far-reaching. A popular saying claims that, if your followers exceed 100, your influence is equal to that of an internal publication. Likewise, if your followers exceed 10,000, your influence is equal to a magazine. But if your followers surpass 10,000,000, you can be regarded as a TV station (Yan & Yu 2011). With the nature of high speeds and low costs, Weibo has demonstrated its great potential in social mobilization and mass incidents.

Moreover, once a blogger's identity is verified, it will attach a 'V' after the blogger's name, which means verified. Therefore, once a 'V' is seen after a celebrity's name, they know this is a real celebrity, not a fake. For this reason, some bloggers tend to be verified to increase their authenticity. Internet celebrities become famous due to the popularity of their content. Their "celebrity" status is measured by internet search results, page views of their sites, media coverage, and Weibo followers. Many internet celebrities have millions of followers and some write provocatively about sensitive social and political issues to spark discussion, thus influencing the ideas of the followers and the direction of certain events. Thus a group of influential and well-known microbloggers has emerged with diverse backgrounds, such as businessmen, scholars, lawyers and journalists. Many have fans exceeding millions, but by far the most popular microblogs among Chinese netizens are those created by Chinese celebrities and movie stars. To follow their idols, increasingly more netizens are opening Weibo accounts. Therefore, active recruiting is part of the host companies' strategy to increase the number of accounts so as to boost revenues from commercial advertisements.

Weibo answers the question "what's happening" without the limitations of time and place. Even basic mobile phones have access to Weibo. Importantly, messages posted on Weibo can be accessed by the broader public, thus the person posting the message and its audience do not have to know each other. This type of feature can mobilize like-minded individuals quite easily, therefore, differing from the traditional social network sites.

There are four popular Weibo services in China: Sina Weibo, Tencent Weibo, Souhu Weibo and Netease Weibo. Among them, as noted, Sina Weibo is the most popular with the largest population of Weibo users. It is important to note that, when Chinese people say "Weibo" they are commonly referring to Sina Weibo. Sina is one of the biggest commercial internet corporations in China with close relationships to the government (Bandurski 2014). For the government, Sina is considered an 'insider' and is therefore easy to control. For the users, it is a commercial institution and has market credentials. This dual identity has enabled the Sina microblog service to monopolize the microblog market (Tong & Lei 2013).

In order to analyze the state regulation of Weibo, it is important to examine Sina Weibo, and its close liaison with the Chinese party-state. Twitter has achieved great success in Western society, and was also initially available in China; however after large-scale riots in Xinjiang in mid-2009 it was unable to formally enter the Chinese market for fear of dissemination of dangerous content (Wauters 2009). Thus the Chinese government decisively blocked Chinese netizens' access to Twitter. However, the great potential of the technological market, induced Chinese internet companies to emulate Twitter and to introduce a number of domestic microblog service providers initiated by Fanfou, an independent microblog service website. Soon after, other websites such as Jiwai, Digu and Zuosha followed in Fanfou's footsteps to enter the market between April and July of 2007. These non-approved microblogs were soon censored and blocked. Moreover, the reason that these early attempts never gathered momentum was largely because they preceded the arrival of the smartphone revolution, which would make social media so pervasive (Bandurski 2014). The iPhone launched in November 2007 and the Android platform, the following year.

Soon after the previously mentioned microblog platforms were shut down in 2009 because of the lessons learned from other countries, the Sina Corporation, the largest Chinese internet portal, was permitted to open its own microblog service, Sina Weibo, in late 2009, with its relatively close links to government enabling a much broader Weibo account usage. As noted, Sina Weibo is subordinate to the Sina Corporation, which is an economically significant company running the Sina web portal, one of the most popular websites in China and offering a range of blogs and news services. Its relations with the government have been described as a "cadre-capitalist alliance" (Lagerkvist 2006). The Sina Corporation enjoys the support of the state and at the same time, complies with state regulations, for example, working closely with the state authorities to filter search results and block unwanted information.

It is also noteworthy that new audience configurations have been produced by Weibo and other social media. Every individual has groups of 'friends' or 'fans' who are able to see their continually changing updates as Weibo automatically circulates updated information to audiences. The audience make up is constantly changing. Significantly, Weibo has broken the traditional modes of one-to-one or top-down communications, instead, producing an asymmetric mode of one-to-many. The "fan" also covers a range from close friends to celebrities. In terms of content, Weibo has embraced everything from the individual level to the national level, individual life, social news and political news. In 2012, Weibo administrators implemented a rigorous measure—the real-name registration (RnR) system requiring audiences to register with their real names or other identity numbers to the service provider for government verification. Unregistered users can only view posts but cannot create content. Student-run internet discussions experienced tight control during the SARS crisis, for example, and the eliminating of anonymity allowed audiences a voice without fear of punishment by authorities (Weber & Jia 2007, p. 784). These control measure ensure that the participants closely adhere to Party orientation and promote social bonds especially on political criticism and sensitive topics.

Weibo's Power. Weibo has indeed given the masses "a tantalizing taste of power" (Sainsbury 2012). It has proven its capacity to initiate wide discussions about issues of various sorts that may be ignored by traditional media (Tong & Lei 2013). This gives rise to the question of whether this new space for public discussion and public scrutiny of those in positions of power and privilege, could be described as a public sphere. Some assert that the internet and its related technologies hold the potential to produce a public sphere, and the rise of online activism indeed confirms the political uses of the internet and the idea that civil society in China is gradually evolving (Sullivan & Xie 2009; Yang 2009). There is no doubt that with new media features such as easier access to alternative sources of information and its potential to break down the hierarchical information flow, Weibo has indeed transformed previous communication. It often breaks down the boundaries, whereas in the past, internet use had been strictly confined within the social and political limits set by the party-state.

Despite the fact that people use Weibo in many ways in their daily activities, such as individual entertainment, social interaction and commercial activities as with Twitter and other social media used in Western countries, Weibo is also a potential channel for netizen's expression of views on social and political incidents. Weibo has also been used to expose social problems and injustices; the government then follows the online chat, sometimes with a corrective impact on government policies. Therefore, many dramatic incidents have been first exposed through Weibo posts, especially in recent years. Examples of this are easily found. According to the Public Opinion Research Centre of Renmin University of China, the internet incidents that most stimulate the frayed nerves of netizens or society are outlined in eight categories, such as corrupt officials or social inequality, but generally focus on the constant development of social conflicts (China News 2009).

Since its emergence, Weibo has been widely used for a variety of purposes and has provided millions of users a platform to voice an unprecedented diversity of opinions on national events and beyond. One striking example is how it has demonstrated its immense power of mobilization in assisting to save abducted children. The Weibo campaign in China to find abducted children started in 2011, initiated by Yu Jianrong, a rural expert with the Chinese Academy of Social Sciences, in the form of a snapshot microblog, in which netizens collect and share photos, information and clues on the internet to fight kidnappers. In the campaign, Weibo users directly post images on Weibo, and these images are circulated numerous times with Weibo's forward function, one of Weibo's innovative functions. This campaign attracted hundreds of thousands of followers within a few weeks, and various government agencies also became involved. Finally, many missing children were found.

In another example of the power of Weibo, in October 2010, a 22-year-old man named Li Qiming, driving a car, struck and killed one person and injured another on the campus of Hebei University. When arrested, Li Qiming yelled out to the angry crowd that had gathered, "Go ahead and sue me, my father is Li Gang". Li Gang was the Deputy Director of the local police department. This event quickly stirred a public outcry on Weibo, with millions of online comments. "My father is Li Gang" quickly became a popular internet expression referring to the misdeeds of the privileged second generation children of officials, as China's netizens believed that the events reflected the arrogance of these offspring of powerful figures. Li was finally punished appropriately. The punishment was clearly attributed to the dramatic outcry assisted by the rigorous discussions on Weibo.

In a similar example, in February 2013, the arrest of Li Tianyi on a charge of gang-rape sparked a tremendous debate on Weibo. Netizens wrote with great anger about his behavior. Li Tianyi is the son of a Chinese General, Li Shuangjiang, a 72-year-old senior military official known for his patriotic songs. Li's mother, Meng Ge, is also a well-known singer in the China's People's Liberation Army (PLA). Many Chinese followed the case closely, shocked by the behavior of the children of China's elite. Finally, the 17-year-old Li Tianyi was sentenced to 10 years in jail in September of 2013. Public opinion was said to have influenced the outcome of the trial, given the long history of light sentences previously handed out to children of the elite. Many such cases have been documented in the scholarly literature and media reports from within and outside China.

In addition, many other stories from all over the country appeared on Weibo, including forced demolitions, police violence, toxic plants, corruption scandals and even reports of propaganda bans. In January 2013, an event later dubbed the "Southern Weekly New Year's greeting incident" took journalists from the traditional printed news press to Weibo (Gao 2013). *Southern Weekly*, a newspaper based in the southern province of Guangdong respected for its investigative journalism and relatively liberal voice in the Chinese media sphere, published its annual New Year's special editorial on January 3, 2013. But it was found that the original content of the editorial was interfered with significantly by the Propaganda Department officials of Guangdong Province and several errors were shown in the paper. The issue evoked strong dissatisfaction among newspaper staff towards the years of government censorship, and inspired them to issue statements on Weibo to protest, demanding the resignation of Tuo Zhen, the propaganda chief of Guangdong province. Weibo users rushed to post messages about *Southern Weekly* in an effort to thwart online authorities. Newspaper staff then went on strike to protest against censorship, and gathered tens of thousands of advocates outside the Southern Weekly headquarters holding up signs demanding freedom of expression and constitutional rights. On Sina Weibo, numerous users posted and reposted messages about this incident as well as open letters, petitions and other support, both for the paper itself and for free speech. Some statements were signed by hundreds of journalists, lawyers and students demanding freedom of speech (ibid.).

In addition to functioning as a public expression platform, Weibo sometimes serves as a news resource. With its unmatched technological access, on some occasions, the traditional media have adopted pictures or sources from Weibo. With its special features, social incidents based on sporadic reports on traditional media or from casual "chats" on social media, could occasionally transform into big events on Weibo.

This behavior has a precedent, and as the *Christian Science Monitor* reports: "The government's tight control of the internet has spawned a generation adept at circumventing cyber roadblocks, making the country ripe for a technology-driven protest movement" (Morozov 2009, p. 10). It is also illustrated that even major Western news organizations such as CNN get information from social networking and social media sites including Twitter. Furthermore, just as Twitter has been considered a powerful media outlet or a 'microphone for the masses' (see Murthy 2012), the professional media has become more tolerant and open in acquiring breaking news from tweets.

Demographic Analysis of Weibo Users. Since its introduction in 2008, Weibo has developed into a major channel of public opinion within a very short time. This technology has widely permeated in Chinese society, as illustrated by its growth figures. 2010 was considered the "inaugural year of Weibo", and since then it has become the first choice for the Chinese netizens as a site on which to disclose and disseminate information, and has profoundly changed the conventional agenda-setting method. Stories include forced demolitions, land acquisition, environmental protests, official corruption, police violence and many other public crises. According to the *2010 China Weibo Annual Report* released by Shanghai Jiao Tong University (SJTU), eleven of the top fifty significant public events in China were originally reported on Weibo (China.org.cn 2010). It was said that Weibo has quickly replaced other online forums and blogs to become the primary site for public discussion on the internet. In 2011, China entered a stage of explosive growth in Weibo usage, with the number of users rising by over 296 percent in 2011 to 250 million users, an increase from 63 million at the end of 2010. In other words, within one year, almost half of Chinese netizen populations were using Weibo (CNNIC 2012). From 2012 onwards, Weibo users increased steadily, and China became the country with the greatest number of social media users, 274 million by the end of June of 2012 (Liu 2012). Weibo has consolidated its leading position in the communication process, by fulfilling a variety of public needs, including entertainment, leisure, social interaction and commercial activities, steadily drawing large and diverse audiences.

By June 2013, Chinese Weibo users reached a peak of 331 million as increasingly more agencies and public figures made use of this platform for public discussion. Although there is still no completely accurate number of regular users of Weibo, within the entire population of 1.4 billion, 331 million is still a relatively small number and therefore cannot be seen as representative of the whole population. This fact must be considered when drawing conclusions about the extent and impact of Weibo users in creating or contributing to a potential public sphere.

There are also further aspects to Weibo usage which must be taken into account when calculating its impact, not the least its abilities to diminish reputations through scandal. According to the *2013 Annual Report on Development of New Media* (Tang et al. 2013), one third of Weibo's most discussed issues are rumors. Weibo experienced a significant shift in December of 2013 with both scale and frequency of use declining to 281 million. This was attributed to two reasons: one, poor social network marketing; the other, the impact of competitors (CNNIC 2013). The number of Weibo users continued to decline in 2014. Some scholars specializing in China's social media have even migrated from Weibo to another new online platform, WeChat, which connects individuals and creates smaller, more intimate communities than Weibo (Bandurski 2014). However, Weibo continues to be valuable in other respects, particularly in the fields of public opinion management, user behavior predictions and network marketing (CNNIC 2014). Based on the existing data of Weibo development, it is therefore significant to examine how Weibo is utilized by the Chinese government for public opinion management and to consolidate control, as will be shown in the following chapters.

However, the CNNIC reports do not provide a breakdown of demographic figures of Chinese Weibo users. Therefore, the data on Weibo users is principally drawn from the *Annual Report on Development of New Media in China* (2010–2017), which is a series of annual reports written and edited by the Institute of Journalism and Communication of the Chinese Academy of Social Sciences. This is viewed as a credible source in China that compiles annual research results on new media, comprehensively tracking new media developments and publishing at the forefront of new media investigation. From its first report in 2010 to now, the *Annual Report on Development of New Media in China* has provided a detailed analysis of the demographic features of Weibo users for eight years. It is notable that each year's report also offers predictions on China's new media, a clear indicator of the government's future focus. This section collects and analyses the data from the annual reports to look at the demographic structure of the Weibo users in China, including differences in gender, age, education, occupation, income and geographic locations, which are outlined below.

A. Gender and Age Composition. Similar to the current overall gender division among Chinese netizens, the number of male Weibo users is roughly equal to that of females. Thus, gender disparity is not a significant factor in the use of Weibo. The dominant age group of Weibo users across both genders is 10–39 years, accounting for approximately 80 percent of the total users, which means that young people have an absolute advantage. Although this group is low education-based in general, the 10–39 age group also includes university students and young professionals, such as journalists, artists and political activists who are more outspoken on social media and likely to have significant influence. Therefore, this age group is still crucial in the Weibo sphere in public expression.

B. Educational Background and Income Disparity. People with lower than high school level education make up approximately three quarters of users. Only an estimated 20 percent of Weibo users have attended college or have any higher education. This is consistent with the Chinese Academy of Social Science report that "over two thirds of internet use in China concerns entertainment, and…the main preoccupation of the educated urban-dwellers who are the bulk of internet users is the enjoyment of consumerism" (Castells 2009, p. 285). The pursuit of democracy in China's new media landscape is, as Castells suggests, the concern of "a tiny intellectual minority". Other scholars contend that Weibo is an apolitical space where popular topics are mainly entertainment based (Sullivan 2012). Weibo users tend to show more concern for everyday life matters such as health, employment or food safety rather than state or international politics, although according to the *2013 Annual Report on Development of New Media* (Tang et al. 2013), there was an intense debate about constitutional issues in May 2012. However, the number of comments on this issue was only 2.25 million. By contrast, the number of comments on employment issues was 24.57 million, the number of comments on pension issues was 23.73 million, medical issues, 47.97 million, and even the socially "hot topics" of the offspring of officials and the rich elites, totaled 41.64 million. These statistics remind us that the internet today is the site for expression of diverse interests, not all of them rationally expressed. The fact that Weibo is only accessible to a small fraction of the population produces a virtual public space that does not however, in key respects, meet the fundamental criteria of a public sphere. This will be analyzed later in this book.

As to the income of users, low income and "no income" groups are the majority, with over 90 percent of Weibo users said to be earning a monthly salary less than 5000 yuan (US$ 833). This is understandable because the majority of users are students, supported by their parents. But it also appears that the mainstream Weibo users are not necessarily the expected middle-class demographic.

C. Occupational Structure and Geographical Locations. At the same time, Weibo users also have a diverse occupational background, including government officials, entrepreneurs, experts, migrant workers and famers. However, students make up the largest group, constituting about one third of users, presumably because students have more leisure time and have the basic internet knowledge to regularly access Weibo.

From a geographical perspective, it has been reported that Weibo users are mainly concentrated in the economically developed eastern regions such as Beijing and Shanghai, as well as first or second-tier cities (categorized according to importance in political, economic and other social activities). This geographical skewing of users towards the urban further reinforces Weibo's lack of representativeness of the whole nation. The concept of the "digital divide" still applies, with many Chinese from rural areas excluded from accessing Weibo because of poor infrastructure, low incomes and even lower literacy rates.

In summary, Chinese Weibo users overall present the characteristics of less educated citizens, youth-oriented, on low incomes and concentrated in the big cities. This certainly does not represent the entire Chinese population. Based on a random sampling approach to representative and reliable statistics on Chinese microbloggers to examine regularity of usage, one study finds that 57.4 percent of the accounts' timelines are empty (Fu, Chan & Chau 2013). It is plausible that many Weibo users simply surf Weibo without producing content, that is, without personally engaging by entering into the discussion. Among the 12,744 samples, 86.9 percent had not made an original post in a seven-day study period. The study showed that a significant portion of Weibo accounts are inactive in terms of contribution, and only a small group of microbloggers were responsible for creating a majority of content and for engaging the attention of other users.

Typological Analysis of Weibo Users. In comparison with other country's online counterparts, Chinese netizens are more eager to consume and to produce information online (Yang 2009), and Weibo, which is tailored for the Chinese market, is able to attract many participants. Compared with previous media such as bulletin board systems (BBS) and blogs, Weibo has particular advantages, such as its two-way interactive communicative modes. Using Chinese celebrities as its earliest growth strategy for marketing, Sina Weibo has attracted increasingly more registered users. A number of individuals and agencies have opened Weibo accounts including celebrities, politicians, ordinary people, net stars, government staff, public intellectuals, businessmen and media agencies. No matter what kinds of benefits Weibo brings to them, as a platform for communication, it is able to fulfill their requirements. I will provide a typological analysis of the Chinese Weibo in this section to show that Weibo has been widely acknowledged for its potential benefits to all levels of society: at the individual, organizational and national levels. These benefits can be categorized into seven types based on the author's content analysis, while acknowledging that this type of categorization may not be absolute. In a short period of less than a decade, Weibo has been widely adopted by the public for various purposes.

A. Individual Use—Ordinary People. As noted, on this platform, individuals are able to upload 140-character posts, along with pictures, video clips, music and links. Other users can then repost, share or comment on these posts. Some Weibo users use it as a platform for informal chatting, sometimes sharing intimate details of their personal life. One can read other people's posts without becoming friends with those people. Therefore, it is quite convenient for people to read others' posts and share information. Others talk about politics and current affairs. Still others use it for organizing political and social campaigns, and Weibo has demonstrated its immense power for mobilization.

B. Individual Use—Celebrities. Sina Weibo has a bigger fan base than any other social media outlet in the world. Its earliest strategy was to attract celebrities, including movie stars, public intellectuals and businessmen, who are able to attract wider audiences. More and more celebrities started to use Weibo for its potential value to them, such as communicating with their fans and for self-promotion. Celebrities are from a range of backgrounds, including international movie stars such as Jackie Chen, Zhang Ziyi, and Jet Li; sports stars including Yao Ming and Tian Liang; and business elites, like those of Pan Shiyi and Ren Zhiqiang. Even some foreign stars such as Tom Cruise and Justin Bieber joined Weibo in order to interact with fans in China. Celebrities often post their life pictures and thoughts on Weibo to have a more personal interaction with fans. Hence, Weibo has become an important source of entertainment news.

Some celebrities not only offer personal information to the audiences on Weibo, but also actively comment on current events. Yao Chen, a high-profile and award-winning actress in China, is such an example. Yao has more fans (analogous to "followers" on Twitter) on Weibo than anyone else in China with over 32 million. She has had many prominent television roles in China, including as a communist spy in the series Lurk and White-collar Girls, which made her a household name and is appealing to advertisers. However, she has devoted much of her energy to people's welfare and has provided online advocacy for them, including issues such as stolen children, poverty and exploited migrant workers, which has made her a grassroots icon and attracted a number of followers.

C. Domestic and Foreign Organizational Use—Education. Many educational organizations also implement a strategy of marketing on Weibo to amplify their influence. Weibo has been used by universities, such as the School of Management at Fudan University, to engage with the public and promote its programs, which often have close connections with enterprises and high-level executives. Meanwhile, Weibo has also been used by foreign universities for marketing and promoting: many Australian universities for example, have a presence on Weibo for a number of beneficial reasons. Universities use Weibo to post program information, including awards, presentations and important events. They use Weibo to build alumni connections, so encouraging alumni and former staff to get involved. It also helps with public engagement, building rapport and relationships with the targeted students for potential recruitment.

In this way, Weibo has indeed facilitated globalized communication between individuals and organizations.

D. Domestic and Foreign Organizational Use—Commerce. As with other media, Weibo has become a major boon for businesses. There have been many enterprise accounts on Weibo in recent years. In addition to its thought-provoking functions and public information, Weibo offers a convenient way to promote corporate brands and products to China's rapidly expanding economy and society, and is the fastest way for companies to conduct marketing and advertising. It is also seen as an effective way to reach consumers in less-developed cities and rural areas.

With China's burgeoning consumer-oriented middle class, international fashion and luxury brands are beginning to grasp this potential. Some foreign companies see Weibo as a good opportunity to promote brands in the Chinese market and to directly communicate with their target customers. Weibo also provides a platform for the companies to monitor and detect public opinion about their brands so as to provide immediate feedback.

E. Domestic and Foreign Organizational Use—Non-Government. The development of Non-Government Organizations (NGOs) in China over the past three decades has been very rapid (Morton 2005). China's rapid economic development has brought huge economic success while also incurring serious problems and social challenges. Hence, the Chinese government encourages the participation of NGOs to deal with these problems. The One Foundation, founded by actor Jet Li in 2011, is a public fundraising foundation which claims to be independent. The One Foundation has actively used Weibo to amplify its influence and good public image. For example, after the devastating earthquake that shook Ya'an on April 20, 2013, the foundation received wide public support and sent many volunteers to assist with search and rescue efforts. At the same time, the One Foundation proactively uses the Weibo platform to collect donations in emergencies. It frequently releases detailed contribution information on Weibo to improve its transparency. In addition, in such emergencies as the earthquake, it interacts frequently with the public to participate in resettlement efforts.

As well as domestic NGOs, a number of international NGOs have also registered on Weibo, including the World Health Organization (WHO) and the International Committee of the Red Cross for health promotion.

F. Government Use—Chinese Government Weibo Site. The first official government Weibo site was established by the provincial government of Yunnan in November 2009 (PDPOM 2011). Within a few years, the number of government Weibo sites increased rapidly. Government Weibo sites now exist across the country from peripheral areas to metropolitan cities, though the government online activities are more active in bigger and richer provinces (ibid.). Different agencies including public security organs, health departments and government organs at various levels, environment departments and judiciary departments have all opened Weibo accounts. But more than one-third of all government Weibo sites are maintained by offices and agencies responsible for public security (PDPOM 2013). For example, Ping'an Beijing (Safe Beijing), which is maintained by the Beijing Municipal Public Security Bureau, has a large number of followers.

G. Foreign Politicians' Use of Weibo. Weibo has also been a useful communications tool for foreign politicians. For example, some Australian politicians have embarked on public relations strategies to build a bridge with local Chinese communities. Though statistically speaking, their efforts are on a small scale (Jiang 2013); their influence is profound in its ability to create a better public image and to strengthen mutual understanding with a rising China. For example, former Australian Prime Minister Kevin Rudd joined Sina Weibo to reach out to Chinese people (ibid.). Kevin Rudd frequently posts comments on Weibo and has attracted tens of thousands of "fans". As a Mandarin Chinese speaker, Mr Rudd signed off as "Lao Lu", or "old Lu", an intimate way to address veteran workers in China. His Chinese name is widely known as Lu Kewen, which was adopted by him during his student days at the Australian National University (The Sydney Morning Herald 2012).

Conclusion

This chapter lays out the background of the social media to be examined in this book. The development of the internet and Weibo has indeed penetrated every aspect of Chinese people's lives, contributing significantly to an era of emancipation and empowerment within some parts of Chinese society. It could be argued that for these social sectors, Weibo has enabled multiple versions of the public sphere. At the same time, the Chinese government has ceaselessly developed the internet since the 1990s for its own purposes, both expansionary and regulatory. However, the long-term effect of China's internet regulation remains to be seen. Therefore, it is significant to examine the parallel tracks of internet development and control in China, not only because it is the country with the world's largest population and is a rising political and economic power, but because of the government's "ambivalence" towards the democratizing aspects of internet and social media. This paradox was first proposed by Tai (2006) as the theoretical model of "fragmented authoritarianism" to capture the changing dynamic between the role of mass media in Chinese society and the government control of information.

The ever-increasing number of netizens shows that the Chinese people rely heavily on the internet and Weibo, in particular. However, when analyzing the demographics of Weibo users, the dimensions of gender, education, income and age all play an important role in determining whether Weibo users constitute a sufficient number, and a coherent user base, to be considered participants in a public sphere. Some analysts are not predicting a strong future for Weibo, due to declining usage, fragmentation of information and a growing lack of interest by users in general content (Wu 2013), and suggest that Weibo's "carnival era" may be ending. But in fact, Weibo has been considered as an important and dynamic battleground by the government to regulate new media and guide public opinion (Tang et al. 2014).

Beyond the bureaucratic regulatory apparatus and apparent blockade of certain non-domestic services, the Chinese government keeps pace with information regulation on the internet. The regulatory measures, ranging from passive monitoring to active regulation (discussed in Chapter Four), reflect the underlying government strategies behind these strategic processes. In this way, the theory of governmentality is particularly helpful to illustrate the changing role of the authorities in the regulation of the internet and Weibo. While it is true that Weibo has been allowed greater openness, freedom and interactivity than other internet and social media sites, the overall strategy of the authorities, seen through a lens of governmentality as formulated by Foucault, is one of strategic instances of openness within a larger framework of control.

As a public, interactive information platform, Weibo has the unique advantage of offering instantaneous communications to citizens who wish to express their public opinion, or eye witness accounts of major events, a function which is playing an essential role in changing the pattern of China's communication ecology (Tang et al. 2014). As social media increasingly penetrates all walks of people's lives, including social, political and commercial fields, it is argued that the next ten years will be a critical period for the development of new media in China. In this process, an essential measure from the authorities' point of view is ensuring safety and security for new media by further strengthening overall planning and official oversight. This point was affirmed by the establishment of the Central Network Security and Information Technology Leading Group on February 27, 2014. Therefore, in dealing with the challenges to China's national security posed by social media, and Weibo in particular, the Chinese government has gradually adopted an overall strategy to regulate and participate in social media in order to ensure overall security. The next chapter will therefore explore the Chinese government's adaptive regulatory measures towards Weibo, evolving from the strict controls of the past to a more fluid and evolving set of regulatory responses.

References

Abbott, J. 2001, 'Democracy@ internet. Asia? The challenges to the emancipatory potential of the net: Lessons from China and Malaysia', Third World Quarterly, vol. 22, no. 1, pp. 99–114.

Bandurski, D. 2014, 'Anti-social media: How China's censors stay one step ahead of freedom', Global Asia, vol. 9, no. 2, pp. 16–25.

Callaghan, G. 2009, 'Remembering Tiananmen', The Australian, 15 May, viewed 22 September 2014, <http://www.theaustralian.com.au/news/remembering-tiananmen/story-e6frg6n6-1225712617852>.

Castells, M. 2009, Communication power, Oxford University Press, Oxford.

China Daily. 2003, 'Sun Zhigang's brutal killers sentenced', China Daily, 10 June, viewed 20 April 2013, <http://www.chinadaily.com.cn/en/doc/2003-06/10/content_168514.htm>.

China News. 2009, 'Analysis on the eight hotspots of the network public opinion', China News, viewed 25 June 2013, <hotspotshttp://www.chinanews.com/gn/news/2009/03-26/1619940.shtml>.

China.org.cn. 2010, 'Micro-blogging increasing rapidly in China', China.org.cn, 30 December, viewed on 20 May 2014, <http://www.china.org.cn/china/2010-12/30/content_21643214.htm>.

CNNIC. 2012, 'Statistical reports on the internet development in China, the 29th survey report', January, viewed 2 July 2014, <http://www.cnnic.net.cn/hlwfzyj/hlwxzbg/201201/P020120709345264469680.pdf.>

CNNIC. 2013, 'Statistical reports on the internet development in China, the 32th survey report', July, viewed 2 July 2014, <http://www.cnnic.net.cn/hlwfzyj/hlwxzbg/hlwtjbg/201307/P020130717505343100851.pdf>.

CNNIC. 2014, 'Statistical reports on the internet development in China, the 33th survey report', January, viewed 4 July 2014, <http://www.cnnic.net.cn/hlwfzyj/hlwxzbg/hlwtjbg/201403/P020140305346585959798.pdf>.

CNNIC. 2018, 'Statistical reports on the internet development in China, the 41st survey report', January, viewed 24 January 2018, <http://www.cnnic.net.cn/hlwfzyj/hlwxzbg/hlwtjbg/201801/P020180131509544165973.pdf>.

Diamond, L. 2010, 'Liberation technology', Journal of Democracy, vol. 21, no. 3, pp. 69–83.

Ferdinand, P (ed.). 2000, The Internet, democracy and democratization, Frank Cass, London.

Forsythe, M. 2011, 'China's spending on internal police force in 2012 outstrips defense budget', Bloomberg News, 6 March, viewed 20 September 2011, <http://www.bloomberg.com/news/2011-03-06/china-s-spending-on-internal-police-force-in-2010-outstrips-defense-budget.html>.

Fu, K-W, Chan, C-H & Chau, M. 2013, 'Assessing censorship on microblogs in China: Discriminatory keyword analysis and the real name registration policy', IEEE Computer Society, vol. 17, no. 3, pp. 42–50.

Gao, H. 2013, 'A press renaissance? The legacy of China's "Southern Weekend"', The Atlantic, 11 January, viewed 22 September 2014, <http://www.theatlantic.com/international/archive/2013/01/a-press-renaissance-the-legacy-of-chinas-southern-weekend/267081/>.

Hachigian, N. 2001, 'China's cyber-strategy', Foreign Affairs, vol. 80, no. 2, pp. 118–133.

Harwit, E & Clark, D. 2001, 'Shaping the internet in China: Evolution of political control over network infrastructure and content', Asian Survey, vol. 41, no. 3, pp. 377–408.

Hu, Y. 2010, 'Micro-revolution: From Twitter to Sina Weibo', New Weekly, p. 315.

Jiang, Y. 2013, 'The use of Weibo to connect Chinese communities in Australia by Australian politicians', Asia Pacific Public Relations Journal, vol. 14, no. 1 & 2, pp. 69–84.

Kahin, B. 1997, 'The U.S. national information infrastructure initiative: The market, the web, and the virtual project', in Kahin, B & Wilson, E (eds.), National information infrastructure initiatives: Vision and policy design, The MIT Press, Cambridge, MA, pp. 150–189.

Kahn, J. 2002, 'China toughens obstacles to internet searches', The New York Times, 12 September, viewed 10 October 2013, <http://www.nytimes.com/2002/09/12/international/asia/12INTE.html>.

Lagerkvist, J. 2006, The Internet in China: Unlocking and containing the public sphere, Lund University, Lund.

Lee, K. 2011, Weibo gaibian yiqie (Microblog: Changing Everything), Shanghai Caijing University Press, Shanghai.

Liu, S. 2012, 'China tops world in microblog user numbers: Report', Global Times, 9 October, viewed on 20 June 2014, <http://www.globaltimes.cn/content/737076.shtml>.

Lu, W, Du, J, Zhang, J, Ma, F & Le, T. 2002, 'Internet development in China', Journal of Information Science, vol. 28, no. 3, pp. 207–233.

M2 Presswire. 2011, 'Research and markets: Rising use of internet spurs growth in online advertising market in China', M2 Presswire, 15 September, viewed 30 June 2013, <http://www.m2.com/m2/web/page.php/contactus>.

MacKinnon, R. 2009, 'China's censorship 2.0: How companies censor bloggers', First Monday, vol. 14, no. 2.

MacKinnon, R. 2011, 'China's "networked authoritarianism"', Journal of Democracy, vol. 22, no. 2, pp. 32–46.

Morozov, E. 2009, 'Iran: Downside to the "Twitter Revolution"', Dissent, vol. 56, no. 4, pp. 10–14.

Morton, K. 2005, 'The emergence of NGOs in China and their transnational linkages: Implications for domestic reform', Australian Journal of International Affairs, vol. 59, no. 4, pp. 519–532.

Murthy, D. 2012, 'Towards a sociological understanding of social media: Theorizing Twitter', Sociology, vol. 46, no. 6, pp. 1059–1073.

Orcutt, M. 2012, 'A peek behind China's 'great firewall'', MIT Technology Review, 13 June, viewed 15 July 2013, <http://www.technologyreview.com/view/428170/a-peek-behind-chinas-great-firewall/>.

Pan, P. 2006, 'The click that broke a government's grip', Washington Post, February 19, viewed 23 September, 2013, <http://www.washingtonpost.com/wp-dyn/content/article/2006/02/18/AR2006021801389.html>.

Papacharissi, Z. 2002, 'The virtual sphere: The internet as a public sphere', New Media & Society, vol. 4, no. 1, pp. 9–27.

PDPOM. 2011, '2011 nian Xinlang zhengwu weibo baogao (2011 Report on Sina Government Microblogs)', <http://wenku.baidu.com/link?url=yCLmhf9zqfbL1DYksZBOBBvNHkhHeZitgenfOueLYakrvfvpdNQYNN4fDyHooiQr8M2Mf54tuh1YeFkVI3UrPGk9EzK0VBqXjYsdR9nx9zO>.

PDPOM. 2013, '2013 nian Xinlang zhengwu weibo baogao (2013 Report on Sina Government Microblogs)', <http://yuqing.people.com.cn/n/2013/1226/c210118-23952286.html>.

Qi, Y. 2000, 'The current situation and prospect of Chinese information resources on the Web', Social Science Computer Review, vol. 18, no. 4, pp. 484–489.

Richburg, BK. 2011, 'In China, microblogging sites become free-speech platform', The Washington Post, viewed 22 May 2013, <http://articles.washingtonpost.com/2011-03-27/world/35260490_1_weibo-free-speech-posts>.

Sainsbury, M. 2012, 'Weibo giving the masses a tantalising taste of power', The Australian, 22 October, viewed 3 July 2013, <http://www.theaustralian.com.au/media/weibo-giving-the-masses-a-tantalising-taste-of-power/story-e6frg996-1226500238244>.

Shane, PM. 2004, Democracy online: The prospects for political renewal through the internet, Routledge, London.

Sullivan, J. 2012, 'A tale of two microblogs in China', Media, Culture & Society, vol. 34, no. 6, pp. 773–783.

Sullivan, J & Xie, L. 2009, 'Environmental activism, social networks and the internet', The China Quarterly, vol. 198, pp. 422–432.

Tai, Z. 2006, The Internet in China: Cyberspace and civil society, Routledge, New York.

Tang, X, Wu, X, Huang, C & Liu, R (eds.). 2013, Annual report on development of new media in China 2013, China Social Sciences Academic Press, Beijing.

Tang, X, Wu, X, Huang, C & Liu, R (eds.). 2014, Annual report on development of new media in China 2014, China Social Sciences Academic Press, Beijing.

The Sydney Morning Herald. 2012, 'Rudd's latest game of Chinese whispers: Join Weibo', The Sydney Morning Herald, 23 April, viewed 22 September 2014, <http://www.smh.com.au/federal-politics/political-news/rudds-latest-game-ofchinese-whispers-join-weibo-20120422-1xfdh.html>.

Tong, Y & Lei, S. 2013, 'War of position and microblogging in China', Journal of Contemporary China, vol. 22, no. 80, pp. 292–311.

Villeneuve, N. 2006, 'The filtering matrix: Integrated mechanisms of information control and the demarcation of borders in cyberspace', First Monday, vol. 11, no. 1.

Wan, W. 2014, 'Chinese President Xi Jinping takes charge of new cyber effort', The Washington Post, 27 February, viewed on 20 July 2014, <http://www.washingtonpost.com/world/chinese-president-takes-charge-of-new-cyber-effort/2014/02/27/a4bffaac-9fc9-11e3-b8d8-94577ff66b28_story.html>.

Wauters, R. 2009, 'China blocks access to Twitter, Facebook after riots', TechCrunch Daily, 7 July, viewed 15 March 2013, <http://techcrunch.com/2009/07/07/china-blocks-access-to-twitter-facebook-after-riots/>.

Weber, I & Jia, L. 2007, 'Internet and self-regulation in China: The cultural logic of controlled commodification', Media, Culture & Society, vol. 29, no. 5, pp. 772–789.

Wong, Poh-Kam. 1997, 'Implementing the NII vision: Singapore's experience and future challenges', in Kahin, B & Wilson, E (eds.), National information infrastructure initiatives: Vision and policy design, The MIT Press, Cambridge, MA, pp. 24–60.

Wu, C. 2013, 'Weibozoudaoshengsicunwangjiaochakou (Weibo has come into an intersection between life and death', Beijing Business Today, July 17, viewed 2 April 2014, <http://www.bbtnews.com.cn/news/2013-07/17000000252410.shtml>.

Xiao, Q. 2011, 'The battle for the Chinese internet', Journal of Democracy, vol. 22, no. 2, pp. 47–61.

Yan, J & Yu, W. 2011, 'How should government officials respond in the microblogging era', Banyuetan (Half Monthly Talk), viewed 5 May 2014, <http://sms.banyuetan.org/yqsm/yqyd/110711/47024.shtml>.

Yang, G. 2006, 'Activists beyond virtual borders: Internet-mediated networks and informational politics in China', First Monday, special issue #7, <http://journals.uic.edu/ojs/index.php/fm/article/view/1609/1524>.

Yang, G. 2009, The Power of the internet in China: Citizen activism online, Columbia University Press, New York.

Yu, H. 2009, Media and cultural transformation in China, Routledge, London and New York.

Zhai, I. 2012, 'Crackdown begins on microblog activities in China', South China Morning Post, viewed 21 May 2013, <http://www.scmp.com/article/719736/crackdown-begins-microblog-activities>.

Zheng, Y. 2008, Technological empowerment: The Internet, state, and society in China, Stanford University Press, Stanford.

· 4 ·

TRANSFORMATIVE REGULATORY MEASURES OF WEIBO

Introduction

Since the rise of the internet, countries including China have embraced it widely for various purposes. The internet has exerted immeasurable impact on the cultural and political spheres of almost every nation. China is not alone in applying what can be seen as a double standard towards the internet, using the technology to promote its economy, while carefully monitoring its use and ultimately retaining tight control over information flows. Even the world's most seemingly democratic nations like the USA or Germany still have limits on what the internet is allowed to do, finding ways to persuade, patrol and police cyberspace (Gerhards & Schäfer 2010). Similarly, other authoritarian countries such as Cuba also accept the principle that internet technology will bring benefits in priority areas while using it as a platform for close monitoring of political activities instead of overtly cutting their country off from the internet (Sun 2010, p. 3). Within Asia, countries such as Malaysia and Singapore observe a similar principle (Diamond 2010; Lee 2010).

Since the internet continues to offer the potential for online protest and threats to governance, the Chinese authorities remain vigilant as to whether such virtual activism serves simply as a harmless outlet for venting resentment or as a means for potentially mobilizing anti-government protests in the street. The Chinese government has over time built an elaborate system of internet regulation, restricting information flow from outside China and closely monitoring information inside the country. The notorious Great Firewall was erected in 2003 as a virtual boundary, as a part of what the Ministry of Public Security called the "Golden Shield Project" that started in 2001, drawing a dividing line between Chinese cyberspace and the outside world. In addition, the Chinese authorities have established a comprehensive system of filtering keywords which have the potential to cause instability. For example, social media sites such as Twitter, Facebook, and YouTube have already been blocked by the Great Firewall off and on for several years. Rather than a single firewall, the Great Firewall consists of a range of regulatory measures, including the use of human agents overseeing specific sites.

The history of Weibo may be short, but its expansion has been breathtaking in scale and impact. With political stability of primary importance to the Chinese authorities, especially after the 'Occupy Wall Street' movements and the Arab Spring uprisings, potential social protests have become a serious issue for the government giving the Chinese leadership a vital stake in regulating information. In response, the authorities have developed multiple tools for regulating online information, moving beyond the Great Firewall. The Chinese state's disciplinary information-regulating technologies are therefore no longer simply illiberal strategies, such as internet censorship or arrest. This study examines the Chinese state's evolving role in information regulation through its proactive and selective application of new technology. It aims to illustrate in a more nuanced way, the changes in the ongoing centralized political dominance of the CCP over Weibo, based on new styles of regulatory practices developed to address the particular challenges of Weibo.

Chinese internet censorship has received a great deal of attention in the international media, from Western governments, and from the international human rights community and increasingly from academia. With the increasing importance of Weibo in the daily life of the Chinese people, it is necessary to explore how the Chinese Communist Party specifically responds to and regulates Weibo among other social media. This chapter reviews previous research on both regulatory control and government functioning to explore how a soft-authoritarian mode of control (Roy 1994) has emerged over Weibo.

This chapter therefore offers a socio-cultural and historical account of how the Chinese government has governed Weibo from the advent of the internet to the present participatory era known as web 2.0. It focuses on the government's efforts to develop new and sophisticated regulatory methods in response to the Weibo era. In the early stages of Weibo, the state took a number of authoritarian measures such as hard censorship to tighten its control of Weibo with the purpose of maintaining strong control over this medium. There was clear oversight over information relating to potential political activity. However, the nature of Weibo's challenges, specifically its instantaneous communication leading to large scale responses, required the government to adopt more sophisticated control measures than ever before. Admitting the power of the internet to bypass political control, the chapter shows how the Chinese government has been perceptive in introducing legislative measures and other oversight techniques specifically to regulate Weibo. It examines how online interventions and manifestations of government are really about providing internet users with degrees of carefully structured freedom, while at the same time tightening the more permanent and potent structures of political regulation.

Recent years have seen a new relationship develop between the CCP and Weibo, a new negotiation between the state and the citizens. The relationship between the government's active use of Weibo and its conventional regulatory strategies for controlling Weibo is supplementary rather than oppositional in the sense of traditional regulations. China's information control regime has necessarily adapted to Weibo, creating an entirely new state of play between the controllers and the controlled. In order to illustrate the changes that have led to this situation, this chapter will firstly examine China's traditional internet controls, regulations and protocols and then review their evolution in response to Weibo. Finally the chapter will explore the outcomes of this more sophisticated version of state control. In summary, this chapter will draw a panoramic view of social media in China, while carefully investigating its continuously updated censorship methods.

Early Conventional Weibo Regulation in China

The rise of social media and the widespread dissemination of information through Weibo aroused unexpected management pressures on the Chinese government (Tong & Lei 2013). In response, the Chinese authorities developed a variety of measures to maintain control, with three types of long-standing censorship of expression identified in Chinese social media (King, Pan & Roberts 2013): The first of these is the previously mentioned Great Firewall, which, while blocking access to information flow into China, did not place new restrictions on the expression of the Chinese people, as they could easily find alternative media platforms through which to express themselves. The second measure to regulate the flow of information on social media was "keyword blocking", which had only very limited effect on freedom of speech as netizens were still able to use other subtle forms of expression such as analogies, metaphors or satire. Beyond the first two barriers to freedom of speech, the third measure involves censors reading and manually removing information that they find objectionable.

Since the arrival of social media, the Chinese government has continued in its efforts to control the medium. Recently the authorities issued a number of severe legal measures to prevent the spreading of irresponsible rumors and to threaten offenders. For example, in August 2013, a well-known online commentator, Charles Xue, was put under administrative detention by Beijing police for alleged involvement in prostitution. With more than 12 million followers on Sina Weibo, Xue, a Chinese-American venture capitalist, admitted that being an internet celebrity had made him feel like an emperor. He admitted to spreading irresponsible internet posts because "the army of supporters who blindly defend me made my vanity expand and I spread some irresponsible information which misled the users" (Xinhua Daily Telegraph 2013). To illustrate his power, he said that a simple post asking for donations for a particular cause could draw more than a million yuan (US$13,000) in less than a week. In addition, Xue had "cooperated" with an environmental expert—Liangjie Xia, to spread fabricated information supposedly in the name of science on Weibo, thereby expanding Xia's popular influence on the sale of water purification products.

On August 20th, 2013, two influential web figures, Qin Zhihui (Known as Qin Huohuo in cyberspace) and Yang Xiuyu (known as Lierchaisi in cyberspace), were detained by Beijing police on criminal charges for "starting quarrels and provoking trouble" and "illegal operation of a business" (Beijing Times 2013). Initially they had spread a series of rumors on Weibo to attract attention and to build an increasing number of followers. In March 2010, Qin and Yang launched a lucrative business called the Beijing Erma Interactive Marketing and Planning Company (for which no website could be found). This was a Chinese "water army" (*shuijun*) company paid by other companies to artificially generate grassroots online activity for their benefit. Erma's client services included web marketing, creating scandals or events and deleting negative comments from online forums. Qin and Yang successfully fabricated scandals including accusations that the government had given a large sum of money as compensation to a foreign passenger who died in the '7-23' Wenzhou bullet train crash on the 23rd July 2011. Qin explained his industry strategy later: you need to "rock" netizens and make them feel as if they are acting as judges in an "unjust society" (Thomas 2013). On April 17 2014, they were sentenced to a 3-year jail term with two years on a defamation charge and another year for affray.

According to a judicial interpretation of the criminal law issued by China's highest court and prosecutor on September 11, 2013, social media users would be charged with defamation or a possible three-year prison term, if posts which contain rumors or offensive content are re-posted more than 500 times or viewed by at least 5,000 internet users; several detentions on this basis have since been reported as the government cracks-down on the spreading of rumors (Kaiman 2013). This campaign was initiated as President Xi Jinping's newly installed government stepped up its harassment of dissidents, showing signs of reinforcing the Party's grip over the internet (ibid.).

Arrest has been another typical longstanding form of censorship. For example, on September 17, 2013, a 16-year-old junior school student from Tianshui, in the north-west of China's Gansu Province, was arrested because of a number of his posts on Weibo, generated great debate. The official reasons for the arrest of this student were that he had used Weibo to spread rumors inciting people to disturb the social order, seriously interfering with public security (China News.com 2013). In his posts, the student questioned an unnatural death case in which some facts may have been officially concealed. As Tai (2006, p. xix) states, in China, there is no judicial independence, therefore, courts sometimes collude with government officials. Chinese netizens may question what they perceive as unfair by taking issues into the 'virtual court of appeal' on the internet, thereby influencing public opinion. It is noteworthy that all the posts written by the junior school student used question marks to express uncertainty. Therefore, after the boy was arrested, many mainstream media reported on and remarked on this case, questioning the legitimacy of this arrest.

Apart from the direct arrest of cyber-dissidents to demonstrate control over the internet, the Chinese government has also waged a "guerrilla war" (Bandurski 2008) against these dissidents. One of its strategies in this war has been the use of China's growing armies of Web commentators, known as the Fifty Cents Party, which involves individuals receiving 50 cents in Chinese currency for each anonymous message they post supporting the government (Shirk 2011). These messages create the impression that the tide of social opinion supports the government, therefore encouraging the public to conform to these views, so presumably reducing the possibility of oppositional collective action (ibid.). The commentators of the Fifty Cents Party are said to be trained and financed by Party organizations to have only one mission: to safeguard the interests of the Communist Party by infiltrating and policing a rapidly growing Chinese internet (Bandurski 2008). The strategy of deploying commentators to try to neutralize undesirable public opinion and to disseminate pro-state propaganda illustrates a shift from direct control of information to management and manipulation of information, "from simple repression and propaganda to an increased use of spin" (Abbott 2013, p. 8). In addition, it is said that there are two million 'internet opinion analysts' employed by the authorities to monitor China's vast online population (Boehler 2013). These 'internet opinion analysts' mostly consist of government employees whose task is to dissect public opinion on local issues and to identify accusations of corruption and poor governance by trawling through blogs, microblogs, and social networks via text messages and written posts and social networks (ibid.). This method of deploying thousands of internet "police" in many cities is only one of the weapons used by the Chinese government in its battle to control the Chinese people's hearts and minds (Xiao 2007). The practice of hiring these commentators was allegedly started by local governments who had found it hard to control public opinion. They could not rely on Beijing to monitor and block every single piece of news about their localities, so they came up with their own solution (Bristow 2008).

More recently though, a variety of specific censorship strategies have been initiated targeting Weibo. First, the service provider, Sina Weibo's computer system scans each Weibo post before it is published. As a result, for example, it is impossible to find on Weibo, the name of Ai Weiwei, the globally recognized artist, who was detained by the government for more than a month because he used Twitter to voice his dissatisfaction with the present state of the country. Nevertheless, a collection of his blog posts and Tweets has recently been published in book form for Western audiences (Ai 2011). However, Weibo users are automatically prevented from posting politically sensitive words such as "Ai Weiwei". When you enter this name as a keyword in the search engine, it will generate the message such as "According to relevant law and policy, the result of 'Ai Weiwei' is not shown".

The second channel to censor posts is through blocking a successfully uploaded entry from being viewed by others or Weibo may delete an entry several hours or days after the manual after-post censoring process.

On several occasions, the censored posts are adorned with pictures of Jingjing and Chacha, internet police cartoon characters which pop up on users' screen on various web sites. These images provide links to the internet police section—the Public Security Web site. Whenever people find any illegal information online, they can click to this site to report it. In 2007, these two animated cartoon figures, Jingjing and Chacha first appeared as the cartoon mascots of the Public Security Bureau's Internet Monitoring division: their names play on *jingcha*, the Chinese two-character phrase for police.

There has been much discussion on when and why content is blocked on Sina Weibo. Findings show that outlying areas such as Tibet or Qinghai provinces, normally risk more censorship than eastern areas like Beijing. Additionally, in these areas, "sensitive terms" are more likely to be deleted over varying time intervals. It could be as immediate as four minutes or as long as four months (King, Pan & Roberts 2013). However, compared with posts that criticize the leadership, the Chinese government shows more concern over texts that could be inciting collective action. In other words, negative posts that criticize the state and the leaders are more often tolerated by the censors. Censorship intervention focuses more on "curtailing collective action by silencing comments that represent, reinforce, or spur social mobilization, regardless of content" (King, Pan & Roberts 2013, p. 326). Sometimes both criticism of the government and the advocating of collective action are censored (ibid.). Following the Wenzhou high speed rail crash, for instance, internet content providers were asked to censor any critical postings (MacKinnon 2009).

Though the state has been implementing a variety of severe regulatory measures on Weibo since its inception, ranging from direct deletion, the arrest of those posting inappropriate material, or countering 'attacks' by the Fifty Cents Party, the strategies for managing this site have evolved significantly. Such an evolution was necessary to match Weibo's ever-evolving information technologies, which enabled Chinese citizens with creative means to bypass official censors, such as using homonyms or metaphors to evade control, therefore creating flaws or loopholes in the state regulatory mechanism. Strategic information control on Weibo becomes more significant with respect to sensitive topics related to politics and the government, as Weibo users tried a number of ways to express themselves at these moments (Sullivan 2012). In this way, the authorities allow certain conversations on approved topics to continue online, while deleting or blocking posts and other information it deems detrimental to the CCP's ability to rule (Young in Chen 2006). Despite diverse strategies by Weibo users to bypass control, the government counters with regulatory strategies to uphold its overriding interest in maintaining political stability. The biggest challenge arises through collective actions of the public; therefore the government chooses different control strategies in response to varied social media content that could be viewed as challenging state power. These censorship strategies may be very direct as each measure is still subject to direct control, or they may take the form of "technologies of power", which position individuals in relation to the dominant power (Foucault 1991). While censorship measures have been long-standing in China, more recently (and triggered by Weibo), the authorities have developed a new era of censorship measures that are much more sophisticated. Apart from the well-documented conventional strategies of control such as censorship and increased monitoring, the Chinese government also uses more subtle but potentially more effective ways to continue to exert influence over social media in order to reinforce control (Weber & Jia 2007, p. 772), as the old-style regulation system cannot work as effectively for internet censors to deal with Weibo's services that process enormous amounts of information (ibid.). Hence, China's industrious internet censors have to develop new tactics. In the next section, this study will examine increasingly subtle means of soft control over social media in what Foucault (1988a) calls the "technologies of the self", whereby individuals regulate their own behaviors through autonomy or self-restraint.

It is obvious that the primary role of the government in the early stages of Weibo was purely and directly one of regulating information control. Gradually, the state's tactics in managing Weibo have become much softer, so appearing to be more liberal. As the next section illustrates, the government also proactively utilizes and involves itself in Weibo to carry out certain activities that it wants to make public. In order to better communicate with the public, for example, government agencies set up institutional Weibo accounts; therefore, in addition to (but separately from) its authoritarian measures to regulate Weibo, it uses the same forum to apply what appear to be liberalizing strategies to openly communicate with the public.

Transformative State Control Through Weibo

Government Application of Weibo. Since the flourishing of social media, many countries have used it for various purposes, with the emergence of Weibo in China, in particular, providing a platform for individuals to comment freely on events, to transmit their views instantaneously and in the process, to exercise their citizenship. An indication of the seriousness with which the Chinese government views Weibo, and the opportunities it presents, is the expanding number of Weibo accounts held by Chinese officials. In the current mobile and pluralized society, Weibo appeals to the Chinese government in a number of ways. It serves as a release valve, allowing the public to "let off steam", or it can channel public discourse to support the government's policies and agendas, or even increase government legitimacy by building a more open and responsive image.

Facing the power of the rebellions seen in the Arab Spring, states including China have still not prohibited the spread of new communication technologies; rather, they have taken a proactive attitude. The rapid development of social media applications (e.g. twitter or microblogs) is helping the US and Canadian governments to better communicate with their peers and citizens, positing Government 2.0 as the new shape of government (Reddick & Wigand 2010; Eggers 2007). China is no exception. Alongside these evolving state measures to exercise greater control over social media content, there has also been increasing evidence that the internet can also be a powerful tool to accomplish the government's own goals—a tool that the state can employ in its ongoing public relations efforts, which knowing cyber analysts at the China Media Project have dubbed the "Control 2.0" mode of keeping order online (Bandurski 2010). The Chinese party-state has currently made every effort to integrate Weibo into its new public management strategy (Noesselt 2013a, 2013b).

Social media tools have been increasingly adopted by the government for various purposes, for example, governments harness new technologies to enhance information exchange with citizens, while local governments in America use different kinds of social media to communicate with residents to support better preparation for emergencies. Police departments use Weibo to share information with their peer departments and to communicate with netizens to acquire clues to break cases and in response to emergencies (Eggers 2007; Heverin & Zach 2011). This method is also adopted by the Chinese government, with an increasing number of government agencies and officials opening Weibo accounts to allow a channel for interacting with citizens. Government Weibo accounts have been registered by officials and departments to deal with a wide range of matters, such as public security, publicity, justice, education and sports. Among the various government agencies, police departments from various levels have emerged as the most active players in opening Weibo accounts.

Government Weibo has spread widely and rapidly in China over the past few years. In Shanghai, Fudan University's "Public Opinion and Communication Research Lab" in 2011, implemented the first domestic "China's Government Weibo Research Report", which notes that government Weibo sites are those related to government and public affairs (Zhang & Jia 2011). Since the launch of government Weibo in China, it has played an increasingly important role in the field of providing information in emergencies, setting public issues, gathering social resources and generating public opinion. The year 2011 was labeled "the year of government Weibo in China", with "microblogging politics" becoming a popular trend. The rise of government Weibo has helped to improve the responsiveness and transparency of governance. Because of its efficiency and improved service, some officials' influence has been greatly improved. In the meanwhile, the Chinese authorities are willing to use government Weibo as a watchdog to monitor the officials' behaviors at different levels, particularly at the local level. It is seen by the government as better to identify the problems in advance and to try to fix them before they give rise to popular unrest.

The government also uses Weibo to mobilize social support for its own advantage. Due to the increasing influence of Weibo, the Party leadership must pay attention to public comment. Weibo is indeed a barometer for the public mood. As noted, an awareness of the importance of Weibo in information dissemination and its widespread influence has seen many Chinese authorities open Weibo accounts for their own purposes. The Chinese government has changed its tactics to make good use of the platform to achieve maximum influence. Increasingly more government agencies and officers reach out to citizens through Weibo by sharing information, gaining feedback and building relationships with stakeholders (Wigand 2010). The government is always seeking more effective uses of this platform. It increases its use of the site as an arena in which to communicate with the public because it benefits both Chinese society and its people by promoting transparency within the government. If 2011 was the year of opening Weibo accounts for government departments, then 2012 was the year of using Weibo to interact with the people (Zhu, Shan & Hu 2011). For example, nationwide police forces used hundreds of Weibo accounts to urge people to protest peacefully during the Diaoyu Island dispute earlier in 2012.

Traditionally, the Chinese government treats the media as its 'throat and tongue'; similarly, the government has taken the same attitude to Weibo. It has been highlighted in the report that the "Weibo national team" has risen since 2012, with the "mouths and throats" of the Xinhua News Agency, People's Daily, CCTV and other central media constantly opening Weibo accounts and trying to dominate the "micro discourse" of Weibo (Tang et al. 2013). From 2012 onwards, the Xinhua News Agency opened Weibo accounts such as @Xinhua View, @Xinhua Europe. The People's Daily followed suit, opening an account, @People's Daily, whose followers have exceeded the subscription number of the People's Daily.

In scrutinizing the use of Weibo by government officials and departments, it appears that the government's goal in using Weibo in this way is twofold, not only to make the governing process more convenient, but to emphasize the government's commitment to build a more effective bureaucracy and a more transparent government.

Additionally, certain internet incidents have shown that online exposure of social issues by Weibo users can lead to the government reversing decisions, with officials occasionally even arrested and charged with corruption. At this point, the government has the same goal as the citizens. The purpose is to help the government to realize its goal of becoming a transparent government within the framework of what is helpful for government control and political stability. Since top provincial officials are appointed by the central government, it is necessary for the latter to know whether the local officials perform their jobs well, as the poor implementation of policies and provision of social goods could stir up public resentment and threaten the CCP rule. The responses by the central authorities to Weibo users' exposures of wrongdoing by these provincial officials could thus be categorized at two levels: firstly, they address the problem, and secondly, they exercise a governmentality approach which "start(s) by asking what authorities of various sorts wanted to happen, in relation to problems defined how, in pursuit of what objectives, through what strategies and techniques" (Rose 1999, p. 20).

Such examples of the decline in the credibility of the government is increasingly a subject of government concern, therefore there is increasing public discontent towards it, as a report published on public opinion by the People's Daily Public Opinion Monitoring office (PDPOM) in December 2011 shows. In this way, social conflicts among different social strata have been increasing, owing to the government credibility crisis and the global financial crisis. Therefore, the government must become more transparent and responsive to public demands, and government Weibo should serve as a bridge between the government and its citizens (Zhu, Shan & Hu 2011).

In addition, PDPOM has published detailed and comprehensive reports examining government Weibo every year since 2011 (PDPOM 2011, 2012, 2013). It offers an annual outline of the use of Sina Weibo by government agencies and individual Party cadres. Generally speaking, government Weibo has been widely used by a variety of government agencies and departments, including police, transport and public health. It compares government Weibo use by officials on a geographical basis, and according to levels of officials' seniority, as well as by agency. It draws conclusions about the successes and lessons learned from government Weibo. As it says, government Weibo is currently spread all over the country, however, online activities and applications are more diverse in big cities and richer provinces (PDPOM 2012).

It is important to note that the application of government Weibo varies among different sectors. As far as the police Weibo account is concerned, its early adoption is associated with the size of government, internet penetration rate, regional competition and learning and upper-tier pressures (Ma 2013). It also indicates the size and power of the police presence. By the end of October 2012, a total of 100,151 government Weibo accounts were opened, with 66,830 government sites and 33,321 sites of government officials. The Chinese state dramatically increased its use of Weibo platforms to interact with the public in 2013 (PDPOM 2013). In addition to previously established sites by government departments, courts and prosecutors, committees of local people's congress and political advisory bodies, it is noteworthy that a total of 77 Central Party ministries opened Weibo sites as well. It is an echo of government policy that government at various levels should actively explore the use of government Weibo to disseminate information (ibid.). According to the PDPOM annual report there are also rankings of the most influential Weibo sites by government agency and by specific officials, including the number of followers, volume of posts and the effectiveness of communication. From these figures and the efforts they reflect, it is reasonable to conclude that the Chinese government intends to play a very active role in making government Weibo a ubiquitous feature of politics in China.

The figure below indicates the rise in government Weibo and the breakdown of sites by agency and individual official.

By December 2012, the number of official Weibo accounts had risen to 170,000 on Sina Weibo. Compared with past propaganda modes, Weibo encourages interaction between the government and the people and empowers the people with a greater space for expression (People.cn 2012). This has shown that the Chinese government has become far more adept, responsive, subtle and versatile in its approach to information control (Noesselt 2013a, 2013b).

This had been announced in 2010 when the government issued a White Paper saying that it would make full use of the internet for developing education, alleviating poverty, conveying state information and providing services to the public (ibid.). Among these fruitful activities, posting official advice on Weibo is the first step for the government in effectively using this platform, where it simultaneously allows microbloggers to provide advice to the government.

At the end of 2012, three predictions were made regarding its developing trends: 1) Government Weibo will become more scientific and more standardized compared with that of 2012, which could still be characterized as somewhat of an experimental phase for government Weibo. More standardized Weibo practices would be seen in 2013 with the implementation of rules and standards on how to use Weibo appropriately. 2) Government Weibo is intended to become more youth-oriented. Young people are clearly the majority users of Weibo, therefore the operators of government Weibo accounts should strive to better harness the participation of energetic and passionate youth. This would change the style and operational procedures of government Weibo accounts. 3) Government Weibo would expand into new areas; therefore there would be a vast increase in Weibo usage both at the high level of government ministries and at the very grassroots level (see People.cn 2012). In 2013, in terms of quality, it was expected that "government Weibo" would expand further into new areas such as industry and administration, to expand the government's provision of information and to strengthen the social management of innovation.

Government Weibo to Improve Transparency. As mentioned, the use of government Weibo has a number of purposes, and one of the primary purposes is to improve transparency. During the huge transition of the Chinese socio-economic change, notable social disparities have emerged; therefore, social stability and public safety are highly emphasized in China. During the early era of e-government, some scholars doubted the potential and progress of China's e-government to 'serve the people' (Zhang 2002). In the current Weibo era, the Chinese government has in fact progressed significantly in better serving the people by openly recognizing the importance of online public opinion. In June 2010, it issued a white paper on the internet in China, stating that "the authorities attach great importance to social conditions and public opinion as reflected on the internet, which has become a bridge facilitating direct communication between the government and the public" (see Yang 2011).

The effectiveness of this commitment to two-way communications between government and the public has been strongly reflected on the Weibo sites of local governments. The government's emphasis on the state's agenda-setting role is true to the original e-government project, which declared agenda-setting as its most important role (Zhang 2002).

On August 22, 2013, the so-called "trial of the century" of the former top politician, Bo Xilai, was carried out by the Intermediate People's Court in Jinan, in eastern China's Shandong province. Bo was charged with bribery, embezzlement and the abuse of power. While trials of Party officials have usually been held in secrecy, these trial proceedings, remarkably, were broadcast live online on Sina Weibo, for the first time in Chinese legal history. Despite certain critiques that the "real-time" Weibo broadcast was actually selective and not genuinely real-time, it is nevertheless noted by China's official media outlet, the People's Daily, as an example of "historical transparency and of the openness of China's rule of law" (Zhang 2013). This five-day trial attracted more than 590,000 followers on Weibo, and it is extolled as a significant benchmark for social media's role in increasing transparency in the Chinese justice system, at least when it comes the trials of Party officials (ibid.).

In the process, Weibo broke down the previous bureaucratic modes of communication, and it was helpful for the government to gather public opinion in response to the trial. Central government takes overall responsibility and oversight for social stability and political legitimacy on the international stage, serving to monitor and curb local government behaviors. Therefore, Weibo is a forum of "transparent technology", which creates new possibilities for exposing and challenging the abuse of power, and for monitoring the abuse of power. The use of Weibo in this way also offered a means of simultaneously prioritizing while limiting and defining the message and the policy behind it. This tactical use of technology by the Chinese government, of co-opting a public communications space, is a remarkable example of governmentality, as conceptualized by Foucault. The Weibo broadcast becomes a tactic of governing, designed to shape the hearts and minds of the Chinese to conform to desired cultural and political molds (Foucault 1988a, 1988b). It embodies the notion of governmentality, defined as "the calculated direction of human conduct and behavior" (Dean 1999, p. 2).

According to the statistics noted earlier, approximately half of the activated government Weibo sites are launched by police departments, which steadily account for the top ten prestigious government Weibo sites (Zhang & Jia 2011). The launch of police Weibo may contribute significantly to sharing information with their peer departments, enabling the government to rebuild its social image and retrieve and consolidate public trust during emergencies. For example, in releasing and exchanging information with peer departments and citizens it assists the police to acquire clues that can resolve cases, and it helps to solve long-standing social problems such as saving abducted children (often boys), which has been discussed in Chapter Three.

Fighting Corruption in Order to Improve Its Image. Weibo can also help the government to weed out corruption and to produce more sophisticated propaganda. Preventing corruption strengthens the government's legitimacy, while smarter propaganda is able to improve the government's image. Some scholars have noted that the central government actually allows ordinary people to expose the corruption of ordinary officials (China.org.cn 2013), because the moderate governance of corruption can help to restore the deteriorating image of the Party and to maintain social stability, which is consistent with government interests. In this way, providing a further example of public online scrutiny of a group previously protected, Weibo has been used to bring corrupt government officials to account. Zhou Jiugeng, the director of Nanjing's property bureau, was fired after pictures of him appeared on the internet in 2008 wearing an expensive Vacheron Constantin watch, a luxury purchase assumed to be beyond his salary. On August 26, 2012, the wrong doings of Yang Dacai—an official in Shaanxi province appeared online. His behavior sparked an outcry when pictures posted on Weibo showed him smiling while visiting a traffic accident site where 36 people had died. This was followed by images showing that he was also wearing a luxurious watch that critics considered he would not have been able to afford on his salary. Chinese internet users discussed his alleged corruption on Weibo and other online forums, requesting the local government dismiss Mr Yang, after which, he was indeed sacked by provincial officials for serious wrongdoing.

Government legitimacy is the capacity of a government to justify its rules and increase their acceptance by the people (Gilley 2005). In the early days of the internet, the Chinese government promoted e-government projects and allowed a certain level of online participation in order to build legitimacy (Lagerkvist 2010; Boas 2006). In current China, by contrast, a variety of factors enable a critique of the regime's legitimacy, such as the strategically permitted rise of liberalism and increased exposure of social problems, such as corruption and social inequality, which diminish political legitimacy (Guo 2003; Wong 2004).

In 2013, a crash on one of China's new high-speed rail lines killed more than 40 people. The news was broken on Weibo by an eyewitness, which was followed by a furious online reaction to the government's handling of the crisis. Senior railway ministry officials resigned, and the then Prime Minister, Wen Jiabao, made a public apology. As this case embodies, the exposure of corruption on Weibo is an important element in this analysis, with a number of local officials having been forced to resign after being exposed on line. At the same time it illustrates how the central government can reassert its control over the governing authorities, which includes improving the quality of surveillance and the commitment to the elimination of corruption. It therefore illustrates a transformation in governance. The new technologies are powerful instruments for increasing transparency and accountability. In examples of new media events such as the 2013 train crash, a triangular relationship between media, citizens and government creates a new kind of power allocation mechanism. Such events ultimately transited from the new media platform to seize the avid attention of the traditional media. Hence, after such a fermentation period, it could be responsible for the formation of strong public opinion pressuring the government and urging officials to resolve problems immediately. Such a triangulation, from online witness-based media exposure to traditional media to government, could become a new path for the state's governance model.

In light of these developments, many government officials have opened Weibo accounts. Borrowing the concept of the *panopticon* as previously mentioned, the government officials are exposed to the public, and at the same time it is an effective measure to strengthen both supervision and a sense of self-regulation, with those online users uncertain of whether they themselves are being scrutinized in the process, so choosing to self-censor, just in case.

The Chinese government is not naturally the opponent of internet incidents, sometimes it tacitly favors them. Morozov (2011) argues that occasionally, online campaigns succeed precisely because the government sees the aims of such campaigns as being in line with the government's plans. Thus the Chinese state intends to take advantage of the power of the internet both to implement its politics and to prolong its rule. On some occasions the government and the citizens share the same interests and goals, such as in cases of online nationalism or anti-corruption efforts. Online activism and the government are not always in opposition, when society and the state are in accord. The current level of graft and embezzlement in China means that the leadership needs such collaboration more than ever (China.org.cn 2013). Faced with this challenge, the leadership is seeking to enhance the state's performance by developing a new concept of administrative work. President Xi Jinping launched an anti-corruption campaign shortly after taking over as China's leader and vowed to tackle both "flies and tigers"—meaning both top officials and lower cadres.

The problem of corruption is indeed a serious situation; even the People's Daily claims that:

> Although corrupt elements are only a small handful in the Party, they have seriously tarnished the image of the Party among the masses, adversely affecting the relationship of the Party with the masses and undermining general political stability for reform and development. (People's Daily 2013)

The government now allows more space for exposing various forms of malfeasance, such as corruption, so making visible the fact that the government has shifted to a "people-centered" approach to governance (Zheng 2008, p. xvi). The leadership has committed to fight corruption, especially since Xi Jinping became General Secretary of the Chinese Communist Party Central Committee. As noted, Xi invested much of his political capital in this initiative to root out the tigers (high-ranking officials) and flies (mid-level or junior officials). However, as scholars point out, the campaign against graft is basically a centralized high-level effort, which is costly and only occasionally yields results. Nevertheless, overall, the power of media and civil society working together is prominent in increasing transparency and reducing the costs of monitoring the bureaucracy (Pei 2014).

Civic Uses of Government Weibo for Publicising Information. The innovative and diffused adoption of Weibo by government has been affirmed by some scholars (Ma 2013). The proliferation of government Weibo marks another stage in the progress of China's e-government project, although it does not, as some suggest, mark any major or radical shift in the party-state's internet strategy (Noesselt 2013a, 2013b). The adoption of Weibo by governments could indeed be considered a straightforward approach as a form of technology for better governance. While many studies show concern over the application of new media technologies as part of e-government, the remaining chapters of this book explore the adoption of Weibo by the Chinese government as marking a change in the state's control methods. The background to this change is the tremendous socio-economic transformation from a central planned economy to a market-oriented economy from the late 1970s, which has greatly changed the philosophy and operation of the government.

The government websites are certainly used to provide basic information or to offer online services, but the emergence of Weibo, enabling government officials to gradually open Weibo accounts, has changed its previous style of interaction. The term "technologies" suggests a particular approach to the analysis of the activity of government interaction with and using Weibo in China. The primary factor here is to minimize the risk of weakening existing political control, while engagingly publicly online. On one level, as described earlier, government employs the internet to varying transparent ends. For example, police make use of Weibo to catch murderers in China.

At the same time, from another perspective, social media often assists authoritarian rulers in regulating civil society and stifling dissent. Weibo simultaneously contributes to a wider discourse that could make government more accountable. Noted author, Wen Huajian, author of China's first microblog novel, *Love in the Age of Weibo*, argues that "since Weibo, information in Chinese society has changed; it's become more transparent, more direct, and sensitive topics like the frequent clashes between residents and local governments over forced demolitions are widely debated on Weibo" (see Hewitt 2012). Examples could be found easily, such as the Yihuang self-immolation protest in Jiangxi province in 2010, which is another case of Chinese online public opinion changing the course of an event. To protest against the demolition, three Zhong family members set themselves on fire and jumped off the roof of their house. When two of their relatives tried to travel to Beijing to make their grievances heard by the central government, they were chased and stopped by local police. Hiding and locking themselves in the airport restroom, they called a reporter from Phoenix Weekly, who then made "live" broadcast of this incident, which attracted an audience of millions (Chan 2010).

With authoritarianism deeply-rooted in its polity, China lacks reliable mechanisms to take the public pulse on key issues. It must turn to the internet for help, where it is much easier to detect and gauge public opinion. On some occasions the online discourse of 'mass incidents' appearing on Weibo can reinforce government legitimacy. However, the impact of online communication on government legitimacy is relative and depends on specific cases (Tong & Zuo 2014).

On January 28, 2013, the Ministers of the Beijing Municipal Propaganda Department began requesting cadres to "use Weibo" and to make it actively play a positive role (PDPOM 2013). In the meeting, it reported that Beijing's internet development action would be developed and implemented, taking new media as a strategic basis on which to build a world-class portal. It was also requested that a management system based on real names would be introduced for mobile phones. The 60,000 people within the publicity team for Beijing were urged to make good use of the new media and to give positive guidance on the big issues of the day in connecting with the more than 200 million people outside the system (ibid.). This shows that the Chinese government wishes to adopt Weibo as a tool or technology to be utilized, as consistent with their own goals.

Forms of Control

Jiang (2010) adapted the concept of authoritarian deliberation from an offline environment to an online one to indicate the central role the Party plays in defining the boundaries of online discourse. It can also be described as a phenomenon of "networked autocracy", in which netizens have the freedom to post comments about social problems so that the central government will, it is hoped, react to solve them (MacKinnon 2010).

This book argues that the concept of governmentality underlies the Chinese authorities' regulation of Weibo, tactically emphasizing the active engagement of the subject in the process of government or governance, instead of being seen simply to exercise its sovereign power. This marks a shift from governance to governmentality. In other words, the government has multiple motives for engaging in social media and Weibo in particular: national prosperity, harmony, virtue, social order and above all, discipline (Rose 1996, pp. 134–135). As Dean (1999, p. 20) puts it, "rather than displacing discipline or sovereignty, the modern art of government recasts them within this concern for the population and its optimization (in terms of wealth, health, happiness, prosperity, efficiency), and the forms of knowledge and technical means appropriate to it". The essential aspect of government is as Foucault (1991, p. 95) states, the "introduction of economy into political practice", in other words, to bring an economic logic to the governance process.

These shifts have taken place over a number of years. In late 2007, Cai Mingzhao, a Vice Minister in charge of government information policy and regulation, emphasized that Chinese online media in all forms must "have a firm grasp of correct guidance, creating a favorable online opinion environment for the building of a harmonious society" (Bandurski 2007). In May 2012, in the China-Singapore forum "Leadership Development in the New Media Environment", Li Yuanchao, the then Central Organization Department Minister, stated that the Chinese government should adhere to a proactive, open and tolerate attitude towards the new media…and to continuously improving the ability to use the new media to strengthen public opinion, promoting social cohesion and consensus (People's Daily 2012).

Another of the multiple strategies for the regulation of internet use by the Chinese government adopts some highly discursive political terms to impact on the internet. Meanings regulate and organize conduct and practices: they help to set the rules, norms and conventions by which social life is ordered and governed. They are, therefore, what those who wish to govern and regulate the conduct and ideas of others seek to structure and shape (Thompson 1997, p. 1). Weibo control on mainland China is therefore not only carried out through various laws or administrative regulations, which are considered non-liberal practice in a non-liberal state; it is also carried out through liberal practice. Such liberal practice in a non-liberal state therefore reveals the change in government attitudes toward technology.

Obviously it is impossible for the government to have total control over every detail of the internet. While direct censorship of the internet is subject to much criticism, especially in annual human rights reports, attempts to exercise censorship become more implicit than explicit. This hints that the government controls Weibo not with a single method but through plural methods. That is to say, the government uses different strategies to regulate different types of content on Weibo. The following sections will examine such varied and subtle methods.

The Delegation of Censorship to Private Sectors. Apart from China's well known censorship efforts such as the Great Firewall, there are a number of "self-discipline" requirements for China's internet companies, and the government delegates a large part of the censorship and surveillance responsibility onto the Chinese internet private companies themselves (MacKinnon 2010). All internet and mobile companies are held responsible for everything their users post, transmit or search. McKinnon compares this with the rule of "intermediary liability" in America, where a service acts as an "intermediate" conduit (ibid.). Managers and employees of internet companies are also expected to censor user-generated content, though there is wide variation from company to company (MacKinnon 2009).

For the sake of security, Weibo service providers are asked to exercise control, and they "must establish an internal censorship department to filter sensitive posts" (Fu, Chan & Chau 2013, p. 43). For example, Sina, which owns Weibo, claimed in response to these government requirements, to have hired a thousand people to monitor Weibo (ibid.). On January 20, 2010, a joint statement called the "Public Pledge on Self-Discipline for Copyright in the Internet" was issued. In this document, companies such as people.cn, xinhua.cn, sina.com, china.com among other companies totaling 101 in Beijing alone, were addressed. It asserts that the internet service providers should shoulder a certain level of social responsibility, abiding by state press law and relevant policies in order to keep a healthy order of internet development (people.com.cn 2010).

Since it is impossible for the Chinese government to police millions of Weibo users, it has therefore delegated a censorship role to the private sector. According to the Washington Post, which obtained a list from one private company in China, journalist Philip Pan (2006) observed: "of 236 items on the list, 18 were obscenities, the rest were related to politics or current affairs." However, the "block list" is not handed down by the government, rather it is devised or understood by the companies themselves to censor and monitor user content in order to meet the government's expectations (MacKinnon 2008, p. 38).

In response to the government's request that companies censor information, every year internet executives are officially rewarded for their 'patriotism'. The rhetoric is all about the "strength and confidence of the Chinese internet" and "harmonious and healthy internet development" (MacKinnon 2010). This is very important because though the government regulatory bodies issue directives to companies on what kind of information should be controlled—it cannot guarantee 100 percent deletion of all suspect information and opinions, that is, this goal is unachievable on the internet (MacKinnon 2008), and the extent and the methods of censorship vary from company to company (Villeneuve 2008).

However, despite the advantages that the internet brings, such as enhanced social interaction, providing information services and greatly facilitating the exchange of views, it also brings problems, such as commercial fraud, malicious attacks and the spreading of rumors. Therefore, it should be realized that the network is not the land of the extrajudicial, because online words and deeds may intentionally or unintentionally violate the law; moreover, they may also cause personal or social harm. Regulation of this issue is the prerequisite to building the foundation of public order and good morals.

All of these measures, from a governmentality perspective, can be seen as undertaken by the government itself. In addition, government also requires the companies to play a role in "hard" censorship. Apart from the "outside" censorship carried out by internet police or other government officials, the internet companies are required to exercise censorship to delete or prevent certain information written by Chinese users from being published. Weibo operators, for example, are required to join in these control measures by the authorities both by the government and by companies to ensure that the search engines, chatrooms, forums and blogs to comply with government censorship. In other words, the Chinese government has de-centered or distributed some censorship power throughout Chinese society.

Self-Mind Control. In 2012, the Supreme People's Procuratorate, deputy Party Secretary, Hu Zejun, contended that the government should construct and use new media to seize the "commanding heights" of information dissemination (People.cn 2012). Foucault describes as structures of governmentality, the use of multiple procedures and the techniques, the art or knowledge that a government applies to promote willing compliance rather than directly employing brute force (Foucault 1991, pp. 102–103). In this way, the actions of subjects become voluntary.

The previously discussed Bo Xilai trial represents the new relationship between the Chinese government and Weibo, in co-opting the media platform to demonstrate its transparency and commitment to root out corruption, while using the platform to achieve a sophisticated political purpose. The Chinese government has therefore pre-emptively taken advantage of the new media to set the agenda ahead. In other words, instead of the traditional passive response to online protests, the Chinese government has learnt to seize the initiative in the battle with the citizens. The government uses social media not only to publicize Party principles, a traditional approach; a new level of government control emerges when the government defines this use of social media as a healthy internet culture. By implication then, what the government does not consider a healthy internet culture is dangerous to the participants. The government therefore expects users of social media to decide what a healthy internet culture is and to stay within those boundaries. This means the government adopts a strategy of personalizing mind control (the technologies of the self) in a completely new way.

At the same time, the government regularly issues regulations to tighten the government's grip on the internet while successfully transferring the responsibility to the users. These types of internet regulation are a kind of illiberal governmentality—where internet and social media users are directed into making preferred statements and choices via the legislative codes. These legal codes and policies are employed by regulatory authorities to "shape, normalize and instrumentals the conduct, thought, decisions and aspirations of others" (Miller & Rose 1990, p. 82). Several examples have emerged in the last few years. With the rise of internet celebrities, China issued seven bottom lines to promote social responsibility among microbloggers and to regulate online codes of conduct, namely that they would monitor:

1. Laws and regulations;
2. Socialist system;
3. State interests;
4. Citizen's legal rights;
5. Social and public order;
6. Morality;
7. Truth of information.

With a wide variety of information on the internet, the new seven bottom lines, according to the People's Daily, could "rectify the chaos of the internet full of saliva, rumors and violence" (Liu 2013). On August 10, 2013, the Forum on Social Responsibilities of Internet Celebrities was held in Beijing. The lead sponsor was the State Internet Information Office, an agency charged with guiding, coordinating and supervising online content management. The Director of the National Internet Information Office, Lu Wei, expressed "Six Hopes" for the internet, including that internet celebrities should shoulder more social responsibility, because their words and actions affect more people online; that network celebrities should consciously safeguard national interests, and actively play the role of contributing to national cohesion with positive energy, encouraging more users to contribute to the great rejuvenation of the Chinese nation (The Economist 2013).

In order to better regulate the online accountability of ordinary people, there are two ways in which the state has attempted to address it. The first is through education of those using the medium. One example of this strategy is the implementation in 2013 of the "Sixteen Opinions on Strengthening and Improving Ideological and Political Work of Young College Teachers", which is a document, issued by the central government to China's young university teachers, as a subtle way to show the proper use of internet tools and enhance the sense of responsibility in speech. A close examination of the "Opinions" reveals several restrictions that could potentially hinder the process of information flow and limit the freedom of speech with the purpose of promoting ideas of political identity and emotional identity in socialism with Chinese characteristics, which also uphold the "correct" political direction. For example, one piece of information from the "Opinions" is to make full use of television, campus networks, mobile news, Weibo and other channels to actively occupy the ideological and political work. The target is young university teachers, as they are an "important force in the development of higher education, as their age is close to students, therefore, they play an important part in influencing students' thinking and behaviors", according to the statement of the "Opinions". Facing difficulties in managing the implementation of the policies, the government has "adopted SNS [social network services] and combines these with the existing network resources, netizens and more channels to build a better electronic government for the rapid expansion of SNS in the future" (Tong & Lei 2013). While the Twitter revolution happens in some countries where state apparatus does not give full attention to this, most authoritarian states are now "moving in the opposite direction, eagerly exploiting cyberspace for their own strategic purposes" (Morozov 2009). The Chinese government has realized that it is an intellectual task to know how the internet fits the Chinese political and social environment. Twitter, which is not allowed in China, could be seen to some extent as part of these "agents of change" in the way the governments respond to postings (Morozov 2009, p. 12). This is an example of what Rose (1999, p. 4) contends: that in addition to the traditional practices of formal statements, documents and speeches, government practices attempt to frame conduct in a variety of ways to achieve larger objectives.

Since the Information Office of Yunnan Province opened the first provincial-level government Weibo in November 2009, soon afterwards, Xinjiang, Beijing and Shaanxi have also encouraged local government and government officials to open Weibo accounts (Ma 2013). The Vice Minister of Central Publicity Department, Wang Chen, expressed support for government Weibo, claiming governments should publicize the Party's principles and policies, actively "occupying" microblogging platforms to develop a healthy internet culture (Xinhuanet.com 2013).

As Rosen (2010, p. 510) argues, despite government control, internet users still "find ways to circumvent and subvert government restrictions". Chinese internet users have evolved sophisticated forms of political expression, including political satire and criticism of the state, without facing harsh repression (Esarey & Xiao 2008). As Yang (2009, p. 49) argues, in the evolution of the

Chinese internet-control regime, government control strategies have recently become more proactive, and (as this book argues), multilayered and governmentalized. In this new game, social media users adopt new rules in the new game. For example, they use different methods to bypass control. The widely seen cartoon creature called the "grass mud horse" (the name in Chinese is homonym for an expletive) as a way of protest. The word "river crabs" sounds very similar to the word of Hu Jintao's political philosophy harmony (*hexie*). This smart use of word play "has become an icon of resistance to censorship and this form of subversive expression and cartoon videos may seem a juvenile response to unreasonable rule" (see Diamond 2010, p. 74). As Yang (2009) notes, "online communities with strong collective sentiments…can generate effective offline action" (pp. 180–181), and "although democracy as a political system remains an ideal and not a reality, at the grassroots level, people are already practicing and experimenting with forms of citizen democracy" (pp. 220–221). The decentralized nature of the internet has the potential for the netizens to resist in a "safer" environment. Throughout his book, Yang (2009) shows how individuals have used a number of strategies to circumvent censorship and to play in a "world of carnival, community and contention" (ibid., p. 1). These strategies include a full range of satire, irony and parody against the state.

The internet itself is simply a technology, a medium which is neutral. Whether online activism succeeds depends on the outcome of the game between government and the citizens. On most occasions, it depends on the 'degree' to which material is accepted by the government. Weibo's new mode of communication has enabled, and it could be argued, required the government to update and evolve its traditional means of censorship. The way that government uses technologies to strengthen censorship of Weibo plays out often in discrete multiple procedures. A small and uncontroversial element of the process of governing can be particularly instructive (Colebatch 2002, p. 419). As Rose (1999, p. 31) argues, "it is, most often, at this vulgar, pragmatic, quotidian and minor level that one can see the languages and techniques being invented that will reshape understandings of the subjects and objects of government, and hence reshape the very presuppositions upon which government rests".

Conclusion: Beyond "Control 2.0"

Most governmentality literatures have focused on its impact on China's economic development in social lives in different fields. Nevertheless, the transformation of China's political system from the highly integrated and all-inclusive state to the empowering of local government authorities has significant implications for the understanding of information control and regulation of China's Weibo. Although the long-term effect of internet regulation remains to be seen on Weibo, ranging from technical restrictions of filtering to demanding that the internet service providers monitor content, to arresting individuals who violate the law, the ever-evolving information technologies make it possible for the authorities to keep pace with the varying tactics of Weibo users. This has been the case from the passive responses in the past to actively taking initiatives in the present. Both government and Weibo users continue to evolve their strategies to match one another.

In summary, the government implements different strategies for different content on Weibo. Weibo autonomy has not, however, emerged in its place. Rather, the mode of state control as a soft-authoritarian mode of control (Roy 1994) has taken shape on Weibo. The key feature of this control is that the state controls Weibo flexibly, selectively and proactively, in a subtle way. It will apply direct and intensive control when it feels necessary and use subtle and invisible control when it feels other methods are unnecessary.

However limited the Chinese state's sophisticated forms of governance may be, as Castells (2009) argues, for most Chinese the causes of democracy and liberal values are only "abstract ideals", and only relate to "a tiny intellectual minority". In some Western countries, Twitter and other social media are not necessarily regarded as channels for political expression, but in China, they are. Problems raised by the internet are not from the internet itself, not technological problems, but the problems of current political structures and operational modes. Many countries are trying to answer this question of how to absorb the internet into political structures and adapt to its social and political development.

With respect to Weibo governance, the perspective of governmentality offers a good optic for analyses. First, the term was originally developed as a tool to study the process of governing. The application of governmentality is aimed at studying those practices of government that employ rationalities to think, make decisions and govern. Second, in the process of social media development in China, governmentality offers a good reference point for social media research, as this study considers political contexts first before analyzing the social media, because it is not complete to attempt to understand the role of any media in any political process without thinking about the surrounding political environment. This chapter (and those following) presents a new approach, which recognizes the government's point of view: that it is necessary to understand the need for flexible oversight and censorship of Chinese Weibo.

With the emergence of new media, especially Weibo, the government's regulatory attitude has changed from reactive to proactive. The next chapter will reveal how the government's policies and actions exert influence on Weibo. Rather than direct control through censorship of social media, the following chapters present detailed case studies that examine the subtle and strategic methods of control, the "invisible" actions of government officials that are best described by Foucault's governmentality. These chapters examine the paradoxical situation in which the Chinese government allows individuals to disseminate rich information on this social media site, while limiting their freedom of speech or tightening controls over society. This study considers the foundation of this kind of control as one of 'strategic censorship'. For example, government documents or policies may offer one view of government interest or intent. The fact remains that state authorities will still monitor the internet closely and make good use of it for the optimization of those policies.

This chapter has outlined the reasons why the government tightens internet control under the guise of internet freedom. Internet incidents can be manipulated by the Chinese government to promote its political integrity, which is a form of governmentality. The government works hard to enforce internet censorship while simultaneously encouraging Weibo to criticize to a certain degree. China's systems of internet censorship, as well as other control measures, are "effective enough that the picture of the world seen by the average Chinese internet user is skewed in the regime's favor" (MacKinnon 2008, p. 33). While the Chinese government encourages the use of Weibo, it serves as an efficient outlet for people to complain about government corruption or inefficiency. However, the nationwide e-government strategy is an example of the Chinese government using Weibo as a tool or mechanism for feedback, receiving complaints and suggestions. Currently, China's goal still remains a focus on economic development, but the precondition for this is the preservation of social stability (*weiwen*). With the rising social dissatisfaction in some sectors of Chinese society, the Chinese government effectively takes Weibo as its battleground to minimize the possibility of social mobilization in the real world.

The popularization of the internet was intended to bring some hope for a weakening government monopoly over information and to some degree, to democratize communication in general. At the same time, however, the government also intends to remain a step ahead as far as control is concerned. In this way, there is an interweaving of freedom and control coexisting in China's cyberspace. Under particular circumstances, the freedom does not result from the technology itself, but represents genuine freedom from government rationalities. In this way, internet-based communications democratize public communication within particular social, political and economic contexts. The larger picture sees the government using Weibo successfully to construct cultural identity.

Chapters Five and Six will offer case studies to illuminate the tactics of governmentality in order to better understand why some Weibo spaces are more liberalized and open than others and the role of the government in continuing to lead in shaping public opinion.

References

Abbott, J. 2013, 'Introduction: Assessing the social and political impact of the internet and new social media in Asia', Journal of Contemporary Asia, vol. 43, no. 4, pp. 579–590.

Ai, W. 2011, Ai Weiwei's blogs: Writings, interviews, and digital rants 2006-2009, MIT Press, Cambridge.

Bandurski, D. 2007, 'State Council vice-minister reiterates control as top priority of Internet development in China', China Media Project, 4 December, viewed 4 January 2013, <http://cmp.hku.hk/2007/12/04/763/, accessed 4 January 2009>.

Bandurski, D. 2008, 'China's guerrilla war for the Web', Far Eastern Economic Review, 15 July, viewed 20 April 2014, <http://samgeall.com/post/42314921/far-eastern-economic-review-chinas-guerrilla-war-for>.

Bandurski, D. 2010, 'Listen to the citizens, and control them', China Media Project, 22 June, viewed 20 June 2014, <http://cmp.hku.hk/2010/06/22/6281/>.

Beijing Times. 2013, 'Qinhuohuo wangluo heishehui zaoyao beiduan (Qinhuohuo network triad was terminated)', Beijing Times, 21 August, viewed on 22 June 2014, <http://epaper.jinghua.cn/html/2013-08/21/content_20370.htm>.

Boas, TC. 2006, 'Weaving the authoritarian web: The control of internet use in nondemocratic regimes', in Zysman, J & Newman, A (eds.), How revolutionary was the digital revolution? National responses, market transitions, and global technology, Stanford Business Books, Stanford, CA, pp. 361–378.

Boehler, P. 2013, 'Two million "internet opinion analysts" employed to monitor China's vast online population', South China Morning Post, 3 October, viewed 20 October 2013, <http://www.scmp.com/news/china-insider/article/1323529/two-million-employed-monitor-chinese-public-opinion>.

Bristow, M. 2008, 'China's internet "spin doctors"', BBC News, 16 December, viewed 12 May 2013, <http://news.bbc.co.uk/2/hi/asia-pacific/7783640.stm>.

Castells, M. 2009, Communication power, Oxford University Press, Oxford.

Chan, Y. 2010, 'Microblogs reshape news in China', China Media Project, 12 October, viewed 23 September 2013, <http://cmp.hku.hk/2010/10/12/8021/>.

Chen, X. 2006, 'Dynamics of news media regulations in China: Explanations and implications', Journal of Comparative Asian Development, vol. 5, no. 1, pp. 49–64.

China News.com. 2013, 'Lvshi: Bei xingju chuzhongsheng yanlun he qunzhong youxing wu yinguo guanxi (Lawyer: Speech of the arrested junior student has no cause effect with mass demonstration)', China News.com, 22 September, viewed 20 October 2013, <http://www.chinanews.com/fz/2013/09-22/5304163.shtml>.

China.org.cn. 2013, 'Weibo: An eye on corruption', China.org.cn, March 11, viewed on May 5, 2013, <http://www.china.org.cn/china/NPC_CPPCC_2013/2013-03/11/content_28201650.htm>.

Colebatch, HK. 2002, 'Government and governmentality: Using multiple approaches to the analysis of government', Australian Journal of Political Science, vol. 37, no. 3, pp. 417–435.

Dean, M. 1999, Governmentality: Power and rule in modern society, Sage, London.

Diamond, L. 2010, 'Liberation technology', Journal of Democracy, vol. 21, no. 3, pp. 69–83.

Eggers, WD. 2007, Government 2.0: Using technology to improve education, cut red tape, reduce gridlock and enhance democracy, Rowman & Littlefield Publishers, Lanham.

Esarey, A & Xiao, Q. 2008, 'Political expression in the Chinese blogosphere: Below the radar', Asian Survey, vol. 48, no. 5, pp. 752–772.

Foucault, M. 1988a, 'Technologies of the self', in Martin, LH, Gutman, H & Hutton, P (eds.), Technologies of the self: A seminar with Michel Foucault, The University of Massachusetts Press, Amherst, pp. 16–49.

Foucault, M. 1988b, 'The political technology of individuals', in Martin, LH, Gutman, H & Hutton, P (eds.), Technologies of the self: A seminar with Michel Foucault, The University of Massachusetts Press, Amherst, pp. 145–162.

Foucault, M. 1991, 'Governmentality', in Burchell, G, Gordon, C & Miller, P (eds.), The Foucault effect: Studies in governmental rationality, Harvester Wheatsheaf, Hemel Hempstead, pp. 87–104.

Fu, K-W, Chan, C-H & Chau, M. 2013, 'Assessing censorship on microblogs in China: Discriminatory keyword analysis and the real name registration policy', IEEE Computer Society, vol. 17, no. 3, pp. 42–50.

Gerhards, J & Schäfer, MS. 2010, 'Is the internet a better public sphere? Comparing old and new media in the USA and Germany', New Media & Society, vol. 12, no. 1, pp. 143–160.

Gilley, B. 2005, 'Political legitimacy in Malaysia: Regime performance in the Asian context', in White, LT (ed.), Legitimacy: Ambiguities of political success or failure in East and Southeast Asia, World Scientific Publishing Co. Pvt. Ltd, Singapore, pp. 28–41.

Guo, B. 2003, 'Political legitimacy and China's transition', Journal of Chinese Political Science, vol. 8, no. 1 & 2, pp. 1–25.

Heverin, T & Zach, L. 2011, 'Twitter for city police department information sharing', Proceedings of the American Society for Information Science and Technology, vol. 47, no. 1, pp. 1–7.

Hewitt, D. 2012, 'Weibo brings change to China', BBC News, 31 July, viewed 12 November 2013, <http://www.bbc.co.uk/news/magazine-18887804>.

Hu, Y. 2010, 'Micro-revolution: From Twitter to Sina Weibo', New Weekly, p. 315.

Jiang, M. 2010, 'Spaces of authoritarian deliberation: Online public deliberation in China', in Leib, E & He, B (eds.), The search for deliberative democracy in China, New York, NY: Palgrave, pp. 261–287.

Kaiman, J. 2013, 'China cracks down on social media with threat of jail for "online rumors"', The Guardian, 10 September, viewed 10 October 2013, <http://www.theguardian.com/world/2013/sep/10/china-social-media-jail-rumours>.

King, G, Pan, J & Roberts, M. 2013, 'How censorship in China allows government criticism but silences collective expression', American Political Science Review, vol. 107, no. 2, pp. 326–341.

Lagerkvist, J. 2010, After the internet, before democracy: Competing norms in Chinese media and society, Peter Lang, Bern.

Lee, T. 2010, The media, cultural control and government in Singapore, Routledge, New York.

Liu, W. 2013, 'China draws seven "red lines" in the sand for internet conduct', Context China, 9 September, viewed 10 October 2013, <http://contextchina.com/2013/09/china-draws-seven-red-lines-in-the-sand-for-internet-conduct>.

Ma, L. 2013, 'The diffusion of government microblogging: Evidence from Chinese municipal police bureaus', Public Management Review, vol. 15, no. 2, pp. 288–309.

MacKinnon, R. 2008, 'Flatter world and thicker walls? Blogs, censorship and civic discourse in China', Public Choice, vol. 134, no. 1–2, pp. 31–46.

MacKinnon, R. 2009, 'China's censorship 2.0: How companies censor bloggers', First Monday, vol. 14, no. 2.

MacKinnon, R. 2010, 'Are China' demands for Internet "self-discipline" spreading to the West?', McClatchy News Service, 18 January, viewed 6 November 2013, <http://www.mcclatchydc.com/2010/01/18/82469/commentary-are-chinas-demands.html>.

Miller, P & Rose, N. 1990, 'Political rationalities and technologies of government', in Hanninen, S & Palonen, K (eds.), Texts, contexts, concepts: Studies in politics and power in language, Finnish political Science Association, Helsinki, pp. 171–183.

Morozov, E. 2009, 'Iran: Downside to the "Twitter Revolution"', Dissent, vol. 56, no. 4, pp. 10–14.

Morozov, E. 2011, The net delusion: The dark side of internet freedom, Public Affairs, New York.

Noesselt, N. 2013a, 'Microblogs and the adaptation of the Chinese party-state's governance Strategy', Governance, vol. 27, no. 3, pp. 449–468.

Noesselt, N. 2013b, 'Microblogs in China: Bringing the state back in', GIGA Working Papers.

Pan, P. 2006, 'The click that broke a government's grip', Washington Post, February 19, viewed 23 September 2013, <http://www.washingtonpost.com/wp-dyn/content/article/2006/02/18/AR2006021801389.html>.

PDPOM. 2011, '2011 nian Xinlang zhengwu weibo baogao (2011 Report on Sina Government Microblogs)', <http://wenku.baidu.com/link?url=yCLmhf9zqfbL1DYksZBOBBvNHkhHeZitgenfOueLYakrvfvpdNQYNN4fDyHooiQr8M2Mf54tuh1YeFkVI3UrPGk9EzK0VBqXjYsdR9nx9zO>.

PDPOM. 2012, '2012 nian Xinlang zhengwu weibo baogao (2012 Report on Sina Government Microblogs)', <http://yuqing.people.com.cn/n/2012/1203/c210118-19770124.html>.

PDPOM. 2013, '2013 nian Xinlang zhengwu weibo baogao (2013 Report on Sina Government Microblogs)', <http://yuqing.people.com.cn/n/2013/1226/c210118-23952286.html>.

Pei, M. 2014, 'Crucial stage in anti-graft campaign', China Daily, 23 April, viewed 2 July 2014, <http://www.chinadaily.com.cn/china/2014-04/23/content_17470123.htm>.

People.cn. 2012, '2012 nian Xinlang zhengwu weibo baogao (2012 Report on Sina Government Microblogs)', People.cn, viewed 3 December 2013, <http://yuqing.people.com.cn/n/2012/1203/c210118-19770124.html>.

People.com.cn. 2010, 'Renminwang deng 101 jia wangzhan qianshu <hulianwang banquan zilv xuanyan> (Public pledge on self-discipline for copyright in the internet)', 20 January, viewed 20 October 2013, <http://culture.people.com.cn/GB/22226/68486/68496/10809154.html>.

People's Daily. 2012, 'Zhongxin xinmeiti huanjing xia lingdaoli jianshe luntan zai jing juxing (Sina-Sigapore forum on leadership building in the new media environment held in Beijing)', 10 May, viewed on 18 December 2013, <http://paper.people.com.cn/rmrb/html/201205/10/nw.D110000renmrb_20120510_5-03.htm>.

People's Daily. 2013, 'Fanfu changlian guanxi dang he guojia shengsicunwang (Anti-corruption is vital to the Party and the state)', 30 January, viewed on 5 May 2013, <http://opinion.people.com.cn/n/2013/0130/c1003-20367836.html>.

Reddick, CG & Wigand, FDL. 2010, 'Adoption of web 2.0 by Canadian and US governments', in Sharda, R & Voß, S (eds.), Comparative E-Government, Springer, New York, pp. 161–181.

Rose, N. 1996, 'Governing "advanced" liberal democracies', in Barry, A, Osborne, T & Rose, N (eds.), Foucault and political reason: Liberalism, neo-liberalism, and rationalities of government, University of Chicago Press, Chicago, pp. 37–64.

Rose, N. 1999, Power of freedom: Reframing political thought, Cambridge University Press, Cambridge.

Rosen, S. 2010, 'Is the internet a positive force in the development of civil society, a public sphere and democratization in China?', International Journal of Communication, vol. 4, pp. 509–516.

Roy, D. 1994, 'Singapore, China, and the "soft authoritarian" challenge', Asian Survey, vol. 34, no. 3, pp. 231–242.

Shirk, S. 2011, 'Changing media, changing China', in Shirk, S (ed.), Changing media, changing China, Oxford University Press, New York, pp. 1–37.

Sullivan, J. 2012, 'A tale of two microblogs in China', Media, Culture & Society, vol. 34, no. 6, pp. 773–783.

Sun, H. 2010, Internet policy in China, Lexington Books, UK.

Tai, Z. 2006, The Internet in China: Cyberspace and civil society, Routledge, New York.

Tang, X, Wu, X, Huang, C & Liu, R (eds.). 2013, Annual report on development of new media in China 2013, China Social Sciences Academic Press, Beijing.

The Economist. 2013, 'Big Vs and bottom lines: Authorities move against some of China's most vocal microbloggers', The Economist, 31 August, viewed 10 October 2013, <http://www.economist.com/news/china/21584385-authorities-move-against-some-chinas-most-vocal-microbloggers-big-vs-and-bottom-lines>.

Thomas, N. 2013, 'China's two greatest Internet rumour mongers and "black PR" philanderers arrested', DANWEI: Tracking Chinese media and Internet, viewed 15 March 2014, <http://www.danwei.com/chinas-two-greatest-internet-rumor-mongers-and-black-pr-philanderers-arrested/>.

Thompson, K. 1997, 'Introduction', in Thompson, K (ed.), Media and cultural regulation, Sage, London, pp. 1–7.

Tong, Y & Lei, S. 2013, 'War of position and microblogging in China', Journal of Contemporary China, vol. 22, no. 80, pp. 292–311.

Tong, J & Zuo, L. 2014, 'Weibo communication and government legitimacy in China: A computer-assisted analysis of Weibo messages on two "mass incidents"', Information, Communication & Society, vol. 17, no. 1, pp. 66–85.

Villeneuve, N. 2008, 'Search monitor project: Toward a measure of transparency', in Chavez, C, Repas, MA & Stefaniak, TL (eds.), A new way to communicate with residents: Local government use of social media to prepare for emergencies, International City/County Management Association, Washington, DC.

Weber, I & Jia, L. 2007, 'Internet and self-regulation in China: The cultural logic of controlled commodification', Media, Culture & Society, vol. 29, no. 5, pp. 772–789.

Wigand, F. 2010, 'Twitter takes wing in government: Diffusion, roles, and management', Proceedings of the 11th Annual International Digital Government Research Conference on Public Administration Online: Challenges and Opportunities, pp. 66–71.

Wong, L. 2004, 'Market reforms, globalization and social justice in China', Journal of Contemporary China, vol. 13, no. 38, pp. 151–171.

Xiao, Q. 2007, 'China censors internet users with site bans, cartoon cop spies', San Francisco Chronicle, 23 September, viewed 3 July 2013, <http://www.sfgate.com/cgi-bin/article.cgi?f=/c/a/2007/09/23/INCLS80LO.DTL>.

Xinhua Daily Telegraph. 2013, 'Daishoukao de 'xuemanzi' tan 'da V' xinlu (Charles Xue with handcuff talks about 'big V')', 16 September, viewed 20 January 2014, <http://news.xinhuanet.com/mrdx/2013-09/16/c_132722998.htm>.

Xinhuanet.com. 2013, 'Wangluo mingren shehui luntan zai yangshi xinzhi juxing (The Forum on Social Responsibilities of Internet Celebrities)', 10 August, viewed 12 November 2013, <http://news.xinhuanet.com/local/2013-08/10/c_116892078.htm>.

Yang, G. 2009, The Power of the internet in China: Citizen activism online, Columbia University Press, New York.

Yang, G. 2011, 'Technology and its contents: Issues in the study of the Chinese Internet', The Journal of Asian Studies, vol. 70, no. 4, pp. 1043–1050.

Zhang, J. 2002, 'Will the government "serve the people"? The development of Chinese e-government', New Media & Society, vol. 4, no. 2, pp. 163–184.

Zhang, Q. 2013, 'Microblogging the Bo Xilai trial: Transparency or theatre?', BBC News, 23 August, viewed 25 August 2013, <http://www.bbc.com/news/world-asia-china-23806657>.

Zhang, Z & Jia, J. 2011, 'Chinese government microblogging study', Journalism Review, no. 6, pp. 34–39.

Zheng, Y. 2008, Technological empowerment: The Internet, state, and society in China, Stanford University Press, Stanford.

Zhu, H, Shan, X & Hu, J. 2011, 'China internet public opinion evaluation report', People's Daily, <http://yuqing.people.com.cn/mediafile/201112/29/P201112290936031431493992.pdf>.

· 5 ·

WEIBO BROADCAST OF THE BO XILAI TRIAL

> The trial of former official Bo Xilai is a significant benchmark for social media's role in increasing transparency in the Chinese justice system, at least when it comes the trials of Party officials. (Zhang 2013b)

Introduction

The political ousting of Bo Xilai, former member of the CCP and secretary of the Chongqing branch, a high-ranking political official identified as a neo-Maoist populist, marked a significant turning point in China's political history. Earlier studies have examined cultural and economic fields through the lens of governmentality. This study, however, will apply the concept of governmentality to the political field, integrating representations of political figures and events in Chinese social media, notably Weibo, taking the Bo Xilai trial as a case study. This trial also marked an unprecedented moment in China's judicial history; and in the way that the social media platform, Weibo, was used for a live broadcast of the trial, which made it the first open trial in Chinese history. The Chinese government's long held tight regulation of both traditional media and new media, including Weibo, meant that it was paradoxical to see Weibo broadcast the Bo Xilai trial, showing a transparency which would be more expected in liberal societies. Previous scholarship has already illustrated that the governance strategies of the Chinese government have demonstrated certain liberal and democratic elements since the reform and opening up in late 1970s (Sigley 1996; Jiang 2012). Until this event, these liberal signs were limited to the cultural and economic sphere, and the Chinese government still held tight controls in the political field. However, the case of the Bo Xilai trial has successfully demonstrated that both the appearance of transparency and tight political control can coexist on Weibo.

In this light, the Bo Xilai trial shows the government's strategic balance between providing information and censorship on Weibo. In the process, the government opened a larger space for public discussion and indicators of increasing transparency. This chapter discusses the "mixture" of both locking and unlocking the political sphere, as a tool and technology of governmentality, intended to fulfill political ends. In thinking about the correlation between governmentality and the Bo Xilai trial in China, this study argues that it is problematic and insufficient to merely equate the conduct of the Bo Xilai trial with Western liberalism. The continuous enforcement of Weibo regulation and other types of control in the new media era have indeed strengthened a more authoritarian Chinese government. However, this chapter argues that the party-state is deliberately using a number of sophisticated strategies and calculations through moderating and censoring the Weibo service, in order to reduce the risks that may arise from such controversial events as the Bo Xilai trial. In contrast to previous academic analysis of censorship on Weibo, which has frequently used ideas of state surveillance (Xiao 2011), the conduct of the trial embodied the paradox of Weibo: that it is both free and open and can be highly monitored. The Chinese government's deliberate intermingling of freedom and control on Weibo, in other words, neither authoritarianism nor liberalism, has reflected the government's rationality, calculation and instrumentalisation.

To describe the use of Weibo during the Bo Xilai trial, this book draws on Foucault's concept of governmentality, referring to a range of activities and calculations to guide or shape the conduct of people (Burchell, Gordon & Miller 1991, p. 2). This chapter contends that both liberal ideals and authoritarian practices could be seen in the regulation of Weibo during the Bo Xilai trial, and both these ideas and practices claim to govern in the name of freedom (Dean 2002, p. 58).

Background of the Bo Xilai Trial

Bo Xilai is a former government official and an offspring of one of China's first revolutionary leaders, Bo Yibo, one of the "Eight Immortals" of the CCP. He made significant achievements as the mayor of Dalian and governor of Liaoning province, and was subsequently promoted to be China's Minister of Commerce from 2004 to 2007. In the next five years from 2007 to 2012, he served as a member of the Central Politburo of the Chinese Communist Party (CCP) and secretary of the CCP's Chongqing branch. He became known for the campaigns he initiated against mafia gangs, for improving social welfare and strengthening economic growth. Significantly, Bo also launched the "red culture" movement in June 2008 to celebrate the CCP's 90th birthday and to promote revolutionary songs that aimed to retrieve the spirit of China's revolutionary era, a campaign that was subsequently adopted by many other cities. His promotion of egalitarian values was known as the "Chongqing model". Bo gathered a national following through his highly publicized campaigns to eradicate organized crime, called *da hei* (smashing black) and his extolling the values of the Mao era. Thus he became a star of what is called the Chinese New Left. He drew support from the masses and from the working classes who had been disaffected by corruption and were the victims of wide income gaps.

Bo's political career had been very promising; however, it came to an abrupt end after his deputy mayor and police chief, Wang Lijun, sought asylum at the United States' consulate in Chengdu. He was sentenced by the Chengdu City Intermediate People's Court to 15 years in prison for abuse of power and bribe taking (Xinhua News 2012a). More specifically, Wang had allegedly been involved in the murder of British businessman, Neil Heywood, by Bo's wife, Gu Kailai, and a family aide, Zhang Xiaojun. The Wang Lijun incident led to a thorough investigation of Bo. After the new CCP leadership came to office, Bo was stripped of all his Party positions and expelled from the Party. His fall resulted from an international scandal involving the death of a British businessman, possibly a spy, a case in which his wife, Gu Kailai, was convicted of murder and his Police Chief implicated.

On August 22, 2013, the so-called "trial of the century" of Bo Xilai was carried out by the Intermediate People's Court in Jinan, eastern China's Shandong province, where he was charged with bribery (some $3.3 million), embezzlement estimated at $817,000 and the abuse of power in covering up the murder of Heywood. Bo was found guilty and sentenced to life imprisonment. Finally he was deprived of his political rights for life. The display of openness surrounding the trial was highly unusual in the Chinese legal system in recent decades; the last such 'public' trial in 1981, when the trial of Mao Zedong's wife and other members of the "Gang of Four" was televised. Historically the trials of Chinese Party officials have been kept secret. Yet despite scant information being released at the hearings into charges against Bo's wife, Gu Kailai, and former police chief, Wang Lijun in 2012, the Bo Xilai trial proceedings were broadcast online on Sina Weibo for the first time in Chinese legal history. The Jinan courthouse opened its own official Weibo account, publicly disseminating courtroom transcripts and other relevant information. During the five-day trial from August 22 to 26, the court released 160 posts in the form of explanatory texts, video evidence and images of complete trial transcripts to a huge audience. Some posts were forwarded hundreds of thousands of times. The Sina Weibo posts updated steadily through the trial, including details on testimony, photos and even an audio clip from a key witness. The widespread, interactive and highly-influential Weibo platform vividly showed the cross-examination and debate between the prosecution and the defense, as well as the final statement of the defendant, all of which helped the public to understand the proceedings of the case as early as possible.

The trial was considered as an unprecedented display of transparency for a trial in China, and therefore drew massive attention from the Chinese public. As the days progressed, followers of the court's Weibo account increased from 40,000 to over 300,000 (People.cn 2013). Some posts were retweeted tens of thousands of times. Finally, the court rejected nearly all of Mr. Bo's defense arguments, convicting him of bribe-taking, embezzlement and abuse of power. He was sentenced to life in prison. The court released the handing down of its decision on Weibo and soon followed with a photo of Mr. Bo in handcuffs. During the trial, Weibo became the main platform for public discussions about the trial. Within the period, more than 1.8 million posts were made about the Bo Xilai trial, the highest number of posts about a specific issue to ever appear on Weibo. The most intense discussions occurred especially on the first and last days of the trial. Within Dean's framework of four dimensions for the rationality of government practices, the visibility of government is of great importance (1999, pp. 30–33), therefore, the visible, real time trial of Bo Xilai on Weibo allowed the government to show great transparency.

On August 18, 2013, the Jinan Intermediate People's Court publicly announced online that the trial of Bo Xilai would be held at 8:30 am on August 22. Soon it attracted a great deal of attention, with more than 20,000 Weibo users re-tweeting this post. The court disseminated detailed accounts of the lively exchanges between the judge, the prosecutor, the defense lawyer, witnesses and Mr. Bo himself. In comparison to the attitude towards sensitive information in the past, this announcement was an important signal that the party-state had chosen to bring the sensitive information further into the public light than ever before.

Weibo Broadcast Breaks the Official Media Monopoly

The Bo Xilai trial saw live microblogging, apparently breaking the information monopoly of judicial control in China. Scholars contend that the number of details in the Bo scandal released to the public by the regime is a clear reflection of the "much more complex, interactive and pluralistic public sphere in China" (Lewis 2013). From the trial opening on August 22 to the final judgment on September 22, Weibo was seen to be the main source of information rather than the major commercial sites, such as Sina, Sohu, and Tencent. The news was produced based on information directly released by the Jinan Intermediate People's Court. After the court's Weibo information such as audio, video and texts had been watched and edited by journalists, the news became the main content of the news portals. However, according to the analysis of eight official newspapers including the People's Daily, conducted by Zhang and Zhou (2013), the information generated by live microblogging was not shared with the traditional media. Due to the sensitivity of this case, the news in these eight newspapers was supplied exclusively by the Xinhua News Agency. The only difference between the material at source and publication was made to the headlines to highlight particular news values (ibid.). Therefore, despite the fact that live Weibo provided sufficient information about the trial, local media continued with its custom of following the line of the official media such as Xinhua News or the People's Daily (ibid.).

The complete "openness" to the public of the Bo Xilai trial on Weibo displayed signs of liberal governing, in that such liberty of public access is considered a central feature of liberal political thought (Dean & Hindess 1998, p. 4), which "conceive(s) the freedom of the governed as a technical means of securing the ends of government" (Dean 1999, p. 15). In this light, such an approach, if seen as a calculated act, still allows the shaping of public conduct and actions within a context of perceived freedom.

By contrast, there was embarrassingly little mainstream media coverage of this trial. The government only allowed several journalists from the Party's media outlets of the Xinhua News Agency to attend the hearings, while other journalists were required to wait in a designated area in a hotel nearby. Thus, most journalists had to turn to Weibo to reproduce information from the court's official Weibo account. The Phoenix TV (Hong Kong) news anchor even looked down at her mobile phone on a live program to check the Weibo updates of the trial when she was on air. Later she commented on her Weibo site, that putting her head down to find the latest information is better than having your head up with nothing to say.

Perhaps surprisingly for a mostly domestic political event, although heightened by the extenuating murder of a foreigner, the dramatic downfall of Bo Xilai made headlines across the world. This five-day trial attracted more than 590,000 followers on the official account of the Jinan Intermediate People's Court (@jinanzhongyuan), and has been praised as a significant benchmark for Weibo in increasing transparency in the Chinese justice system, particularly when it comes to the trials of Party officials (Zhang 2013b). This case has also been considered a turning point in China's legal history. The trial of Bo Xilai via Weibo has been widely appraised by the Western media, such as The New York Times, The Age and the BBC. And the court's use of the Weibo format has demonstrated the new Chinese leadership's determination to display transparent governance. During the trial, by disseminating its proceedings on Weibo, the Chinese government is demonstrating what it means to govern a nation, and in so doing, boosts the government's political confidence. It also demonstrated unusual flexibility during the trial in allowing the transmission of Weibo posts longer than 140 characters by those commenting on the trial. This was temporary, but was nevertheless a reflection of the government's disposition relating to all matters concerning the trial. It also increased the directness and accuracy of all reporting of the trial, so diminishing the chances of rumour spreading.

Selective Transparency as a Tool of Governing

Sina Weibo Used for Broadcast of the Trial. The authorities' unexpected openness about the trial—by showing the trial as it happened and the fact that Weibo was followed by millions of Chinese directly or through news reports drawing on Weibo, reflected the government's calculations. The completely new aspect of the conduct of the trial was that it appeared on Weibo, the social media platform the government most wants to control. There are multiple reasons for the choice of Weibo: first, the scale of the exposure, as Weibo has greater influence than any other media. In addition, unlike TV, which the public conceives as pre-made for performance, live broadcast on Weibo was seen as credible. The trial broadcast on Weibo fulfilled the public expectations of local people and the international community to seek the truth, using "technologies of truth", defined as "popular logics for establishing facts" by Rose and Miller (1992). At the same time, it has demonstrated the Chinese government's transparency with nothing to be concealed. If the Chinese government "managed" the event in some ways, on Weibo, as some critics have claimed, then it could be described as a triumph for governmentality. This is a considerable evolution from the earliest censorship of the case as it first came to light, with the direct censoring of sensitive words. When scandals involving Bo Xilai and his wife Gu Kailai first took place in 2012, Weibo censors actively and immediately worked to delete relevant posts, even those whose language had been modified to avoid control (Benney 2013). It has been suggested that during sensitive moments, Weibo censors actively work to delete and suppress relevant posts. This rigid regulation of the past stands in stark contrast to an open trial of the key perpetrator, believed to have been broadcast live. This could arguably describe skilled governmentality at work.

In order to fully analyze this idea, it is necessary to examine the close relationship between Sina Weibo and the Chinese party-state. The norm is that non-approved microblogs are censored and blocked. Twitter was launched in 2004 and was initially available in China until 2009 when it was permanently blocked after large scale riots in Xinjiang in mid-2009 involving Han Chinese and ethnic Uighurs in Urumqi, the capital of Xinjiang (Wauters 2009). Twitter and Youtube immediately and actively conveyed the information online, which seriously frustrated the Chinese government's efforts to control the news (The Telegraph 2009). Therefore, while the authorities made efforts to neutralize the news, audiences actively shared the news and images from Twitter. Soon afterwards, Twitter became inaccessible in China. A number of domestic microblog services such as Fanfou and Digu were also shuttered at that time (though they reappeared later in 2010), as Chinese authorities apparently believed that the riots were fuelled by the internet, particularly by online forums (Sullivan 2014). However, the fact that Sina Weibo emerged immediately after the riots and has survived, strongly suggests its relatively close links with the government. This is further supported by the fact that

Sina Weibo is part of the Sina Corporation, which enjoys the support of the state. The Sina Corporation is a very economically significant company, running the Sina web portal, one of the most popular websites in China, and also a range of blogs and news services. The cooperative relationship between the state and Sina requires that the Sina Company must conform to the communications regulations set by the state, and the state constantly pressures Sina to ensure its censorship compliance (Chin & Chao 2011).

Expertise Employed to Convince the Public. It is noteworthy that several well-known lawyers and legal experts commented exclusively on the trial on Weibo where the trial transcripts appeared simultaneously. One famous lawyer, Chen Youxi, for example, wrote an 8,000 word essay on his blog, praising the live broadcast of Bo Xilai's trial as sufficiently protecting the defendant's rights and providing objective evidence, noting that the way in which the Xinhua News Agency reprinted all the trial transcripts demonstrated that it was indeed a successful trial (Chen 2013). In his blog, he says:

> ...The openness of today's trial is unexpected, especially with the trial transcripts released simultaneously. The comprehensive record of the trial transcripts is breaking records in the Chinese criminal court, and is deemed to have a profound impact for future trials. In addition, it has provided the direct empirical evidence for this commentary. My overall remarks are: The first day points to a successful trial in spite of several flaws in the investigation of Bo Xilai, which are still unsatisfied and may possibly become long-term risks for this trial. (Chen 2013)

In addition, the unprecedented information it provided eliminated the possibility of rumor spreading. This blog was read more than 160,000 times. Governmentality is perceived as highly credible when it publicly draws on the expertise and commentary of experts in the field, which is doubtless an effective strategy for the government to enhance credibility. The calculations of government reside not only in its political principles, but also in experts and specialists called on to represent it, so verifying the acts of governing (Dean & Hindess 1998, p. 9). It reaffirms that governmentality exists in the medium of thought with multiple and heterogeneous ways to make the world calculable (ibid.). One distinctive characteristic of the governmentality approach in modern government is to "govern at a distance", which refers to both geographic distance and in a constitutional sense to govern "through the activities and calculations of a proliferation of independent agents" (Rose & Miller 1992, p. 180).

This illustrates how the expertise was employed to convince the public of the credibility of the process, in order to ultimately achieve the government's purposes. The next section will consider how, in relation to the coverage of the Bo Xilai trial, the government of China strategically employed both liberal and authoritarian techniques, in innovative ways, to pursue its own ends. The notion of governmentality is a useful framework for examining this approach. It sees government as "an inventive, strategic, technical and artful set of 'assemblages' fashioned from diverse elements, put together in novel and specific ways, and rationalised in relation to governmental objectives and goals" (Dean & Hindess 1998, p. 8).

Coexistence of Transparency and Political Control. Despite appearances, however, the Bo Xilai trial was not totally open and transparent. In strong contrast with the abrupt removal of top leaders in past decades, there are hints of strong political stage-managing in this online case. This section will examine the trial procedures in detail, arguing that selective transparency was used here as a technology of governmentality.

This shocking news of the trial attracted thousands of comments, most of which showed great support for the CCP's obvious determination to fight internal corruption. According to a random sampling of the comments on the trial, the vast majority of users condemned Bo Xilai (Zhang & Zhou 2013). To prevent the spread of rumors or speculation and any possible attempt to express sympathy towards Bo Xilai, Sina Weibo at an early stage blocked the search function for the names Bo Xilai, Neil Heywood, and Wang Lijun. Despite this example of "hard control", Weibo indeed revolutionized the flow of information, with many Weibo users seeking ways to get around the blockade using abbreviations and homonyms in diversified ways (Hewitt 2012a). In addition to the support for fighting corruption, many comments praised the government and showed great support for the current leadership.

Previous comments have shown the periodic omnipresence of the 50 Cents Party (as discussed in Chapter Four). At this time they appeared to act as strong propagandists for the authorities. A series of continuous posts appeared to be written by the same person to convey the impression of the government's determination that in China, people are all equal under the law. Therefore, Bo Xilai had betrayed the national interest and should be subject to heavy punishment. These statements all seemed to have originated from the 50 Cents Party, where their government sponsored messages served the purpose of formalizing and publicly embedding the message the government wished to have conveyed. In this way, instead of deleting comments supporting Bo Xilai directly as in the past, the authorities tried to coordinate the comments. The 50 Cents Party was the agent or tool of government in shaping and reshaping public conduct in practice (Dean 1999, pp. 17–18). This amounts to a regulation of microbloggers' conduct involving the analysis of thought. In this way, the process of government employs various acts of agency and different regulations of thought, operated and embedded in organized ways, as technical means to shape and reshape public conduct in practice (ibid.).

The supportive tone of the comments above suggests that they are from the 50 Cents Party as they set the tone on fighting corruption. They state that no matter how high the political rank, the government and the Party are determined to weed out corrupt officials. It is noteworthy that at the bottom of each page of comments, there was a notice saying that, "To avoid disturbance, the Weibo anti-rubbish system would automatically filter some content". This technical filter has been a longstanding practice of government, a technical aspect regarded as a necessary dimension in public communications (Dean 1999, p. 31). The war between the government and the people over truth and rumor is said to happen every day in China. There was a rumor control team in Sina Weibo, comprised of ten staff, maintaining a 24 hour watch on Weibo, with the purpose of deleting false news and information (China Daily 2011). In 2012, this led to three of China's most influential internet companies—Baidu, Sina and Tencent—pledging to "firmly support and cooperate with relevant government departments in cracking down on and probing web rumors" (Hong 2013). The government employs a range of means, mechanisms and technologies to accomplish its information management goals, especially through including the cooperation of Weibo-based companies to exercise direct censorship. While it is true that the government is heterogeneous to be truly persuasive in all areas of public life, it does not emanate from one single state source, but also requires other agencies to "manage their own behavior" (Dean & Hindess 1998, p. 3).

Noticing the numerous similar comments and the homogeneity of views on Weibo about the Bo Xilai trial and the government's principled approach, many questioned the writers' identities and the intentions of this group of Weibo users. However, these types of anti-Fifty Cents Party posts were not deleted. This reaffirmed the view that the CCP's censorship program aimed more at curtailing potential collective or mobilizing actions rather than silencing negative posts criticizing the state or the leadership (King, Pan & Roberts 2013). In other words, the government's intention may have been both to prevent collective action while at the same time; using Weibo to obtain the views of the populace about specific political events. This type of censorship has been described as 'mediated' (Meng 2010) involving constant negotiations between users, service providers and the state. Another example is that one of the most popular Weibo users, Zuoyeben, made a post making fun of a hand position of Bo Xilai during his trial, meaning "everything is fine". This post was shared several thousand times in less than 12 minutes before Zuoyeben's user account was deleted (see Rauchfleisch & Schäfer 2014). This shows that Weibo makes it possible for the forming of the public sphere in some situations, though within a short period due to strict regulation.

In the days before the opening of the Bo Xilai trial, the Jinan Intermediate People's Court released several pieces of news about its regulations which were unrelated to the trial. However, even comments made by the public on these posts could be seen as connected to Bo Xilai. This reaffirms that the primary reason for the Jinan Intermediate People's Court to open a Weibo account was the Bo Xilai trial.

On 22 August 2013, the history making Bo Xilai trial opened on time. The court regularly updated its public information and released pictures of the Jinan court building as well as the hall of justice in which the trial took place. It first offered basic information about the people and the reporters who would attend and briefly introduced Bo Xilai, providing pictures of him in the court.

It also released long and detailed conversations that took place in the court. By releasing so much factual material about the event at the outset, as it happened, the government was establishing its credibility in telling the truth about the events. This presentation of the truth in strategic ways is endorsed by an analytics of government in which the 'truth' is produced in social, cultural and political practices (Dean 1999, p. 18). In other words, one way of governing others or ourselves is through providing the truth, or what we perceive to be true. Nevertheless, the detailed and unambiguous trial transcripts subsequently posted on Weibo did provide convincing evidence for the conviction of Bo Xilai, thereby offering the justification for the conviction. This transparency eliminated the possibility of rumor. There was no need in this case for the Chinese government to issue its regular reminder to web users that Weibo was not to be used for the spreading of such rumors, and that such conduct could bring severe consequences. In fact, in 2012, when Wang Lijun fled to the American Consulate, it produced a series of public scandals about Bo and another politician Zhou Yongkang, then secretary of the Political and Legal Affairs Committee (also known as the 'second center of power' in the

CCP) and once a resolute supporter of Bo Xilai. Zhou was arrested in 2014 for bribery. The rumors repeatedly raised by foreign reporters of this incident were criticized by Xinhua News as "lacking exact sources of information, making groundless speculations and featuring critical remarks about China's political situation" (Xinhua News 2012b). In this process, new media has played an essential role in the Bo scandal, including breaking news and information before the traditional press, fostering the spread of alternative news and catalyzing broader discussion (Lewis 2013).

From the first day of the trial, hundreds of thousands of people forwarded news of the proceedings online. It is noteworthy that more people "forwarded" on Weibo messages than "commented" themselves, as this seemed to be a safer practice. In addition, the comments which appeared on the trial are basically those criticizing Bo Xilai. There may be two reasons. Firstly, this provides clear evidence that, given the sensitivity of this trial, people tacitly and safely chose the path of self-censorship. Rose and Miller (1992, p. 174) argue that "power is not so much a matter of imposing constraints upon citizens as of 'making up' citizens capable of bearing a kind of regulated freedom". The rigid and constant regulatory measures on social media have rendered people self-aware and self-regulated. Secondly, the function of deletion was still being applied by the government and the companies to censor unwanted information. In fact, on the first day of the trial, for example, the comment function on Weibo was open to everyone. Therefore, there were diverse comments on the Bo Xilai trial, some of which showed support for Bo. However, they were deleted immediately. It shows that the government controls and monitors Weibo closely so that seemingly problematic content can be quickly and effectively censored. But on the second day of the trial, the comment function was closed down by Sina Weibo and comments supporting Bo Xilai deleted immediately. In the larger exercise of government power, the Sina company's compliance with the unavoidable responsibility of regulating information, provided a technology of government with a capacity to 'govern at a distance', as "political forces have sought to utilize, instrumentalist and mobilize techniques and agents other than those of the 'state' in order to govern 'at a distance'" (Rose & Miller 1992, p. 181). It was reported that the server message that appeared on Weibo at this time if one wished to comment was "Server data synchronization has been delayed, please wait 1–2 minutes". Negative comments then disappeared after the waiting period had passed. Thus, all of the remaining comments appeared to be consistently in favor of the widely predicted conviction of Bo Xilai (Zhai & Boehler 2013). Therefore, though

Weibo played an essential role in the Bo case, as it facilitated a broader discussion and potentially provided a public hotbed for rumor spreading, the government believed that these could then be managed through the online trial. In this regard, "the degree to which the details of this scandal have been made public by the regime are reflective of this much more complex, interactive and pluralistic public sphere in China" (Lewis 2013, p. 679).

However, these diverse public discourses in the information age are still closely managed and manipulated by the party-state to selectively tighten or loosen the scope of the public sphere. In fact, monitoring online public opinion also allows government departments such as the police to get involved in limiting speech online. In this context, the crackdown on the internet celebrities in August 2013, immediately before the Bo Xilai trial, is noteworthy. The internet celebrities targeted made televised confessions, and social media users would be charged with defamation or possible crimes if posts which contained rumors or offensive content exceeded certain numbers, as discussed earlier in Chapter Four. This reflects Foucault's view that, in the programs or rationalities of government, a monolithic state is not the only source of power; other ranges of parties which attempt to regulate should be also included. Rose and Miller (1992, p. 180) propose that it includes a variety of independent actors such as philanthropists, doctors, hygienists, managers, planners, parents and social workers, who have played an essential role involved in the governance (ibid.).

Before the findings of the Bo Xilai trial were released, the Jinan Intermediate People's Court also quoted famous sayings from both traditional Chinese culture and English judicial history. For example, it quoted that 'justice must not only be done, but must be seen to be done'. This was another public confirmation of the strengthening of judicial openness and the pursuit of justice. These statements were intended to justify the live broadcast of the trial and to reaffirm its transparency and integrity. In addition, the authorities expressed good wishes for China's traditional Moon festival, reflecting their wishes to be seen to be humane.

However, after the five-day trial concluded, many of the posts of the Jinan Intermediate Court were forwarded from the National People's Courts, instead of its own, reflecting that, given the sensitivity of the issues, the local court maintained consistency with the central government. Freedom to watch and comment on Bo's trial did not mean the absence of power or governance, but was in fact, a technique of governing where the regulation of subjects took place through the bestowing of apparent freedom.

The complex relationship between the social media companies and the government, as noted, has been described as a form of "cadre-capitalist alliance" (Lagerkvist 2010). This could apply to the role of the Sina Corporation in communicating with both the Chinese government and the public, as demonstrated in the Bo Xilai trial. On the one hand, it facilitates censorship within the parapets of the state; on the other hand, it needs to provide entertainment and to offer a free-speech platform to make a profit. It has nevertheless been argued that at higher managerial levels of the corporation, liberal attitudes to free speech are less common. However, in the Bo Xilai trial, we see the apparent signs of liberalism in relation to free speech, although within enforced cooperation with the government.

Though the Weibo comments function was open to the public, censors imposed subtle ways to moderate the debate. Thus, comments remained heavily censored and if one wished to comment it was a sign of political struggle on Weibo, that would be censored and a message will appear saying "sorry, this content violates the Weibo regulations". According to Foucault, the relationship between the technologies of power, which govern individuals through domination and manipulation, and the technologies of the self that allow individuals to manage themselves through autonomy and their own means, is very close. In China, liberal technologies are always accompanied by authoritarian measures, as exemplified by the deleting of comments to "guide" public opinion.

However, on several occasions during the Bo Xilai trial, Weibo posts that expressed sympathy for Bo were not deleted. Therefore, there was still space for people to discuss the trial, and, despite the fact that government at a distance makes good sense for the companies to control Weibo, it still allows the companies to enjoy an apparent advantage of flexibility and subjectivity to deal with the information. A government is a series of deliberations and a calculation, which attempts to shape, guide or regulate the fields for a variety of ends. Government often gives shape to freedom, and concerns the shaping of human conduct and acts on the governed by action or freedom (Dean 1999, p. 15). The way the Chinese government constructs freedom for Weibo users, to a certain extent, entails the government's strategic capabilities for public control.

Government's Determination to Fight Corruption. This action, clearly permitted by government, indicated that it had turned to more subtle and strategic management of public opinion. In the process of government, the part of "state actor" plays an important and significant role in constituting the regulatory order (Colebatch 2002, p. 419). To Dean and Hindess (1998, p. 11), studying government as "the conduct of conduct" includes two methods. One should not only pay attention to the techniques of the authorities attempting to shape and direct the conduct of individuals or groups, but also take the authorities' agenda into consideration. The way the Chinese government preset an agenda on fighting corruption and was determined to make it an open trial, is the way the authorities utilize the technology to guide the population to fit their determinations. It echoes with government officials declaring that social media should take the "commanding heights" (People.cn 2012). This is undeniably a convenient way to enhance credibility and to improve the government's transparency.

Although some posts opposing the government's position appeared, the Sina Company clearly kept them circumscribed within acceptable limits. The comments include a focus on the punishment of corruption of government officials. Though users voicing such negative comments faced many perceived risks, the Weibo platform still served as a conduit for information and as a "safety valve" as Hassid (2012) suggests, for public enquiries during this trial. It provided an outlet to voice anger, criticism or even dissent over particular problems, rather than provoking social turmoil or social activism. Firstly it successfully demonstrated the government's responsiveness to public concerns over sensitive issues. It also confirmed the government's determination to fight corruption. In this way, rather than adopting direct methods of regulating the population, the government chooses to take the concern and optimization of the population into consideration, including the population's wealth, health, happiness and prosperity, by using appropriate technical means to achieve its goals (Dean 1999, p. 20).

Fighting corruption is a common interest in China, and the action of weeding out corruption has long been seen as a safeguard for the national interest and improves the Party's image. As Rose and Miller (2010, p. 279) argue, government is a "problematizing activity", which poses the obligations or problems for the government to address. Therefore, when handling social failings or ills, the ideal government is supposed to rectify them. The problem of corruption has widely been seen as a longstanding social disease that impedes economic growth, undermines Party legitimacy and causes social instability. With greater openness and three-decade economic reform, China has transformed itself "from a centrally planned economy to a socialist market economy in which power and money are widely exchanged" (Broadhurst & Wang 2014, p. 168). This larger context provides a warm bed to breed corruption. The problematization of corruption has posed great challenges to the CCP for its future, which requires a program of action to remedy the problem. China's former President, Hu Jintao, warned that "corruption could kill the Communist Party and called to safeguard party control" (Branigan 2012). For the new leadership, fighting corruption has become a top priority. At the 18th National Congress of the Communist Party of China in 2012, China's newly appointed President Xi Jinping, re-emphasized the risks posed by corruption in his first public address. Therefore, the strategy of emphasizing Bo Xilai's corruption fitted perfectly with the background of fighting corruption in China, which has gained substantial legitimacy. There is a necessary link between the goals of the authorities and the activities of the citizens (Rose & Miller 1992, p. 193).

In this context, the open trial of Bo Xilai was seen as a demonstration of the Chinese government's determination to root out corruption. At the same time, the crackdown on corrupt senior officials could also help to build up new leaders' authority and advance transparency at the beginning of their reign, though it would not take effect in heightening legitimacy within the Chinese state in the long run (Broadhurst & Wang 2014).

Furthermore, much of what was being posted online after Bo's sentencing was supportive of the authorities and their efforts to combat corruption. This seems to be exactly the kind of message that Chinese government intended to get across, that is, that the event and its handling were intended to maximize loyalty to state ideologies and to minimize dissent. The state had shown its masterful skills in agenda-setting to guide public opinion by proposing acceptable and appropriate topics for debate. Meanwhile, it also linked with a notion of the morality of self-government. When one undertakes a moral action, it can be argued that it is an attempt to self-govern, in other words, to make oneself accountable for one's own actions (Dean 1999, p. 12). Hence, the collective condemnation of Bo Xilai and his corruption makes it very clear to people what constitutes good and what is bad. Therefore, it could be considered as a warning or an education to other government officials to "self-govern". Where discipline and control are carried out automatically, without direct policing or overt surveillance, there is a parallel to Bentham's panopticon prison structure (see Foucault 1977): the tower at the center of the prison with wide windows on every side that can open to the inner side of the ring. A supervisor on the tower could easily observe the prisoners inside, and thus this panopticon architecture allows, indeed forces the prisoners to discipline themselves automatically. Therefore, self-governing serves as an act of warning and intimidation and ensures that supervisory and surveillance power, always exists. It has been clearly documented that the Chinese government controls all forms of media in China, including Weibo. But on occasions, censorship of Weibo is known to be relaxed, allowing some space for free speech, particularly in cases of breaking news. Such Weibo-based stories include the case of Guo Meimei, the 20-year-old who claimed herself to be a senior manager in the Chinese Red Cross Society while flaunting her wealth on Weibo, posting photos of herself with expensive items such as jewelry, designer bikinis, Hermes handbags and a Maserati. This incident ignited heated public discussions and suspicions about the corruption and management within state-backed charity organizations.

At another level, the transparency of the Bo Xilai trial had limits. Zhang Zhi'an, a journalism professor at Sun Yet-sen University in Guangzhou, stated that the released transcripts appeared to be edited and censors appeared to have removed many comments on the blog that were skeptical of the justice process (Zhang & Zhou 2013). Though the guilty verdict and the sentencing of the former top politician, Bo Xilai, was considered a mere formality, despite this public reservation about the completeness of the communications transparency, it was nevertheless labeled as a significant step for the Chinese government to have embraced the most popular form of digital communication, Weibo, in the process. The proceedings were considered as an "open trial", but the courtroom was open only to the official media outlet, the Xinhua News Agency—the only approved media outlet for the case. The foreign media was not allowed to attend the trial. This great privilege limited the scope of coverage, maintaining a level of government control, so constituting a strategy and technology of governmentality, designed to shape and guide the hearts and minds of the Chinese to conform to the desired political ends (Foucault 1991). This trial has indeed attracted praise from much of the media for the robust determination of the government to fight corruption (The Economist 2013). However, it has also been critiqued as melodrama for "there were no political signals or messages of reformists triumphing over conservatives, nor even of one political faction crushing another" (Chang 2013). The only thing we could see is the official's failure to properly manage the family affairs (ibid.). While China's official media outlet, the People's Daily, described the trial as representing the "historical transparency and openness of China's rule of law" (Zhang 2013a), other critics noted that the real-time Weibo broadcasts were actually selective and not genuinely occurring in real-time. In addition, the staging of the trial was a powerful and unprecedented example of the way

Chinese authorities have sought to "not merely control social media", but to control opinion leaders, in order to "shape conversations" (Branigan 2013).

The handling of the Bo Xilai trial has also been described as a public relations strategy by David Bandurski of the Hong Kong University Media Project, as it aimed to use this platform to improve its political legitimacy (ibid.). The open trial and real-time Weibo broadcasts were indeed intended to reflect the transparency and openness of China's rule of law. However it is also the case that the authorities have managed to balance openness with control (Zhang 2013a). And it reassured the authorities that it was wise and strategic for the Chinese government to make public access available on a platform with which to monitor and persuade a population during the trial, so allowing the authorities to retain their commanding height. This spectacle of the Bo Xilai trial reaffirmed the importance of Weibo in people's lives. Despite the discounting of duplicate and fake registrations, the massive number of Weibo users continues to be a daunting challenge for a state to maintain its firm grip over information.

Despite the official transparency of coverage of the Bo Xilai trial, it has been widely acknowledged that the Chinese government has never really loosened its control over Weibo and other social media. Its well-known techniques for maintaining control have been illustrated in detail in Chapter Four. Especially since the new leadership took office in 2012, the government has ceaselessly taken up network space. On 27 February 2014, the Department of Central Internet Security and Informatization Leading Group was established to lead and coordinate internet security and informatization work among different sectors, with president Xi Jinpin as the leader of this team. In its first meeting, President Xi pledged to strengthen China's internet security and to build the nation into a strong cyber power. Xi emphasized that network security should be raised up to the height of national security (Zhao & Cao 2014). Subsequently, on April 15, 2014, President Xi held the first meeting of the National Security Committee, declaring that it would adhere to "overall national security", with network security of vital importance.

Timely Involvement of Mainstream Media

As early as 2012, in the wake of the stunning news about Bo Xilai, the headlines of major newspapers in China showed "unwavering public support" towards the central Party leadership's decision. Even the well-known liberal

Guangzhou newspaper, the Southern Weekend, was no exception (Hewitt 2012b). During the first days of the Bo Xilai trial, as previously mentioned, traditional media and official media were muted in the reportage of this trial. As a breaking and sensitive political event, this restraint was understandable. However, as the trial moved into its second and possibly final day, government and Party media outlets published several commentaries that ridiculed Bo over his denials. They fully displayed the government's justifiable reasons for guiding people's opinions in the trial, which, in turn, serves as a form of governmentality. Another state media outlet, Global Times, a subsidiary of the People's Daily extolled the crackdown on Bo Xilai as a victory against corruption by saying that the "high voltage" campaign has showed the government's resolute determination to fight graft which could "correct the Party's style and win people's support" (Global Times 2013). In addition, one commentary in the online edition of the People's Daily stated:

> What is regrettable is that, with regard to the facts, Bo Xilai made a supreme effort to quibble, to avoid the major charges while admitting the minor ones, and almost completely denied the facts of his crimes. (Wong & Ansfield 2013)

These commentaries were also highlighted by CCTV News to reiterate their importance (CCTV.com 2013). It reaffirmed that official media plays a bigger part in "commenting" than "reporting". In relation to big events, the role of official media tends to be more concerned with "guiding" people's judgment to tell right from wrong. It could obviously be seen that its "mouth and throat" function is strengthened in the social media era. The difference is that its use always appears to be very timely and appropriate. It allows enough space for people to discuss first, and then it gives guidance. Official media such as the People's Daily and Xinhua News Agency is always representing the authorities or the voices of handpicked experts, as one part of government whose role is not only to weave a comprehensive web of 'social control', but to enact various attempts to contain conduct through strategies of "education, persuasion, inducement, management, incitement, motivation and encouragement" (Rose & Miller 2010, p. 273). Meanwhile, the editorials and commentaries of the official media are seen as "expert" in this field, helping to assuage the public confusion and guide public opinions. The overriding message from the Global Times, one of the "mouth and throat" organs of the Party, declared that the live broadcast of the Bo Xilai trial could dispel public uncertainties and suspicions by uncovering the truth through Weibo.

> The Bo Xilai case must be a loud alarm, which revealed the central Party's firm determination and confidence to fight corruption. Each type of suspicion should be completely abandoned. The chances of corruption escaping the punishment will become increasingly smaller, which is a big trend and is not only a gust of wind. (Global Times 2013)

This emphasis on "fighting corruption" while maintaining control, embodies the intentions of governmentality, which is to maneuver the conduct of populations according to its "desires, aspirations, interests and beliefs" by "employing a variety of techniques and forms of knowledge" (Dean 1999, p. 11). Since corruption is a severe problem within the CCP and people show great resentment and dissatisfaction towards it, playing up the emphasis of fighting corruption in the Bo Xilai trial was the best strategy. As Rose and Miller (2010, p. 273) contend, a government is constituted with the purpose of articulating the various dreams and strategies of authorities to shape and regulate the beliefs and conduct of others in desired directions by acting upon their will.

Since government is a series of strategies and techniques through which to render programs operable and achievable, there are several programs of government to be deployed, including the complex assemblage of different types of forces—legal, architectural, professional, and other aspects of individuals or groups, to achieve regulatory ends (ibid., p. 281). In addition to the liberal technologies, such as guiding and persuasion, coercive techniques such as punishment and supervision are also involved. The Chinese government has made continued efforts to consolidate control over Weibo, and it is noteworthy that close to the time of the Bo Xilai trial, the Chinese government initiated a campaign of intimidation against China's social media users. Different from the previous anti-rumour campaigns, this time its focus was on high-profile social media figures. Several prominent Weibo figures were detained or interrogated. Meanwhile, warnings were issued to prosecute people for their online activities. These were described by one top propaganda official as "the purification of the online environment" (Chin & Mozur 2013).

These examples included an American investor and "Big V", Charles Xue, who has 12 million followers on Weibo, who was arrested for soliciting a prostitute in August 2013. However, this case was interpreted by some analysts as a warning to other social media stars (ibid.), and an "intimidation strategy" for the purpose of controlling online information (Areddy 2013). Official media, Xinhua news, said "the internet Big V 'Xue Manzi' has toppled from the sacred altar. This has sounded a warning bell about the law to all big Vs on the internet" (Buckley 2013). Mr. Xue publicized posts which criticized toxic food, high prices, low wages and other issues and said, "We have become 'people who tolerate'". This message was reposted by his followers more than 17,000 times and received more than 2000 comments (ibid.). It was also announced that the police had arrested another big V, Qin Zhihui, who specialized in spreading rumors against politicians, celebrities and even Zhang Haidi, a spiritual icon of the country. Finally Qin was sentenced to three years in prison. Subsequently, the propaganda officials pledged publicly to apply seven rules to regulate control. These added to the already existing regulations and laws for governing implemented by the Chinese government. These strong demonstrations of the ability of the government to control also serve to enforce people's self-censorship and self-regulation. Thus, these sophisticated and well-managed government strategies aim to normalize the practice of individuals managing themselves through self-regulation, which Foucault (1988a) called "government of the self".

In this way, in addition to the sovereign power, other forms of strategies are also employed. Thus the central elements of government as a form of power are distinct from the operations of sovereignty.

> With government it is a question not of imposing law on men, but of disposing things; that is to say, of employing tactics rather than laws, and even of using laws themselves as tactics—to arrange things in such a way that, through a certain number of means, such and such ends may be achieved. (Foucault 1991, p. 95)

The opacity and implicitness of censorship in China has made people fear and therefore unconsciously, to self-regulate.

Conclusion

In the Bo Xilai trial, a form of government in charge is found that combines both the characteristics of apparent liberalism in its transparency, and of authoritarianism in ensuring that it realizes its objectives of regulating Weibo through the careful staging of sensitive political events. The witnessing of the trial on Weibo has indeed provided an open and free platform for public discussion, serving as a type of online public sphere in the Chinese society. However, it is highly managed and engineered by the Chinese government. The highly interactive and disseminating nature of Weibo has enabled a large population to talk, which clearly presents a challenge to the government's control over public discourse. Even the New York Times columnist Nicholas

Kristof boldly commented before the trial that "the [Bo Xilai] scandal is the talk of China, and the government has lost control of the narrative" (Kristof 2012). Subsequently the party-state has demonstrated its masterful ability in consolidating its control in sensitive issues. Despite the appearance of a liberal approach, for example, calling on people to fight corruption, it is in fact non-liberalism that prevails, in which it overrides the choices and aspirations of the individual when exercising hard censorship.

The practice of government in its management of the trial is therefore complex. The government takes diverse strategies, procedures, mechanisms and techniques used by authorities to give credibility to official programs and to render them operational (Sigley 1996, p. 473). A certain new openness marked the trial, while at the same time it was always possible to predict the precise outcome of any possible intervention. Thus, in the government's public access management of the trial on Weibo, the authorities were still able to embed sovereign interest and power into the open and free platform of Weibo. They skillfully guided people's opinions and thought when necessary. For the Chinese government, which aims to build a society based on the rule of law, the openness of the Bo Xilai trial offered a perfect opportunity for it to exhibit a high degree of transparency. At the same time, further institutional adaption and openness within the Party are needed to build up its legitimacy (Broadhurst & Wang 2014). It has reflected a greater nuance in how the party-state manages to manipulate the public discourse in the information age. From a macro perspective, despite the Chinese government's traditionally authoritarian methods of censorship in governing social media, in this case it appeared to do the opposite, while actively using Weibo to its own advantage, therefore embodying governmentality.

Despite the fact that Weibo offers a seemingly free and open platform for people to interact and talk, if the Bo Xilai trial and its public debate are seen as indicative, it is in fact not a public sphere. The unified and regulated discussions on the Bo Xilai trial show that it is not a fair and free platform, but a constrained public space. It not only demonstrates the increasing responsiveness of the Chinese government to public concerns, but is also another perfect example of cooperation between the government and Sina Cooperation. Sina Weibo has demonstrated that it is an extension of the government's information monopoly over traditional media, and includes the social media, Weibo. The trial clearly reflected the adaptability of the Chinese government in using Weibo to maximum effect.

The authorities tolerated more openness and freedom in addressing this type of problem, which may spark popular dissatisfaction or suspicion if left unreported. However, despite a degree of openness in the Bo Xilai trial, the transparency was selective. Nevertheless, in the process, the CCP has already taken a giant step toward transparency. On the one hand, it reflects the government's efforts to advance with the times to maintain political stability; on the other hand, it has demonstrated the government's adeptness and increasing confidence in using Weibo to its own advantage. It confirms the former president Hu Jintao's way of "taking the initiative" in shaping public opinion by allowing the state media like Xinhua, CCTV, and People's Daily to report breaking news. After the successful test of releasing information during the May 2008 Sichuan earthquake, Hu paid a visit to the People's Daily and commented: "We must perfect our system of news release, and improve our system for news reports on sudden-breaking public events, releasing authoritative information at the earliest moment, improving timelines, increasing transparency, and firmly grasping the initiative in news propaganda work" (see Bandurski 2008). It seems the government has considered Weibo as another battleground in which to channel correct public opinion.

Online communication about certain topics such as corruption may avoid a crisis. At the same time, it helped to strengthen Xi Jinping's image, so representing a shift in Chinese leadership (Ng 2013).

In its most politically sensitive moments, the Chinese government has often shown a "heavy-handed and traditional-style management" of the media and the internet (Hewitt 2012b). In this sense, Weibo could be considered an extension of the official mouthpiece. Therefore, although the unprecedented transparency of the Bo trial was considered by Kaiser Kuo, Director of International Communications for China's leading search engine, Baidu as "a comparably large and impactful public sphere in China's history" (ibid.), the Chinese government has above all, tried to keep pace with technological change in order to enforce regulation. The use of Weibo during the Bo Xilai trial demonstrated the modern government's control of the conduct of its citizens via seemingly transparent methods, while on the other hand building the government's legitimacy and transparency. The trial was a clever step of the Chinese government to provide openness while retaining control.

This chapter illustrates how authoritarian and liberal measures are integrated into neoliberal technologies in the current Chinese social media context, revealing the intertwining of both authoritarian and liberal tactics in the Bo Xilai trial. The liberal discourse of governmentality has been shown as compatible with the illiberal context of China, because the idea of 'liberalism' here is not a political concept, but a way of self-governing, and an influential rationality of government (Dean & Hindess 1998, p. 7). During the trial, the Chinese government has shown sufficiently skilful and sophisticated techniques to control the conduct of its citizens via seemingly moral, rational and transparent methods. Despite a conventional authoritarian approach to governing, here the government has exhibited a high degree of transparency, which fulfills its purposes. This chapter also argues that the state's manipulation of Weibo during the Bo Xilai trial indeed minimized the chance of reasoned and rational debate, while demonstrating skillfully that it is ever more difficult to evade state control to form a real public sphere.

References

Areddy, J. 2013, 'Bo Xilai's life sentence: The Weibo reaction', The Wall Street Journal, 22 September, viewed 23 April 2014, <http://blogs.wsj.com/chinarealtime/2013/09/22/bo-xilais-life-sentence-the-weibo-reaction-china/>.

Bandurski, D. 2008, 'Propaganda leaders scurry off to carry out the "spirit" of Hu Jintao's "important" media speech', China Media Project, 25 June, viewed 20 April 2013, <http://cmp.hku.hk/2008/06/25/1079/>.

Benney, J. 2013, 'The aesthetics of microblogging: How the Chinese state controls Weibo', Tilburg paper in Culture Studies, viewed 23 May 2014. <http://www.tilburguniversity.edu/upload/e4ef741d-2c6a-4ad9-9b17-32e103332502_TPCS_66_Benney.pdf>.

Branigan, T. 2012, 'China's Hu Jintao warns congress corruption could cause fall of state', The Guardian, 9 November, viewed 20 March 2014, <http://www.theguardian.com/world/2012/nov/08/china-hujintao-warning-congress-corruption>.

Branigan, T. 2013, 'Bo Xilai trial coverage: Controlled by the court, but extraordinary', The Guardian, 23 August, viewed 23 April 2014, <http://www.theguardian.com/world/2013/aug/22/china-open-bo-xilai-trial>.

Broadhurst, R & Wang, P. 2014, 'After the Bo Xilai trial: Does corruption threaten China's future?', Survival, vol. 56, no. 3, pp. 157–178.

Buckley, C. 2013, 'Crackdown on bloggers is mounted by China', The New York Times, 10 September, viewed 24 April 2014, <http://www.nytimes.com/2013/09/11/world/asia/china-cracks-down-on-online-opinion-makers.html?pagewanted=all&_r=0>.

Burchell, G, Gordon, C & Miller, P (eds.). 1991, The Foucault effect: Studies in Governmentality, Harvester Wheatsheaf, Hertfordshire.

CCTV.com. 2013, 'Jianchi fazhi fanfu, jianshe lianjie zhengfu (Adhere to fight corruption, building transparent government)', CCTV.com, 22 September, viewed 22 May 2014, <http://tv.cntv.cn/video/C10437/44fe86327ec44baab8271f8e541213bb>.

Chang, P. 2013, 'Don't be fooled by Bo Xilai's trial', South China Morning Post, 1 September, viewed 3 May 2014, <http://www.scmp.com/comment/insight-opinion/article/1301341/dont-be-fooled-bo-xilais-trial>.

Chen, Y. 2013, 'Successful trial, unsatisfied investigation', Chen Youxi's Blog, 23 August, viewed 2 February, <http://blog.sina.com.cn/s/blog_6b804b510101r7rq.html?tj=2>.

Chin, J & Chao, L. 2011, 'China portal Sina gets veiled Weibo warning', The Wall Street Journal, 24 August, viewed 20 March 2013, <http://online.wsj.com/news/articles/SB20001424053111904279004576526293276595886>.

Chin, J & Mozur, P. 2013, 'China intensifies social-media crackdown: Campaign takes toll on public debate, popular platform', The Wall Street Journal, 19 September, viewed 22 April 2014 <http://online.wsj.com/news/articles/SB10001424127887324807704579082940411106988?mg=reno64wsj&url=http%3A%2F%2Fonline.wsj.com%2Farticle%2FSB10001424127887324807704579082940411106988.html>.

China Daily. 2011, 'Romor-growing pain of Weibo', China Daily, 10 November, viewed 22 August 2013, <http://www.chinadaily.com.cn/2011-11/10/content_14072700.htm>.

Colebatch, HK. 2002, 'Government and governmentality: Using multiple approaches to the analysis of government', Australian Journal of Political Science, vol. 37, no. 3, pp. 417–435.

Dean, M. 1999, Governmentality: Power and rule in modern society, Sage, London.

Dean, M. 2002, 'Liberal government and authoritarianism', Economy and Society, vol. 31, no. 1, pp. 37–61.

Dean, M & Hindess B. 1998, 'Introduction: Government, liberalism, society', in Dean, M & Hindess, B (eds.), Governing Australia: Studies in contemporary rationalities of government, Cambridge University Press, Cambridge, pp. 1–19.

Foucault, M. 1977, Discipline and punish: The birth of the prison, Pantheon Books, New York.

Foucault, M. 1988a, 'Technologies of the self', in Martin, LH, Gutman, H & Hutton, P (eds.), Technologies of the self: A seminar with Michel Foucault, The University of Massachusetts Press, Amherst, pp. 16–49.

Foucault, M. 1991, 'Governmentality', in Burchell, G, Gordon, C & Miller, P (eds.), The Foucault effect: Studies in governmental rationality, Harvester Wheatsheaf, Hemel Hempstead, pp. 87–104.

Global Times. 2013, 'Yishen pan Bo Xilai wuqituxing zhangxian falv gangxing (A trial of Bo Xilai to life imprisonment highlights the rigidity of the law)', Global Times, 23 September, viewed 24 June 2014, <http://www.guancha.cn/HuanQiuShiBao/2013_09_23_174072.shtml>.

Hassid, J. 2012, 'Safety valve or pressure cooker? Blogs in Chinese political life', Journal of Communication, vol. 62, no. 2, pp. 212–230.

Hewitt, D. 2012a, 'Weibo brings change to China', BBC News, 31 July, viewed 12 November 2013, <http://www.bbc.co.uk/news/magazine-18887804>.

Hewitt, D. 2012b, '"Unwavering public support" not quite so easy to find these days', The China Beat, 17 April, viewed 20 April 2014, <http://www.thechinabeat.org/?p=4249>.

Hong, K. 2013, 'China's censorship on Sina Weibo in overdrive after former official Bo Xilai is charged with bribery', The Next Web, 25 July, viewed 12 May 2014, <http://thenextweb.com/asia/2013/07/25/chinas-censorship-on-sina-weibo-in-overdrive-after-former-official-bo-xilai-is-charged-with-bribery/>.

Jiang, Y. 2012, Cyber-Nationalism in China, University of Adelaide Press, Adelaide.

King, G, Pan, J & Roberts, M. 2013, 'How censorship in China allows government criticism but silences collective expression', American Political Science Review, vol. 107, no. 2, pp. 326–341.

Kristof, N. 2012, 'A body, a scandal and China', The New York Times, 21 April, viewed 27 April 2013, <http://www.nytimes.com/2012/04/22/opinion/sunday/kristof-a-body-a-scandal-and-china.html?_r=0>.

Lagerkvist, J. 2010, After the internet, before democracy: Competing norms in Chinese media and society, Peter Lang, Bern.

Lewis, OA. 2013, 'Net inclusion: New media's impact on deliberative politics in China', Journal of Contemporary Asia, vol. 43, no. 4, pp. 678–708.

Meng, B. 2010, 'Moving beyond democratization: A thought piece on the China Internet research agenda', International Journal of Communication, vol. 4, pp. 501–508.

Ng, T. 2013, 'Xi Jinping represents a shift in Chinese leadership style, observers say', South China Morning Post, 8 June, viewed 12 June 2014, <http://www.scmp.com/news/china/article/1256047/xi-jinping-represents-shift-chinese-leadership-style-observers-say>.

People.cn. 2012, '2012 nian Xinlang zhengwu weibo baogao (2012 report on Sina government microblogs)', People.cn, viewed 3 December 2013, <http://yuqing.people.com.cn/n/2012/1203/c210118-19770124.html>.

People.cn. 2013, '2013 nian Xinlang zhengwu weibo baogao (2013 report on Sina government microblogs)', People.cn, viewed 26 December 2013, <http://yuqing.people.com.cn/n/2013/1226/c210118-23952286.html>.

Rauchfleisch, A & Schäfer, MS. 2014, 'Multiple public spheres of Weibo: A typology of forms and potentials of online public spheres in China', Information, Communication & Society, no. ahead-of-print, pp. 1–17.

Rose, N & Miller, P. 1992, 'Political power beyond the state: Problematics of government', British Journal of Sociology, vol. 43, no. 2, pp. 173–205.

Rose, N & Miller, P. 2010, 'Political power beyond the State: Problematics of government', The British Journal of Sociology, vol. 61, no. s1, pp. 271–303.

Sigley, G. 1996, 'Governing Chinese bodies: The significance of studies in the concept of governmentality for the analysis of government in China', Economy and Society, vol. 25, no. 4, pp. 457–482.

Sullivan, J. 2014, 'China's Weibo: Is faster different?', New Media & Society, vol. 16, no. 1, pp. 24–37.

The Economist. 2013, 'Going down fighting: China has been gripped by an extraordinary courtroom drama', The Economist, 31 August, viewed 2 May 2014, <http://www.economist.com/news/china/21584367-china-has-been-gripped-extraordinary-courtroom-drama-going-down-fighting>.

The Telegraph. 2009, 'China riots: Twitter and YouTube frustrate "censorship attempts"', The Telegraph, 6 July, viewed 15 March 2013, <http://www.telegraph.co.uk/news/worldnews/asia/china/5756766/China-riots-Twitter-and-YouTube-frustrate-censorship-attempts.html>.

Wauters, R. 2009, 'China blocks access to Twitter, Facebook after riots', TechCrunch Daily, 7 July, viewed 15 March 2013, <http://techcrunch.com/2009/07/07/china-blocks-access-to-twitter-facebook-after-riots/>.

Wong, E & Ansfield J. 2013, 'As surprisingly open trial begins in China: Fallen politician shows defiance', The New York Times, 22 August, viewed 20 April 2014, <http://www.nytimes.com/2013/08/23/world/asia/fallen-officials-trial-begins-in-china.html?ref=asia&_r=0>.

Xiao, Q. 2011, 'The battle for the Chinese internet', Journal of Democracy, vol. 22, no. 2, pp. 47–61.

Xinhua News. 2012a, 'Wang Lijun sentenced to 15 years in prison', Xinhua News, 24 September, viewed 22 October 2013, <http://news.xinhuanet.com/english/china/2012-09/24/c_131868689.htm>.

Xinhua News. 2012b, 'China voice: Why do rumors repeatedly arise in Bo Xilai incident?', Xinhua News, 29 April, viewed 4 May 2013, <http://news.xinhuanet.com/english/indepth/2012-04/29/c_131560026.htm>.

Zhai, K & Boehler, P. 2013, 'Court's Sina Weibo account promotes one-sided debate on disgraced Bo Xilai', South China Morning Post, 19 August, viewed 20 April 2014, <http://www.scmp.com/news/china-insider/article/1297719/courts-sina-weibo-account-promotes-one-sided-debate-bo-xilai>.

Zhang, Q. 2013a, 'Microblogging the Bo Xilai trial: Transparency or theatre?', BBC News, 23 August, viewed 22 March 2014, <http://www.bbc.com/news/world-asia-china-23806657>.

Zhang, Y. 2013b, 'Fall of a princeling: Bo Xilai's trial by Chinese social media', The Conversation, 30 August, viewed 20 March 2014, <http://theconversation.com/fall-of-a-princeling-bo-xilais-trial-by-chinese-social-media-17599>.

Zhang, W & Zhou, C. 2013, 'Shuangchong shijiao xiade Bo Xilai an tingshen weibo zhibo kaocha (Investigation on the live Weibo trial of the Bo Xilai trial from double perspectives)', Shanghai Journalism Review, viewed 25 May 2014, <http://journalist.news365.com.cn/gybk/201406/t20140605_1082809.html>.

Zhao, L & Cao, Y. 2014, 'Xi looks to a nation of cyberpower', China Daily, 28 February, viewed 25 May 2014, <http://usa.chinadaily.com.cn/china/2014-02/28/content_17311470.htm>.

· 6 ·

PATRIOTIC CITIZENRY IN CHINA'S WEIBO COMMUNITY

> The event, "Ding was here" should be an opportunity to reflect on one's educational attainments… [The self-reflection on this event] made people see a strong appeal to the level of civilization of this society and a conscious reflection on the state. (Li 2013)

Introduction

The quotation is a commentary from the People's Daily, the mouthpiece of China's Communist Party, after the "Ding was here" controversy, which was an internet incident that garnered great debate on Weibo about the Chinese people's national and international image. This event evoked and consolidated strong patriotic and collective sentiments among Chinese netizens. This chapter therefore draws upon this event as a case study, seeking an explanation for this powerful online discourse and illustrating how the party-state attempts to embrace more sophisticated forms of governance to construct an environment for "free" communications space. At the same time, it exemplifies the techniques of "technologies of the self", which Foucault defines as the multiple procedures and art or knowledge that government applies to promote willing compliance rather than directly employing brute force (Foucault 1991, pp. 102–103). This type of governance involves more complex and ambiguous relations between the state and netizens as indicated by this case study.

Drawing from possible explanations from the literature review chapter as well as the samples collected from "Ding was here", this chapter argues that the formation of patriotic sentiment that arose from this case is realized through a variety of technologies. A number of strategies and technologies of rule were adopted by the Chinese government to indirectly guide people's minds in order to ultimately achieve their regulatory purposes. The case will provide a detailed analysis of the tactics of governmentality in shaping microbloggers' patriotic sentiments. Therefore, to investigate the impact of "Ding was here", this chapter presents four sections. The first section introduces the background to the event. The second section describes the "self-disciplinary" aspect of online activities in China—the enforcing of collectivism in cyberspace. The third section illustrates how this control strategy—governing from a distance—is interlinked with the Chinese government's activities. The final section will put this into perspective with an analysis of how the response to "Ding was here" supports the current political framework.

In other words, we need to consider how the cultivation of national identity shapes individual identities through particular strategies. This chapter argues that the emergence of the collective identity that arose from "Ding was here" is particularly congruent with some of the core slogans of the Chinese state. The explanation for this congruence is multi-layered. One is the success of the ideas of collectivism and patriotism, to be understood as the human conduct of everyday life and discourses, utilized to strengthen the reinforcement of the state, ensuring that the role of the Chinese government slogans is to promote political stability and social harmony as called for by former president Hu Jintao. The analysis in this chapter therefore provides insights into how cultural control is exercised in China. The close relationship between technology and cultural control will become apparent through a brief examination of the development of the internet and its regulatory practices in China from the early days of internet use to the era of web 2.0. The sections that follow examine how the internet is being strategically regulated and monitored via the discourse of technological auto-regulation in China.

This chapter also examines how neoliberal governmentality and patriotism are both enabled in Weibo users. Rather than the government acting purely on the basis of power and authority, techniques of "freedom" were also used, allowing individuals to govern themselves to achieve the authorities' ends (Dean 2002, p. 37). This constitutes an important new technique of governing in the social media era in China. The long-term ingrained governmental planning of promoting autonomous choices has framed Weibo users' thinking in order to feel a degree of responsibility for national image and self-steered patriotism. This reinforces one of the most potent methods of enabling and maintaining discipline via the notion of government of the self, through the concepts of patriotism and national image.

Background of "Ding Was Here"

On May 24, 2013, a verified Weibo user named "kongyouwuyi" (Mr. Shen) posted a photo of an engraving in the 3,500-year-old Luxor Temple in Egypt which had been vandalized with Chinese graffiti saying "Ding Jinhao was here". The traveler wrote on the original Weibo post, "It was the saddest moment during my stay in Egypt. I'm so ashamed that I want to hide myself. I said to the Egyptian tour guide, 'I'm really sorry' (Shen 2013). Then we tried to wipe out the shame with tissue, but it was difficult to clear it out, and we could not use water." Immediately, this posting generated a massive online backlash among China's unforgiving netizens. The post was tweeted and retweeted and it sparked a heated discussion in China about etiquette when travelling abroad, with Ding Jinhao becoming the target of Chinese internet vigilantes. By May 25, 2013, there were more than 11,000 comments and as many as 83,000 retweets (Pan 2013). There were diverse online criticisms of the boy and his parents. In addition, there were many debates about Chinese people's travelling etiquette and *suzhi* (quality), saying that Ding's bad manners had damaged the image of the Chinese people.

In the meantime, the post prompted an online hunt for Ding Jinhao, with the internet vigilantes in China soon identifying him. He was a 14-year-old student. On May 25, a netizen revealed Ding's personal information through the aptly named human flesh search engine (to be discussed later in this chapter) and posted it on Weibo, including his date of birth and the school he attended in Nanjing in eastern China's Jiangsu Province. Later that day, Ding's embarrassed parents made a public apology to both the Chinese people and to the Egyptian authorities for their son's wrongdoing. They told the Nanjing-based *Modern Express* newspaper: "We apologize to the Egyptian authorities and the Chinese people who were concerned about the incident. He has realized that he made a mistake, and we beg your pardon; please give him a chance to correct his act" (Hu 2013). Later, on May 26, the official website of the school Ding attended was hacked by vigilante netizens and defaced with a pop-up window on the website mimicking Ding Jinhao's vandalism. Visitors have to click "ok" on a message box which reads "Ding has visited this place" before they are granted access to the site. There were also calls to reflect on education and family influence, with Weibo users condemning Ding's parents for not educating him properly. Netizens argued about whether the behavior lost face for the Chinese people. There were a number of comments abusively attacking Ding himself. Later that day, according to a report from the Xinhua News Agency, the graffiti had almost been removed.

In the following days, there were almost one hundred English reports on "Ding was here" when searched in Google. News agencies such as AFP, Reuters, CNN, the BBC and other influential media, had reported on this event, using widely applied negative terms such as 'destroy' and 'deface'.

In terms of the particular event that led to national embarrassment, one explanation may be that the Chinese state would like to improve China's global image and soft power. With China's economy booming over the past decade, a growing number of the country's residents have become global tourists, fuelled by rising incomes and the relaxation of government restrictions on citizens' ability to travel abroad. According to a CNN report, in 2012, the Chinese have overtaken Americans and Germans as the world's top international tourism spenders, with 83 million people spending a record US$102 billion on international tourism, a 40 percent rise from US$73 billion in 2011 (Cripps 2013b). In 2013, the number of outbound Chinese tourists was more than 90 million for the first time, and is expected to exceed 100 million in the next five years. The number will probably exceed 400 million in the five years following this (Qian & Xu 2013).

In the responses to Ding's incident, there was a tendency for emotional over-reaction, which indicates a lack of confidence and a sense of inferiority or shame within the Chinese nation. However, the dramatic rise in tourists evident in a number of recent reports also suggests that Chinese travellers have replaced the "ugly American" stereotype with what The Atlantic Wire has dubbed the "Ugly Chinese Tourist" (Abad-Santos 2013). And Ding Jinhao is definitely not the first person with such "uncivilized" behavior. The poor behavior of Chinese tourists is often criticized by the media and meets a very strong response. The report from the Atlantic Wire also lists further instances where Chinese people have earned this reputation, such as at the Louvre in Paris, where the sign to warn people not to defecate and urinate on the premises is only in Chinese. There are Chinese tourists visiting the monks and temples in Thailand while disrespectfully wearing shorts. Chinese people are known for talking loudly. Chinese tourists hit the lions in zoos with snowballs and kill crocodiles by throwing objects into their exhibits (Abad-Santos 2013). Moreover, according to this news, there were other similar incidents that caused public outrage in March 2009 when a man from Jiangsu province carved his name in a rock in Taiwan's Yehliu Geopark, and also in February 2013 when a visitor engraved their name in a cauldron at Beijing's Palace Museum.

Following the Ding incident, online posts claimed that Song Yin, said to be a senior reporter with the Hong Kong-based Wen Wei Po newspaper, had engraved similar words in a Dunhuang fresco in northwest Gansu Province. A photograph showing the words: "senior reporter of Wen Wei Po Song Yin was here for research in *lixia* in 2000" (*lixia* is a Chinese solar term referring to the beginning of summer). Wen Wei Po condemned the act, but said there was no such person working at the newspaper (Hu 2013).

This conflict in behaviors is not necessarily a new phenomenon. In 1992, a book called The Ugly Chinaman and the Crisis of Chinese Culture written by Bo Yang, was published in the English-speaking world, which included the author's speeches, writings and media interviews. Initially, this critique of the Chinese was banned in mainland China by Communist Party Officials. It was not until 2008 that Bo Yang's work, which in Chinese is called Ugly Chinese, crossed the seas and entered mainland China. This book described bad manners in Chinese culture, such as the rude, pushy behavior of the crowds, belching, wind-breaking, and spitting. He summarized Chinese people's characteristics as either arrogant or degraded, but certainly without dignity. The author contends that the problem goes back centuries. Bo Yang sharply describes this as "the putrid vat of soy sauce" (his phrase for the unpleasant side of China's otherwise fascinating culture) (Bo 1992). However, improving China's image and also strengthening its soft power could be a possible explanation for this congruence between shameful public behavior abroad and the empowered state agenda promoting China as a civilized nation. It does not quite explain the collective outpouring of emotions of national patriotism. Understanding this involves us in questions relating to the Chinese version of governmentality. These remarks on Chinese people's travelling etiquette showed the problematic of governmentality, that problems do not exist in themselves, rather, they become known "through grids of evaluation and judgment about objects that are far from self-evident" (Dean & Hindess 1998, p. 9). The study of government, then, entails modes of reasoning, employing various kinds of knowledge and agency to function in multiple ways (ibid.).

A Wave of National Embarrassment and National Patriotism

The event of "Ding was here" sparked national embarrassment and a wave of public condemnation. Expressions like "Ding's uncivilized behavior is a disgrace to our entire race" and "This is not only a child's fault. I believe that many adults probably behave as badly. This is a national shame and the Chinese people really need to reflect" are widely seen. This "power effect" is conceptualized by Rose (1999) that "free" actors are subject to new practices to construct identities for citizens to shape their conduct according to responsibility and self-conduct. In this incident, people are neatly divided into exclusive groups: patriots and non-patriots.

Moreover, there were even death threats (Hu 2013). The question on the minds of many at that moment was "why do Chinese people not behave properly?" An editorial of the *People's Daily* Online expressed the belief that "the instance shows our families and schools have failed to deliver to the children something that should be expected first and foremost of any education: moral principles and civic virtues" (Wan 2013).

A small cultural incident about travel etiquette such as this would usually, at most, spark a debate about the citizens' awareness of the need to show respect towards public property and historical heritage. However, in an anonymous online survey conducted by Tencent to answer the question of whether the incident of "Ding was here" made you feel embarrassed and the Chinese people lose face, 85 percent of participants felt that this was true, while only 15 percent felt that it was not.

Here a question can be asked: why did this small travel incident spark such great national embarrassment? China's cultural traditions offer a clear explanation. The Chinese have always cared strongly about appearances, and a level of appropriateness and dignity that they refer to as "face". They never want to lose face; they want always to show their absolute best. Since this behavior happened abroad, national image and pride come into play, therefore, it resulted in an extreme loss of face for the entire Chinese people. The rising economic development and global integration of China in recent years meant that the Chinese people are keen to improve their international image and status. However, in addition to the "loss of face" in this incident, there was a convergence between the public outcry and the government's ongoing efforts to build patriotic sentiment. This outpouring of spontaneous patriotism resonated with the instrumental technologies of government in usually advanced liberal regimes, and more recently used by the Chinese authorities (Rose 1996, p. 53).

In addition to the application of brute force to exercise control, modern government adopts certain strategies, techniques and procedures to render programs operable. In the construction of a strong sense of patriotism, the Chinese government uses a number of technologies to reach its aspirations. For example, inspiring imagination is an essential step for formation of group identity. It has been noted that "all communities larger than primordial villages of face-to-face contact (and perhaps even these) are imagined" (Anderson 2006, p. 6). In this way, communities are distinguished not by uniqueness but by their imagination. It is also true of nation and state. Therefore, throughout modern history, Western civilization and advanced culture have inevitably been "the other" in China's imagination, as contrasted with China reflecting the self-abasement, lack of confidence and aspiration of the Chinese. Particularly in the late nineteenth and early twentieth centuries, China was referred to as the "sick man of East Asia" when it was riven by internal divisions and forced by great powers into a series of unequal treaties. Therefore, to a certain extent, this view reflects the way the Chinese have defined and positioned themselves in different historical periods. It also reflects the way the Chinese conceive their national identity.

The government of the self, in which individuals manage themselves via self-regulation, is an extension of regulation over space and time via "indirect mechanisms" as a part of liberal democratic practices (Miller & Rose 1990, p. 83). Contemporary Chinese government increasingly uses this mechanism to regulate Weibo and other media. This type of control allows the government to achieve its purposes yet "act at a distance", which is "to do things in the center that sometimes makes it possible to dominate at the periphery spatially as well as chronologically" (Latour 1987, p. 232). In this case, the Chinese government has implemented a variety of strategies to cultivate a collective sense of patriotism to shape their individual identities, including the use of Weibo.

Timely Involvement of Mainstream Media

In "Ding was here", the Chinese government closely followed online chats in order to call public attention to travelling etiquette, as even possibly having an impact on government policies. The day after the public outcry over "Ding was here", the CCP mouthpiece, the *People's Daily*, picked it up and made a commentary to maximize its impact (Li 2013). The *People's Daily* commentaries are always seen as highly consistent with the Party principles from the paper that "set the tone for all other media in China" (Yin 2007). It could be seen that the government in fact prompts a popular reaction, and then follows it up. The interaction between mainstream media and Weibo is as follows: In the first step, the public has responded to the initiative to set the agenda, and then the mainstream media will selectively highlight certain cases to re-set the agenda, at the same time enabling the public discussion to reach a peak. Weibo users then widely forward the mainstream media commentaries. The government's responsiveness is a way of control through maximizing the impact of the story for its own purposes.

This incident gained enthusiastic support from the state and state-controlled media, and it is undeniable that this is particularly congruent with some of the core policies of the Chinese state. This event appeared in fact just a few days after China's government had attacked 'uncivilized' tourists for ruining the country's reputation abroad. Several days prior to the Ding Jinhao event, on May 16, at a meeting on a new tourism law of China, a senior Communist Party Official, Wang Yang, one of the country's four vice-premiers, warned Chinese tourists that they should be more polite when travelling, for example, not talking loudly in public, carving characters on tourist attractions, or crossing the road against the traffic lights, and activities such as spitting are considered poor behavior. Wang said that "[i]mproving the civilized quality of the citizens and building a good image of Chinese tourists are the obligations of governments at all levels and relevant agencies and companies". He further stated that Chinese authorities should "guide tourists to conscientiously abide by public order and social ethics, respect local religious beliefs and customs, mind their speech and behavior…and protect the environment" (Cheung 2013). Wang also urged compatriots to project "a good image of Chinese tourists" and advocated for the nation's Tourism Law (ibid.).

Therefore, this case reveals that online opinions easily gain the attention of the traditional media, which could be seen as a method to reinforce the central position of the mainstream media. In this way, the state-controlled, mainstream media remains dominant in "molding" and constructing social responses and public opinion. Prior to national economic reform in 1978, the media was a Party propaganda apparatus (Shirk 2011), but in current times, once the appeal of online public opinion is congruent with government actions, the mainstream media reaffirms the dominance of its traditional function in directing public opinion. In this incident, the netizens influenced the agenda of the conventional media, and then the conventional media maintained the agenda by issuing propaganda commentaries. The function of the conventional media remains to perform a propaganda function in China and to correctly guide public opinion (Rawnsley 2006; Zhang 2006). Therefore, the event of "Ding was here" coincided with the national appeal of issuing tourism law.

Weibo offers a perfect platform for state propaganda expression. Despite the fact that Weibo has exhibited exciting new possibilities for political discussion and protest mobilization, offering citizens new channels for speaking and acting together, it is more effective when facilitating propaganda. Individuals who appear to be expressing their views autonomously assist the government to realize its goals for governing its citizens in a spirit of national patriotism. Political authorities no longer seek to govern individuals in all spheres of their existence, from the most intimate to the most public, as "individuals themselves, as workers, managers and members of families, can be mobilized in alliance with political objectives" (Miller & Rose 2008, pp. 51–52). The Chinese state and its netizens do not confront one another, but respond to this agenda in a spirit of "cooperation"—though this type of relationship is not fixed and is always changing.

In September, immediately before the Golden Week holiday that started on National Day October 1, which is one of the most popular times of year for the Chinese to travel, China's National Tourism Administration publicized an illustrated 64-page 'Guidebook for Civilized Tourism' to instruct citizens on social norms overseas. It could also be accessed by people from its official website. China is not the first country to issue guidelines to travellers. Both locals and visitors on Tokyo subways, for example, will often encounter an ongoing series of 'etiquette tip' posters for consideration on public transport (McNeice 2013). The booklet covers everything from reminders to say "please" and "thank you" and other specific rules of polite behavior in different countries. These books are printed with attractive cartoons and vivid illustrations. For example, do not ask questions like 'where are you going?' when greeting in the UK, and do not pick up your chopsticks before your elder. It also includes advice on etiquette on taking photos, toilet use, and queue jumping. Lessons learned from the globally publicized scandal, the Guide remind visitors, were to respect historical relics, and "not to scribble on, climb on or touch them". The guidebook of civilized tourism was a technique of the self, which served several purposes. It appeared during the Golden Week holiday, a time when the greatest number of tourists would be travelling or preparing to travel, therefore this action was able to immediately improve the tourists' image. Furthermore, it was able to educate and regulate people's behaviors. The 'Guidebook for Civilized Tourism' was distributed by some cities for free. This management of distributing brochures to improve citizens' behaviors demonstrates the amenability of tools in and of government control. As mentioned in Chapter Two, among Foucault's four 'technologies', the latter two of 'technologies of power' and 'technologies of the self' have a 'contact point', which means that technologies of power 'interact' with technologies of the self to bring individuals into subjection (Burchell 1996, p. 20). In this case, government departments produce information handouts to educate the citizens to be "civilized". In addition, public relations experts could be employed to devise a number of advertising campaigns to generate public concern. This is one part of government technologies, which are "the complex of mundane programs, calculations, techniques, apparatuses, documents and procedures through which authorities seek to embody and give effect to governmental ambitions" (Rose & Miller 2010, p. 273).

On October 1, the Tourism Law of the People's Republic of China went into effect attempting to lay out rules to regulate China's tourism industry, addressing issues like tourist safety, unfair competition, price hikes and forced goods purchases, in order to promote sustained industry growth. There are several articles of the new law dealing with tourist behaviors. For example, Article 14 states: "Tourists shall observe public order and respect social morality in tourism activities, respect local customs, cultural traditions and religious beliefs, care for tourism resources, protect the ecological environment, and abide by the norms of civilized tourist behaviors" (Cripps 2013a).

To widen the reach of improving citizen behavior, different media including television and newspapers, were used to broadcast the law. The patriotic sentiment engendered by "Ding was here" echoed by the Communist Party's flagship newspaper, the People's Daily. One day after this incident, in an article with the title of "hands are full but hearts are empty", the newspaper made the commentary that "nowadays, people in China no longer want for food and clothing, and even in the luxury shops abroad, there are advertising posters in Chinese, however, many people feel their hearts are empty because of lacking spiritual support" (Li 2013). In the end, the paper wrote that 'a visit' should become an opportunity to reflect our civilization. The heated discussion on Weibo, the emotions, the shame and the condemnatory tone, enable us to see a strong pursuit of civilization. Only by reflection on China's civilization could its citizens gain respect in the international arena, and move forward on the road to national rejuvenation (ibid.). The way the government takes advantage of the internet incident to educate the public reveals a complicated picture of government networks that have become more adept in setting public agendas and regulating public discourse.

It should be noted, however, that in China, official media such as People's Daily and Xinhua News Agency are what Jiang (2010) defines as "central propaganda spaces" over which "the state has firm if not complete control" (p. 12). It is easier for the state to give direct control over dependent institutions, therefore the content of these media is dominated by state principles aimed at the "guidance of public opinion" (*Yulun Daoxiang*), compliance with official agenda in the central propaganda institutions and is also buttressed through state sanctioned leadership (ibid.). Therefore, it is not surprising that the commentaries from the People's Daily correlate to the government propaganda in this case.

Government intervention through different types of handouts and newspaper editorials help people to behave in socially or culturally acceptable ways. This type of moral regulation is consistent with what Dean (1999, pp. 11–12) proposed as the "moral activity" of the government, as government sets the rules for the people to tell right and good from wrong and bad.

Xinhua News also made comment on this scandal by publishing an article "Why did 'a visit' become a never-ending ghost?" (Mao 2013). It notes that despite the fact that much criticism and reflection constantly takes place in our society, China's citizens are still far from exhibiting the civil behavior of the West. Therefore, every person should reflect on what they should do to make the society more civilized. Since postings from Weibo are quickly picked up by the mass media as "threads" for future propaganda, it suggests that the expression of public opinion on Weibo is able to direct or shape the traditional media agenda on some occasions. Since Weibo provides an effective channel for public expression, a large number of netizens can collectively discuss issues of public concern. Under this circumstance, the Chinese government is able to make effective use of Weibo for the purpose of disseminating 'propaganda'. When the Weibo incident is consistent with the state ideology or guiding thought, it will immediately strengthen its propaganda effect. In this way, while Weibo offers a thread for further public discussion, mainstream media makes its utmost efforts to "reflect" on the incident. This is consistent with Rawnsley's findings that the mass media is obliged to perform a propaganda function in China to "correctly" guide public opinion and maintain the interest of the Party (Rawnsley 2006). Therefore, the fragmented and multifarious postings on Weibo can be transformed by the mass media into a strong public message. It also suggests that the role of the traditional media should not be underestimated. Weibo is likely to follow the pattern set by previous electronic media and will be tamed through regulation to help foster the Party's continuing rule (Hassid 2012). The following section will explore how the congruence between the incident of "Ding was here" and state policy may offer some insights into the complexities of governance in China.

The Chinese State and Media Control

Before moving on to an in-depth analysis of "Ding was here", it may be useful to briefly expand on the institutional aspects of the Chinese state that attempt to regulate the media. The Chinese government has long maintained the tradition of control of public expression, and it is embodied even in the Chinese Constitution. Although the Constitution evolved through the twentieth century, it was set in 1982 by Deng Xiaoping. In Chapter One, Article Twenty-two states: "The state promotes the development of art and literature, the press, radio and television broadcasting, publishing and distribution services, libraries, museums, cultural centers and other cultural undertakings that serve the people and socialism, and it sponsors mass cultural activities". In addition, the state has overarching influence in shaping the country's discourse, protecting public order and controlling public expression. Chapter One, Article One states: "Disruption of the socialist state by any organization or individual is prohibited" (see Winfield, Mizuno & Beaudoin 2000, pp. 326–327).

The Chinese state therefore undertakes a variety of measures to control the mass media by permitting the authorities to control, limit, and restrict information, as well as to diffuse new ideas and values (Zhao 1998). Among them, collective values are expected to give rise to the Chinese emphasis on harmony (ibid.). At the same time, the official discourse of nationalism has focused on patriotism and this term is also a political construction for the purposes of political stability and national unification (Zheng 1999, pp. 88–90). As a political construction, patriotism has entitled various meanings in accordance with different contexts, which as Mao Zedong (ibid., p. 196) argued "the specific content of 'patriotism' is determined by historical conditions." He contends that the theme or nature of patriotism remains a strong national identity. It is argued by Hunt that compared with nationalism, patriotism is much more useful for describing the features of the Chinese to search for a national identity (see Zheng 1999, p. 90).

The next section highlights the state's transformative role in exercising disciplinary technologies over society for this purpose. The governmentality approach directs our attention to the identities through which people are governed; and "practices of government, as much as practices of self-government, or modes of resistance, attempt to specify and fix our identities in definite ways in the service of particular ends" (Dean & Hindess 1998, p. 11). The sense of patriotism can therefore be seen as a construction of identity.

In Anderson's sense, a nation as an "imagined community" is a product of social and cultural construction (2006). Therefore, the enforcement or construction of the Chinese nation's identity has taken a number of steps and strategies. National identity has dual characteristics; with one demanding that the members of the community cultivate a sense of belonging and a self-consciousness of the community, while the other demands that they make the difference between themselves and the outside world (Wang 2008, p. 99).

National identity is not however, a fixed term, but always changeable. In the course of building its national identity, the ways in which the Chinese government promotes certain cultural traits and a national position are products of a particular period. The aspects of national identity under discussion are a product of the Weibo period with the flourishing of new technologies. The Chinese government promotes shared historical memory, unified cultural roots and political discourse to nurture patriotism and to enable the Chinese national identity to stand with pride.

During the Weibo era, the measures the Chinese government has taken to build a nation-state can be seen as attempts to transmit an imaginary and patriotic construct to the masses. These methods involve more subtle and sustained forms of control over populations from which "subjects" can be brought to internalize state control through technologies of the self. These technologies permit "individuals to effect, by their own means, a certain number of operations on their own bodies, on their souls, on their own thoughts, on their own conduct, and this in a manner so as to transform themselves, modify themselves and to attain a certain state of perfection, of happiness, a purity, of supernatural power, and so on" (Foucault 1993, p. 203). In this way, the collective patriotic sentiment arising from "Ding was here", was constructed and fostered by the Chinese state through a number of measures. The next section will analyze the specific measures.

Patriotism Construction of the Chinese State

> It would be wrong to say that the soul is an illusion, or an ideological effect. On the contrary, it exists, it has a reality, it is produced permanently around, on, within the body by the functioning of a power that is exercised on those punished—and, in a more general way, on those it supervises, trains and corrects, over madmen, children at home and at school, the colonized, over those who are stuck at a machine and supervised for the rest of their lives. (Foucault 1977, p. 29)

The specific characteristic of Chinese governmentality is "a mixture of conventional Chinese socialist technologies of government such as 'the mass line' and neoliberal strategies designed to govern through the desires of individuals" (Jeffreys & Sigley 2009, p. 7). Rose (1999) describes the processes of psychologizing involved in the more everyday and practical procedures, systems and regimes of injunction, prohibition and judgment through which human beings come to understand, and act upon their daily conduct (p. 31). One of the most potent and influential means of enabling and maintaining discipline via the government of the self is through the concept of patriotism. The formation of patriotism in the Chinese people's minds has also long been conducted through daily practices. In this case, the automatic responses of national patriotism came as a result of earlier and ongoing work of the government, which has certainly contributed to the public outcry over Ding, if not completely shaped it, in quite a subtle way.

What is new in the era of the technologies of power affecting the conduct of individuals and the technologies of the self is made manifest in the ways Chinese are disposed towards becoming patriotic, brave and loving traditions, thus responsible for national image. Meanwhile, in the process, the Chinese are treated as 'free citizens'. This idea is captured in the team song of the Young Pioneers of China. This song, recited by primary school-going children every day, reads:

> We are the successors of communism,
> Our ancestors inherited the glorious tradition of revolution,
> Love the motherland and the people,
> With bright red scarf fluttering on the chest,
> Not afraid of difficulties, do not fear the enemy,
> Persistently study, and resolutely struggle,
> Bravely move toward victory,
> We are the successors of communism

Patriotic Education. The reaction to the Ding event can be seen as part of ongoing work in China's moral and educative environment. Since coming to power in 1949, the Communist Party has shaped education with Marxism and Mao Zedong Thought as the Party's political ideology of socialism. Even today, it is compulsory for all educational institutions in China to teach political courses such as Marxism and socialist values, including socialism, patriotism and collectivism. Cheung and Pan (2006) argue that although educational institutions have been granted a certain degree of autonomy in the teaching and learning process, the state still holds the power to regulate this autonomy within the socialist framework of China. National education policy with a socialist purpose directs the political framework that enables education to serve the state's political project, ensuring that "policy-makers took effective state-directed educational efforts [political education] to ensure regime legitimacy and the commitment of youth to national development agendas" (Arnove 2010). The Chinese state takes complex strategies, including the shaping of emotional attachment and the promotion of a sense of duty, to construct collective priorities over personal and regional interests in Chinese history and culture (patriotism) as well as China's role at the international level (nationalism) (Fairbrother 2003). In addition, Hong Kong and Mainland Chinese students' patriotic and national orientations and perceptions in his studies are under explicit ideological instruction (ibid.).

Since August 1994, China has formally proposed *suzhijiaoyu*, or Quality Education, which has been associated with ideas of education and proper behavior and has been incorporated into governmental educational and population programs in particular ways (Hoffman 2006) now implemented for almost 15 years. The concept of *suzhijiaoyu* in government education has become increasingly important over the 1990s, eventually becoming one of the guiding principles of education policy (Dello-Iacovo 2009).

Together with the Quality Education framework, the government launched a program of 'patriotic education' in 1994. After the demonstrations in Tiananmen Square in 1989, the Chinese leaders realized that they had to pull China back to being a collective community with common goals in order to enable economic liberation in the wake of opening and reform policy. Therefore, readings on the pre-1949 history of the imperialists' aggression against China returned to the classroom. The Chinese government started a patriotic education campaign in 1992 and poured unprecedented resources into building people's patriotism. Initially, it was only included in primary and secondary schools, but later expanded to high schools and universities, aiming to enhance the patriotism of all Chinese people. In 1995, the government identified 100 patriotic books, films and songs recommended for young Chinese. The 1994 document, "Outlines for Patriotic Education", offered guidelines for teaching patriotism that included both cultural and political messages: the official Party line and Deng Xiaoping's theory of "socialism with Chinese characteristics" were the guiding principles. The purpose of this patriotic education was socialist modernisation and the peaceful reunification of China, as well as to "rejuvenate" China's national spirit and to "reconstruct the sense of national esteem and dignity" (see So 2003, p. 235). Many studies have successfully explored and proved that Chinese political education textbooks helped to unify the diversified population and lead the general public into a national identity (Pykett 2010; Zhao 2014). Through professional disciplines and other forms of expertise, new ways of knowing the self and others can be achieved. In this way, the sentiment of national patriotism reflected in Ding further contributes to the ongoing patriotic education.

Patriotism is an important factor for political legitimacy in China. The concept of patriotism was mentioned by Mao Zedong in his famous speech on 'The Place of the Chinese Communist Party in the National War' in 1938. Mao referred to patriotism as the way of realising internationalism in the war of resistance against Japan. Patriotism became particularly important in recent decades, and it was considered as the Communist Party ideology together with socialism. The Party Central Committee journal, *Qiushi*, published an editorial that gave the official view of Chinese patriotism:

> Patriotism is historically-specific, having different contents under different historical circumstances. Today, if we want to be patriotic, we should love the socialist New China under the leadership of the Chinese Communist Party. (Pye 1996, p. 106)

Soon after the 1989 Tiananmen crackdown, Jiang Zemin launched a series of patriotic campaigns in a speech titled "Carry on and develop the Tradition of Patriotism in New Historical Circumstances". Deng Xiaoping echoed the campaign and with his speech "Revive the Chinese Nation". The CCP boosted the campaign based on an "Outline for the Implementation of Patriotic Education" in 1994.

The compelling characteristic of socialist China is that the state remains an active participant in neoliberal governance (Hoffman 2006). In this way, authoritarian technologies and liberal science technologies are combined or appear interchangeably in the framework of China's governmentality. As Sigley (2004, p. 563) contends, 'authoritarian and illiberal measures are constitutive of the way in which a liberal arts of government operates'. In this way, the "hybrid socialist-neoliberal" model (Sigley 2006), not only includes liberal measures; control is not only exercised through autonomy, the practice of the government is calculated and contested, but also contains illiberal measures. In the Ding event, both liberal and illiberal measures were employed to construct individuals' identities.

In addition to patriotic education, moral education was also implemented. Former Chinese President Hu Jintao said that the young should learn to 'love the motherland' as a key virtue of 'socialist honor' (with harming the motherland being a signal of 'socialist disgrace') (Gries 2004). Moral education that promotes feelings of nationalism should not be equated with 'propaganda', however, a pejorative term in the English language that likens state ideology to brainwashing (ibid.). After years of cultivation and education, people's responsibility and a historical sense of patriotism comes in a large measure, from their inner heart, especially in the younger generations. With the fast growth of the economy and China's increasing importance in the world, people have felt the automatic desire to shoulder historical responsibilities, which can been seen in the examples of earthquakes and other natural disasters by "a volunteerism with a historical understanding of progress" (Kang 2012, p. 931). This type of automatic volunteerism and sense of responsibility is the fundamental reason for the national patriotism shown in the Ding event.

Reviving Confucianism. To construct individuals' identities, the communist regime has flexibly adjusted the content and boundaries of its hegemony over time. It has also constantly created new labels such as "three representations" and "harmonious society". It has been commonly accepted that the three ideologies of New Confucianism, Marxism and Chinese liberalism have dominated the ideologies in China since the beginning of the twentieth century. The relationship between them is complicated. It has been well known that it was difficult to align the two opposite philosophies of Marxism and Confucianism, with the former opposing class hierarchy but the latter accepting class inequity. However, in recent years the CCP has actively promoted the study of Confucianism and adapted certain terminologies into its ideology. Brady (2012, pp. 58–63) divides the CCP's attitude toward Confucianism from the May Fourth era to the present into five stages, briefly saying, that before the opening and reform of 1978, Confucianism was rejected as an old order. Since China's opening to the outside world in 1978, the attitude towards Confucianism has changed, with, for example, increasing numbers of ethnic Chinese travelling to China in search of their roots (*xungen*). Chinese education has long been based on Confucian teachings, which have been considered the philosophical roots and the underlying social traditions for collectivism (ibid.). Confucianism was founded by Confucius, the renowned philosopher, educator and politician who lived from 551 to 479 BCE during the Han Dynasty. Not a religion, Confucius's teachings are basically the practical ethics or moral principles for dealing with daily life, which have long exerted influence in various aspects of Chinese society, such as family and cultural life. Admired for his wisdom, Confucius was followed by a host of disciples who recorded his teachings. Confucianism has special benefit to offer the party-state, for example, the well-being of the people, the notion of unity, and loyalty to the country.

Thus, it has long been considered that one of the significant features of the Chinese culture is "collectivism" (Hofstede 1993). By definition, 'collective' means that a large group of many are tied together into a community through a certain common identity (Wang & Liu 2010). In this sense, people constitute a strong, cohesive group or community often including not only individuals but also their immediate and extended family members. Chinese individuals tend to place their priority on collective interests over individual goals, and evidence shows that the principle of collectivism has displayed a trend towards enforcing unification.

The searching for cultural roots with the enforcement of Confucianism and collectivism, contributes significantly to economic growth. Hofstede and Bond (1988) investigates the reasons for East Asia's outperformance over other countries or regions such as South and Southeast Asia, as well as South America in the late twentieth century, finding that in spite of Maoism, many Confucian values remain strong in the People's Republic [of China] (p. 19).

They summarized a series of core principles of Confucian teachings: 1) The stability of society is based on unequal relationships between people, for example, the basic relationship of ruler/subject, father/son, older brother/younger brother, husband/wife and older friend/younger friend. Thus, it suggests that inequality and power exist in any aspect of the society; 2) The family is the prototype of all social organizations. In this respect, a person should give up his/her individuality so as to maintain the collectivism or the harmony in the family. Further, Hofstede notes that the features of harmony or collectivism could be embodied in maintaining a person's 'face', which means one's dignity, self-respect, and prestige. Losing 'face' or losing dignity is a serious matter in Chinese society; 3) Virtuous behavior towards others consists of treating others as one would like to be treated oneself, which emphasizes people's benevolence or loving; 4) Virtue with regard to one's tasks in life consists in trying to acquire skills and education, being thrifty, being patient and being moderate (ibid., p. 8).

Therefore, in this book, rather than being considered as a strategy merely for collective action, collectivism is recognized as a moral principle, and the acts of one individual, such as "Ding was here", has repercussions for the whole society. Ho and Chiu (1994) point out that while individualism means selfishness and not being obedient to group disciplines, collectivism promotes the care and thought for others, which is helpful to enhance group solidarity. In this sense, the theme of collectivism is congruent with the notion of a 'harmonious society'. However, Confucianism experienced several rises and falls in Chinese history, and it was only adopted by the Chinese government in recent years.

Historically, the CCP denounced Confucianism and traditional culture as "feudal" or an obstruction on China's path towards becoming a modern nation. During the Maoist period of patriotism, traditional cultural heritage was not considered important. It was not until in the 1980s that traditional culture was regarded as an important element of Chinese nationalism, which could be used to arouse patriotic feelings in the citizenry. The CCP is now at the forefront of those who promote a revival of Confucianism. The CCP has embraced the return of Confucianism directly and incorporates some aspects of traditional Chinese thought as mainstream discourse in Chinese society.

Instead of considering Confucianism as 'feudalistic' as previously, it is ironic to see that in the last two decades, Confucianism has re-emerged to "transform the belief-systems of communities and provide models for political and cultural development that guide their modernizing strategies" (Hutchinson 1987, p. 30). And Confucianism was considered as a strong drive for cultural nationalism with the embrace of the market and its economic development focus, for the relaxation of political restrictions gave some space for New Confucianists to show concern for moral order (Guo 2004, pp. 72–74). It helps to construct a national identity which offers a basis for the Chinese to conduct their collective life, and further, for a nation to realize moral regeneration, cultural revival and to restore its self-respect and confidence (ibid., p. 73). This thought was evidenced by a series of measures taken by the Party leaders, for example, the officially sponsored celebration of the 2545th anniversary of Confucius's birth in 1994. Former vice-premier Gu Mu chaired this celebration as Chairman of the China Confucius Foundation, and Jiang

Zemin was also present at this conference and made a speech (Chinakongzi.org 2009). The essence of Confucianism is one of the primary reasons for the formation of collective sentiment concerning national image and pride in response to the Ding event.

The burgeoning of Confucianism is not only seen in political terms, but can also be seen in popular cultural products. Professors of literature and history such as Yu Qiuyu, Yu Dan and Yi Zhongtian, now enjoy popular icon status by giving CCTV lectures on Confucian classics and traditional literature. As media celebrities, they speak of classic Confucian values and historical anecdotes on highly rated TV talk shows and in their best sellers, in a highly entertaining manner. This event of turning the classics of high-culture into profitable products of popular consumer culture is still in "keeping with the state mission of building a 'harmonious society'" (Kang 2012, p. 924).

Yu Dan is an associate professor of film and television at Beijing Normal University with few scholarly credentials before she became famous. Since a 2006 CCTV talk show and the publication of the collection of her lectures, Yu Dan's insights into the Analects, she has achieved instant and enormous success by turning "old Confucian teachings into a Chinese version of 'Chicken Soup for the Soul'" (Ni 2007). It was reviewed by The Guardian as confirming that "the Chinese government is now reviving Confucianism as part of its strategy to promote the 'harmonious society'" (see Kang 2012, p. 925).

From Confucianism to Maoism, the dominant political values in China have all prioritized the collective over the individual. Daily CCP campaigns in the media, in schools and elsewhere, give rise to patriotism. One typical example is 'Article One' of the Rules for University Students in the Capital: "Ardently love the Chinese Communist Party, ardently love the socialist homeland, [and] ardently love the people", and the highest expression of patriotism in China today is to love the Communist Party (see Duke 1985, p. 141). Zheng (1999) contends that there are three reasons that the CCP promotes patriotism: firstly, to enhance political legitimacy; secondly, to maintain political stability; and thirdly, to form national unification (pp. 90–94). Chinese leaders repeatedly reiterate this point. Deng Xiaoping once argued that the Chinese people had their own national self-respect and pride, and it was the highest honor to love their "socialist motherland and contribute all we have to her socialist construction, [and] we deem it the deepest disgrace to impair her interests, dignity and honor" (Deng 1984d, p. 396, cited from Zheng 1999, pp. 92–93).

A distinction between nationalism and patriotism is further drawn by Zheng (1999, p. 93): while nationalism is based on a shared culture and ethnicity, patriotism encompasses "all those legally entitled to be citizens, irrespective of their ethnicity, national identity, and culture", and it does not need an ethnic or cultural foundation.

In response to the changing social and economic landscape in China, the CCP has designated new models to accommodate the current concerns guiding individuals' outlook and behavior. Since 2002, an annual election of the "Top ten people moving China" is held by CCTV, which includes people who generate wide recognition or make great contributions to society. Most importantly, the people selected have to represent contemporary moral directions of the society. Therefore, this program has been regarded as the contemporary Chinese people's spiritual epic. The moral or patriotic imperatives can be widely seen in the official rhetoric. Morality and patriotism are always seen to contribute to building 'spiritual civilization'.

Earlier, in 1996, a questionnaire completed by graduates, found that two thirds of them saw the perceived connections between patriotism and morality. A sample of the responses is as follows:

> Patriotism is an invariable part of virtue. Morality includes patriotism. If a person is not a patriotic person, he will have no morality. (See Agelasto & Adamson 1998, p. 366)

The responses clearly show the effectiveness on the individuals of state-directed patriotic campaigns committed to national agendas. The Chinese tradition, including traditional culture and values, has played an important role in shaping Chinese patriotism since the reform beginning in the late 1970s.

Promoting Political Slogans–National Rejuvenation. The collective sentiment of national patriotism in "Ding was here" could also be seen to contribute to the constant propaganda of political slogans. For example, "National Rejuvenation" has been the keynote of the media since the election of Xi Jinping, the successor to Hu Jintao in 2012. However, the term, national rejuvenation, could date back to the formative period of Chinese nationalism, from the latter stages of the nineteenth century to the early twentieth century. The term became a catchphrase increasingly used during the tenures of Deng Xiaoping's successors, Jiang Zemin, Hu Jintao and Xi Jinping.

Over the years, the CCP leadership has tried other methods to revitalize its ideology using several theoretical principles, such as the former General Secretary Jiang Zemin's theory of the 'Three Represents' and Hu Jintao's 'scientific concept of development' and 'harmonious society'. In 2001, Jiang Zemin declared that the CCP was leading the road to the "great rejuvenation of the Chinese nation", as he introduced the "Three Represents" theory at China's Fifteenth Party Congress in 1997. Jiang declared that the Party would always represent the development trend of China's advanced productive forces, represent the orientation of China's advanced culture and represent the fundamental interests of the overwhelming majority of the Chinese people. Later the Chinese Communist Party amended its constitution at the Sixteenth National Congress in Beijing in November 2002 to include the Three Represents theory as a guiding ideology of the Party together with Marxism, Leninism, Mao Zedong Thought and Deng Xiaoping Theory. On July 1, 2001 at the celebration of the 80th anniversary of the founding of the Party, Jiang delivered a speech stating that:

> Upholding Marxism as the guiding ideology, we have educated the people in patriotism, collectivism and socialism and done much to promote socialist ethical and cultural progress. We have persistently carried forward the fine cultures of all ethnic groups of the country and actively absorbed what is advanced in other civilizations in order to make our socialist culture increasingly flourish. The ideological and ethical standards and the educational, scientific and cultural qualities of the people have kept improving, displaying to the world a new mental outlook of the Chinese nation. (China.org.cn 2001)

In elaborating how to correctly understand and comprehensively fulfill the requirements of the "Three Represents", Jiang proclaimed:

> In light of the new practices and requirements of the times and to satisfy people's needs for spiritual and cultural life, promote cultural innovations, nurture the advanced culture and gather hundreds of millions of people closely around the great banner of the socialist culture with Chinese characteristics. (China.org.cn 2001)

Jiang's successor, Hu Jintao, clearly recognized the importance of constructing the image of 'cultural China'. According to Cao (2011), in the political report to the 17th CCP National Congress in 2007, then General Secretary Hu Jintao, for the first time, gave strategic significance to the notion of soft power. Hu emphasized the importance of culture in international competition, noting that: "In the current world, culture has become critical for national cohesion and solidarity, and it is essential for overall national power". Hu also detailed a number of strategic methods for the fulfillment of objectives on soft power: 'fostering a harmonious culture', 'promoting traditional culture' and 'encouraging cultural innovation and regeneration'. Cao's (2011) discourse analysis of the discursive structure of 'soft power' in China, reveals that soft power discourse is used to articulate traditional values by China's political and intellectual elite. The external dimension of soft power is seen as the natural extension of China's cultural rejuvenation with the purpose of "developing a strong national identity" (p. 12). Hu went further to stress rejuvenation and patriotism. In the speech of 2011 to commemorate the one-hundredth anniversary of the Xinhai Revolution in China, Hu Jintao mentioned rejuvenation twenty-three times. He emphasized the important meaning of the Xinhai Revolution, which overthrew the country's last imperial dynasty, and eventually led to the founding of the Republic of China in 1912. Hu then said that the Chinese people were full of confidence in the bright prospects of the great rejuvenation of the nation. He particularly stressed that:

> To realize China's rejuvenation, it is essential to firmly hold the flag of patriotism. Patriotism is the soul of the Chinese nation and a powerful force mobilizing and uniting the whole nation to strive to revitalize China. (People.com.cn 2011)

This speech was followed by a series of programs called "Road to Rejuvenation", including a popular CCTV television series, a three-volume book and a "song-and-dance epic" at the National Theatre. CCTV's live broadcast was infused with emotionally charged images and narratives of ancient China as the 'Central Kingdom' at the turn of the first and second millennia. In the course of the transition from Mao's revolution to Deng's restoration, two moments are repeatedly described as milestones: one is Mao's 1949 victory, which led to the unification of China and the other is Deng's opening and reform in 1978, which illuminated the path for the Chinese to realize prosperity. Under this circumstance, patriotic pride or sentiment derives to a large extent from China's fast growth into a world power, as there is a dramatic contrast between current day China's development and events in earlier modern history when Chinese people suffered great humiliations and backwardness in the 1840s Opium War (Kang 2012, p. 931).

The slogans promoted by the Chinese government can be placed within a much broader historical and ideological context. The Chinese government deployed strategies for historical-political manipulation in order to achieve better governance. Central to this strategy is the "victimization narrative" of modern Chinese history, in which China is placed in the role of victim of Western aggression and exploitation from the mid-nineteenth century (Gries 2004).

In addition, civic education textbooks are indispensable arenas for the state to reconstruct history and to restore collective memories in order to define a cohesive national identity (Zhao 2014). As Gries (2004, p. 47) argues:

> The 'Century of Humiliation' is neither an objective past that works insidiously in the present nor a mere 'invention' of present-day nationalist entrepreneurs. Instead, the 'Century' is a continuously reworked narrative about the national past central to the contested and evolving meaning of being 'Chinese' today.

It is undeniable that China's long history of fragmentation and imperialist aggression has enabled the state to inculcate the Chinese people with patriotism. Thus, governmentality is best interpreted in this combined application of 'technologies'. The government proposed the discourse of 'national rejuvenation' to open new space to individuals and groups to gain cultural identities and a sense of belonging within the state. The contemporary form of governmentality "operates through the delicate and minute infiltration of the ambitions of regulation into the very interior of our existence and experience as subjects", thus enabling individuals to believe "in making our subjectivity the principle of our personal lives, our ethical systems, and our political evaluations, that we are, freely, choosing our freedoms" (Rose 1999, p. 11). In this way, it is much easier for individuals to internalize these notions and principles, and adhere to the advice and values from government leaders.

The governmentality approach also directs our attention to the identities that arise as part of the process of governing. Practices of government, as much as practices of self-government, or modes of resistance, attempt to specify and fix our identities in definite ways in the service of particular ends. The "dangerous individual" or the "long-term unemployed" as much as the "active citizen" or the "enterprising person" are personal and collective identities "made-up" through particular forms of reasoning and technologies so that they might be worked with and upon to different ends (Dean & Hindess 1998, p. 11). This tactic or mode of governing is interpreted by Burchell (1996, p. 657) as a new form of "responsibilization", in which the individuals or collectives assume active responsibility for their behaviors, including the procedure and the outcome. In this way, the governed are encouraged, freely and rationally, to conduct and regulate them.

Discussion of Patriotism in "Ding Was Here"

With the media-rich post-1980s generation in China, it is possible to interpret the form of patriotism emerging from the incident of "Ding was here", as based on the governance of subjects 'through their own autonomy'. This type of online discourse by a large number of internet users is also manipulated to strengthen the state's hold on power and to improve the Party's image, which is to the government's advantage. The CCP government has actually strengthened its hold on power by adopting political approaches and tactics common in democratic societies but without becoming a democracy (Brady 2012). Moreover, the way the state has allowed its citizens to discuss and circulate views aimed at local and specific issues on Weibo provides an outlet for public outcry and a transmission belt of public opinion (Yang 2011).

We can clearly see in the trajectory of "Ding was here" that this form of governance may be attempting to embrace the aspirations of the Chinese people and to shape them in terms of a cultural identity that is compatible with the continuance of the political status quo. The "Ding was here" event, along with the subsequent criticism of Chinese culture, resonated with what the communist government and Chinese intellectuals believe at this time. This event has been considered as leading to "soul-searching" in China (Wong 2013) where the interest of the masses is congruent with that of the regime, thus ensuring the preservation of the existing system and values.

As mentioned previously, after the photo of the graffiti was posted on Weibo, Ding was found through the Human Flesh Search Engine. The official Chinese news agency, the Xinhua agency, published an article that drew an analogy with internet lynching to describe the human flesh search engine, noting that it is "not the familiar search engine from Baidu and Google, but a search engine employing thousands of individuals all mobilized with one aim, to dig out facts and expose them to the baleful glare of publicity" (Bai & Ji 2008).

Weibo has also been strongly criticized for its human flesh search engine (HFSE) or 'Renrou (human flesh) search engine', which is used specifically by the Chinese media for online searches for people, often with the aim of discrediting them based on unearthing controversial facts. This search engine employs thousands of individuals mobilized by the sole intention of digging out hidden facts and exposing individuals. The practice of the *renrou* search was first used in 2001 and then became a 'buzzword' in 2008, when there was a peak of *renrou* searching. In a dramatic incident, the wife of a man named

Wang Fei committed suicide because of his betrayal, leaving a blog diary behind expressing her despair. Soon, people not only wrote abusive words on the door of Wang's parents' house accusing them of raising their son poorly; they also went to the company where Wang worked, asking that he be dismissed. A story on these "online vigilantes" hunting down an individual also appeared in the New York Times, in which the reporter said that:

> Human-flesh search engines—renrou sousuo yinqing—have become a Chinese phenomenon: they are a form of online vigilante justice in which internet users hunt down and punish people who have attracted their wrath. The goal is to get the targets of a search fired from their jobs, shamed in front of their neighbors, run out of town. It is crowd-sourced detective work, pursued online—with offline results. (Downey 2010)

The human flesh search engine continues to be used widely to reveal the illegal or poor behavior of officials. A recent trend is to focus on specific items of clothing or jewelry worn by officials to assess whether they are profiting from corruption (as noted in the previous chapter). However, the HFSE has more generally been stigmatized for exposing individuals to public humiliation, sometimes out of vigilantism, nationalist or patriotic sentiments, or to break through the internet censorship in China (Fletcher 2008).

When Ding's personal information was exposed, it caused him great harm. His parents said when they made the public apology in the newspaper, "the boy cried the whole night" (Hu 2013). Even worse, the website of the school he attended was hacked by the internet vigilantes as previously mentioned. This clearly indicates that there are irrational behaviors on Weibo that could destroy the basis of a healthy public sphere as described by Habermas. It is not reasonable to let a 14-year-old boy be the scapegoat for a 'disease' that plagues the whole nation. Among the tens of thousands of comments on "Ding was here", there was certainly debate over how uncivilized the behavior was and how we need to maintain ancient heritage, in this case, Egypt's. It is said that anonymity breeds courage, and therefore internet anonymity serves as a refuge for irrational voices and behaviors, which makes for the formation of a 'cacophony' (Hu 2008).

This case reveals the irrational aspect of Chinese netizens where the political and social conditions are not able to guarantee the forming of an ideal Habermasian public sphere—though it probably does not, in fact, exist anywhere—even in Western history. Firstly, the Weibo users do not represent the overall population. Secondly, the theme of each discussion is subject to an agenda-setting function to some extent. Thirdly, online public opinion is heavily influenced by coercion—which has been instilled subtly through education campaigns.

In addition to these factors, there is one further interesting phenomenon. Some comments targeted Ding's family background. Any Chinese person who is able to go abroad on a tour, especially to a place like Egypt, is assumed to be wealthy and rich people are not well liked in China. Many people assume that others who became rich achieved this through corruption or other dubious methods. Hence, there was a lot of criticism of Ding's parents. In current day China, though a large portion of the population has become wealthy, there is a variety of social problems, such as environmental pollution, social injustice as well as the widening gap between the rich and the poor. The social resentment noted in Chapter Four does exist in Chinese people's minds. People express their resentment against those who attain power or wealth. Thus, it is not difficult to understand why some official media has shown concern over social psychology in the Web 2.0, such as expressions of feelings of injustice and resentment.

Conclusion

The analysis of "Ding was here" reveals that in contrast with the direct and hard censorship of the past, the Chinese authorities now engage with social media, notably Weibo, in more subtle ways, yet still with regulatory intentions. China's political ideologies and strategies today are aimed at maintaining state stability and defending the current political system, thus policies and regulations are targeted at maintaining the political status quo. Despite the fact that the Chinese state is considered an authoritarian regime, it employs a number of alternative technologies to shape and normalize the conduct of the Chinese as described in this chapter. Therefore, in the case of "Ding was here", harnessing a strong patriotic passion is a vital step in influencing opinions in favor of the political status quo. In this respect, the Communist Party has used the Quality Education campaign and the Patriotic Education campaign to construct and shore up a patriotism that serves to maintain social stability. This is what Rose (1999) refers to in Governing the Soul, where such techniques have been used within what he terms the 'psy' discipline (such as psychology) to administer the 'controllable' subject with free space. The goal of media governmentality in China, to extend Foucault's point, is to cultivate a well-disciplined, highly moral and politically-compliant citizenry through the arts of re-inventing or sustaining traditions such as Confucianism, collectivism or patriotism to support the construction of national identity.

China's authorities have demonstrated much success with the use of governmentality in the digital age. It can be seen, clearly, that the Chinese leadership has been pro-active with regard to media regulation. Apart from the ability to utilize 'visible' technologies, it also applies codes of conduct on its citizens from a range of social, cultural and political perspectives. The attitude of the Chinese government towards the internet is what Lee (2010) describes as that "in-between narrow path". On the one hand, the state makes good use of the internet to promote strong economic growth, while on the other; it applies sophisticated regulatory technologies to frame and produce discourses for the effective governing of people's minds and souls. As the case of "Ding was here" suggests, Weibo users' attitudes and values are still heavily influenced by the mainstream cultural values of collectivism and patriotism, which show an enforcing trend in the virtual communities. It suggests that Weibo is being used for pedagogical and control reasons under the guise of social media entertainment, by which subtle ideological constructs—such as collectivism and patriotism are being shown on Weibo, which was originally simply a new form of social media. It is noteworthy that the interaction between the mainstream media and Weibo helps the government to set its agenda and to achieve its purposes. In this case, once an online contention reaches a certain level, the government becomes alerted, the authorities then take action to cool down public emotions and to guide the public appropriately. In addition, Weibo provides a platform for the authorities to detect the citizens' views directly and closely.

Therefore, though many studies view social media as offering tools of democracy, much of the traffic on China's Weibo merely serves to spread rumors and irrational or trivial discussions. More significantly, China's Weibo still serves as a tool for supervision by the state, suggesting that social media in China forms at best, a limited version of the public sphere. As Diamond (2010) affirms, if the social and political structure is not ripe for profound change, technology may not lead to democracy. Harnessing Weibo's potential revolutionary power, the Chinese government promotes its development on the one hand, while controlling the medium through carefully "regulated freedom". Thus, despite Weibo's surface appearance as offering a public sphere, it is clearly negotiated within existing political power structures. This study therefore proposes an alternative and original interpretation of the inter-relationship between Weibo and the authorities. In order to maintain both control and a degree of freedom, Weibo is regulated, shaped and governed autonomously through the notion of governmentality, as has been argued in this chapter.

References

Abad-Santos, A. 2013, 'How Chinese tourists usurped the ugly Americans', The Wire, 28 May, viewed 20 October 2013, <http://www.theatlanticwire.com/global/2013/05/how-ugly-chinese-tourists-became-new-ugly-americans/65649/>.

Agelasto, M & Adamson, B. 1998, Higher education in post-Mao China: An ecology of Hong Kong, Hong Kong University Press, Hong Kong.

Anderson, B. 2006, Imagined communities, Verso, New York and London.

Arnove, RF. 2010, 'Reflections on comparative education and international development', Compare, vol. 40, no. 6, pp. 827–830.

Bai, X & Ji, S. 2008, 'Human flesh search engine: An internet lunching?', Xinhua News Agency, 31 July, viewed 20 September 2013, <http://www.cq.xinhuanet.com/2008-07/31/content_13984982_1.htm>.

Bo, Y. 1992, The ugly China man and the crisis of Chinese culture, Allen & Unwin, New York.

Brady, A. 2012, 'State Confucianism, Chineseness, and tradition in CCP propaganda', in Brady, A (ed.), China's thought management, Routledge, New York, pp. 57–75.

Burchell, G. 1996, 'Liberal government and techniques of the self', in Barry, A, Osborne, T & Rose, N (eds.), Foucault and political reason: Liberalism, neo-liberalism and rationalities of government, University of Chicago Press, Chicago.

Cao, Q. 2011, 'The language of soft power: Mediating socio-political meanings in the Chinese media', Critical Arts, vol. 25, no. 1, pp. 7–24.

Cheung, S. 2013, 'Dire manners and "uncivilized behavior" of tourists is harming China's image, admits VP Wang Yang', South China Morning Post, 18 May, viewed 22 August 2013, <http://www.scmp.com/news/china/article/1240206/dire-manners-and-uncivilised-behaviour-tourists-harming-chinas-image?page=all>.

Cheung, KW & Pan, S. 2006, 'Transition of moral education in China: Towards regulated individualism', Citizenship Teaching and Learning, vol. 2, no. 2, pp. 37–50.

Chinakongzi.org. 2009, 'Speech on the 2545th anniversary of Confucius's birth', November 7, Chinakongzi.org, viewed 23 May 2013, <http://www.chinakongzi.org/17zt/gumu/pics/200911/t20091107_5155772.htm>.

China.org.cn. 2001, 'Jiang Zemin's speech at the meeting celebrating the 80th anniversary of the founding of the Communist Party of China', 1 July, viewed 12 July 2013, <http://www.china.org.cn/e-speech/a.htm>.

Cripps, K. 2013a, 'China's first tourism law comes into effect, tourists issued manners guides', CNN, 4 October, viewed 22 October 2013, <http://edition.cnn.com/2013/10/03/travel/new-china-tourism-law/>.

Cripps, K. 2013b, 'Chinese travelers the world's biggest spenders', CNN, 12 April, viewed 22 October 2013, <http://edition.cnn.com/2013/04/05/travel/china-tourists-spend/>.

Dean, M. 1999, Governmentality: Power and rule in modern society, Sage, London.

Dean, M. 2002, 'Liberal government and authoritarianism', Economy and Society, vol. 31, no. 1, pp. 37–61.

Dean, M & Hindess B. 1998, 'Introduction: Government, liberalism, society', in Dean, M & Hindess, B (eds.), Governing Australia: Studies in contemporary rationalities of government, Cambridge University Press, Cambridge, pp. 1–19.

Dello-Iacovo, B. 2009, 'Curriculum reform and "quality education" in China: An overview', International Journal of Educational Development, vol. 29, no. 3, pp. 241–249.

Diamond, L. 2010, 'Liberation technology', Journal of Democracy, vol. 21, no. 3, pp. 69–83.

Downey, T. 2010, 'China's cyberposse', The New York Times, 3 March, viewed 2 April 2013, <http://www.nytimes.com/2010/03/07/magazine/07Humant.html?pagewanted=all&_r=2&>.

Duke, M. 1985, Blooming and contending: Chinese literature in the post-Mao era, Indiana University Press, Bloomington, IN.

Fairbrother, G. 2003, Toward critical patriotism: Student resistance to political education in Hong Kong and China, Hong Kong University Press, Hong Kong.

Fletcher, H. 2008, 'Human flesh search engines: Chinese vigilantes that hunt victims on the web', Times Online, <http://web.archive.org/web/20090304053728/http:/technology.timesonline.co.uk/tol/news/tech_and_web/article4213681.ece>.

Foucault, M. 1977, Discipline and punish: The birth of the prison, Pantheon Books, New York.

Foucault, M. 1991, 'Governmentality', in Burchell, G, Gordon, C & Miller, P (eds.), The Foucault effect: Studies in governmental rationality, Harvester Wheatsheaf, Hemel Hempstead, pp. 87–104.

Foucault, M. 1993, 'About the beginning of the hermeneutics of the self: Two lectures at Dartmouth', Political Theory, vol. 21, no. 2, pp. 198–227.

Gries, PH. 2004, China's new nationalism: Pride, politics and diplomacy, University of California Press, Berkeley, CA.

Guo, Y. 2004, Cultural nationalism in contemporary China: The search for national identity under reform, RoutledgeCurzon, London.

Hassid, J. 2012, 'Safety valve or pressure cooker? Blogs in Chinese political life', Journal of Communication, vol. 62, no. 2, pp. 212–230.

Ho, YF & Chiu, CY. 1994, 'Component ideas of individualism, collectivism and social organization: An application in the study of Chinese culture', in Kim, U, Triandis, HC, Kagitcibasi, C, Choi, SC & Yoon, G (eds.), Individualism and collectivism: Theory, methods, and application, SAGE Publications, California, pp. 137–156.

Hoffman, L. 2006, 'Autonomous choices and patriotic professionalism: On governmentality in late-socialist China', Economy and Society, vol. 35, no. 4, pp. 550–570.

Hofstede, G. 1993, 'Cultures constraints in management theories', Academy of Management Executive, vol. 7, no. 1, pp. 81–94.

Hofstede, G & Bond, MH. 1988, 'The Confucius connection: From cultural roots to economic growth', Organizational Dynamics, vol. 16, no. 4, pp. 5–21.

Hu, M. 2013, 'Schoolboy's Egyptian temple shame', People's Daily, 27 May, viewed 3 June 2013, <http://english.peopledaily.com.cn/90882/8258482.html>.

Hu, Y. 2008, Zhongsheng xuanhua (The rising cacophony), Guangxi Normal University Press, Guilin.

Hutchinson, J. 1987, The dynamics of cultural nationalism, Allen & Unwin, London.

Jeffreys, E & Sigley, G. 2009, 'Governmentality, governance and China', in Jeffreys, E (ed.), China's governmentalities: Governing change, changing government, Routledge, London, pp. 1–23.

Jiang, M. 2010, 'Spaces of authoritarian deliberation: Online public deliberation in China', in Leib, E & He, B (eds.), The search for deliberative democracy in China, Palgrave Macmillan, New York, pp. 261–287.

Kang, L. 2012, 'Searching for a new cultural identity: China's soft power and media culture today', Journal of Contemporary China, vol. 21, no. 78, pp. 915–931.

Latour, B. 1987, Science in Action, Open University Press, Milton Keynes.

Li, H. 2013, 'Hands full with heart empty', People's Daily, 27 May, viewed 22 September 2013, <http://opinion.people.com.cn/n/2013/0527/c1003-21619899.html>.

Lee, T. 2010, The media, cultural control and government in Singapore, Routledge, New York.

Mao, J. 2013, 'Why "a visit" has become a never-ending ghost?', Xinhua News, 27 May, viewed 22 September 2013, <http://news.xinhuanet.com/comments/2013-05/27/c_115916137.htm>.

McNeice, S. 2013, 'Chinese authorities issued guidebook for "civilized tourism"', 10 October, viewed 22 October 2013, <https://www.newstalk.ie/reader/47.339/14831/show_list_0_0/>.

Miller, P & Rose, N. 1990, 'Political rationalities and technologies of government', in Hanninen, S & Palonen, K (eds.), Texts, contexts, concepts: Studies in politics and power in language, Finnish political Science Association, Helsinki, pp. 171–183.

Miller, P & Rose, N. 2008, Governing the present: Administering economics, social and personal life, Polity Press, Cambridge.

Ni, C. 2007, 'She makes Confucius cool again', Los Angeles Times, 7 May, viewed 5 May, 2012, <http://articles.latimes.com/2007/may/07/world/fg-confucius7>.

Pan, H. 2013, 'To ashamed to go to Egypt after the scandal', Xinhua News, 26 May, viewed 23 September, 2013, <http://news.xinhuanet.com/world/2013-05/26/c_124763897.htm>.

Pye, L. 1996, 'How China's nationalism was Shanghaied', in Jonathan, U (ed.), Chinese Nationalism, M.E. Sharpe, New York, pp. 86–112.

Pykett, J. 2010, 'Citizenship education and narratives of pedagogy', Citizenship Studies, vol. 14, no. 6, pp. 621–635.

Qian, C & Xu, J. 2013, 'The number of Chinese outbound tourists will exceed 100 million next year', Xinhua News, 10 October, viewed 24 October, <http://news.xinhuanet.com/world/2013-10/10/c_117649303.htm>.

Rawnsley, GD. 2006, 'The media, internet and governance in China', The University of Nottingham, viewed 3 June 2012, <http://www.nottingham.ac.uk/cpi/documents/discussion-papers/discussion-paper-12-china-media-internet-governance.pdf>.

Rose, N. 1996, 'Governing "advanced" liberal democracies', in Barry, A, Osborne, T & Rose, N (eds.), Foucault and political reason: Liberalism, neo-liberalism, and rationalities of government, University of Chicago Press, Chicago, pp. 37–64.

Rose, N. 1999, Governing the soul: The shaping of the private self, Free Association Books, London.

Rose, N & Miller, P. 2010, 'Political power beyond the State: Problematics of government', The British Journal of Sociology, vol. 61, no. s1, pp. 271–303.

Shen, K. 2013, Source: <http://weibo.com/1440641483/zyfhP0kac?type=comment>.

Shirk, S. 2011, 'Changing media, changing China', in Shirk, S (ed.), Changing media, changing China, Oxford University Press, New York, pp. 1–37.

Sigley, G. 2004, 'Liberal despotism: Population planning, subjectivity, and government in contemporary China', Alternatives, vol. 29, no. 5, pp. 557–575.

Sigley, G. 2006, 'Chinese governmentalities: Government, governance and the socialist market economy', Economy and Society, vol. 35, no. 4, pp. 487–508.

So, AY (ed.). 2003, China's developmental miracle: Origins, transformations, and challenges, M. E. Sharpe, New York.

Wan, L. 2013, 'Boy's graffiti signals lack of values at home', People's Daily Online, 27 May, viewed 30 August 2013, <http://english.peopledaily.com.cn/90882/8260820.html>.

Wang, L. 2008, 'With the dragon as a foil: American imagining of China and the construction of America's national identity', Social Sciences in China, vol. 29, no. 4, pp. 98–112.

Wang, G & Liu, Z. 2010, 'What collective? Collectivism and relationalism from a Chinese perspective', Chinese Journal of Communication, vol. 3, no. 1, pp. 42–63.

Winfield, BH, Mizuno, T & Beaudoin, CE. 2000, 'Confucianism, collectivism and constitutions: Press systems in China and Japan', Communication Law and Policy, vol. 5, no. 3, pp. 323–347.

Wong, G. 2013, 'Egypt temple vandal sparks soul-searching in China', 29 May, viewed 2 August 2013, <http://www.timesofisrael.com/egypt-temple-vandal-sparks-soul-searching-in-china/>.

Yang, J. 2011, 'The politics of the dang'an: Spectralization, spatialization, and neoliberal governmentality in China', Anthropological Quarterly, vol. 84, no. 2, pp. 507–533.

Yin, J. 2007, 'The narrative function of news: A comparative study of media representation and audience interpretation of China-US trade relationship', China Media Research, vol. 3, no. 3, pp. 33–42.

Zhang, X. 2006, 'Reading between the headlines: SARS, Focus and TV current affairs programs in China', Media, Culture & Society, vol. 28, no. 5, pp. 715–737.

Zhao, Y. 1998, Media, market and democracy in China: Between the party line and the bottom line, University of Illinois Press, Urbana, IL.

Zhao, Z. 2014, 'Pedagogization of nation identity through textbook narratives in China: 1902–1948', Citizenship Studies, vol. 18, no. 1, pp. 99–112.

Zheng, Y. 1999, Discovering Chinese nationalism in China: Modernization, identity, and international relations, Cambridge University Press, Cambridge.

· 7 ·

CONCLUSION

Overseas observers and scholars regularly attempt to capture the political implications of the rise of social media in China under the theme of oppressive state control; however, the Chinese government's constant advances in the way it deals with social media should not be underestimated. The state of play between the regime's maintaining of strict information control and its allowing greater freedom of information in China has been richly analyzed by scholars in recent years (Tong & Lei 2013; Yang 2009; MacKinnon 2009), who have concluded with a variety of interpretations. This book contributes to the analysis, reaching a different conclusion than earlier discussions by explaining the occurrence of more open debates on Weibo despite facing strict censorship. Chinese social media culture is so internally complex that it is actually possible for both greater freedoms of information and information containment to take place simultaneously. This paradox is informed by the new context of China's more expansive conversation with the world, which contributes to a subtly changed internal landscape for new media.

This book puts forward a new contribution to the literature on Weibo and democracy through its analysis of governmentality and the public sphere. Instead of taking on either a democratizing role or a non-democratizing reading of Weibo in China, this book outlines both optimistic and pessimistic aspects generated by Weibo use. More significantly, it shows how the party-state has adapted its regulatory measures by offering more apparent freedom for better control.

The Chinese authorities have transitioned from an approach to information regulation which involved a total banning of certain media platforms, including Facebook and Twitter, to a more complex regulation of, for example Weibo, which has posed significant challenges to the authorities. Instead of banning Weibo, the government has allowed a certain amount of "free" space on the platform in order to meet public demands, while at the same time using the platform to meet the state's political aims. Therefore, instead of describing the relationship between the state and Weibo as a binary site of hegemony and counter-hegemony (Tong & Lei 2013), this book provides a critical perspective on both the constructing of the "free" space and of the control of Weibo. This book explores the inherent contradictions present in some discourses on Weibo, and identifies the key regulatory strategies that the Chinese party-state employs to govern the Chinese people's thoughts and conduct. It examines government information regulation through the tools and different tactics which are designed to shape the hearts and minds of the Chinese to conform to desired political goals (Foucault 1991). Through this examination, the book suggests that Weibo primarily offers a public space for communication. It is not a revolutionary tool for potential democratic transformation and cannot meet the definition of a fulfilled public sphere.

Regulatory strategies such as the deliberate suppression, manipulation and strategic release of information interact in complex ways on Weibo. While new forms of government thinking are viewed as unlocking the "old" forms of power and authority, they may produce new versions of the public sphere. Based on case studies, this book argues that the Chinese government's calculated actions to regulate Weibo are based on both existing cultural and institutional practices. This research has therefore been concerned with the multiple spaces of governmentalities: how these spaces are constituted through government practices and how such practices have implications in the production of publics.

In this way, the theoretical models of the public sphere and governmentality are particularly useful for understanding the changing nature of the role of Weibo in Chinese society and the implications for government control over Weibo. Though Weibo claimed substantial space for freedom of expression for the public to express their concerns and to talk about the "hot" issues, such as exposing official corruption and injustice, all of these took place within the government's confined domains. Despite the fact that Weibo users have developed a variety of creative methods to bypass official controls, the Chinese state has relentlessly adapted and refined its strategies to exert control. This ambivalent status for Weibo is well explained by the governmentality model. This study contributes to the literature in that it is not only another application of Western-based governmentality in a non-liberal context, but in addition, it extends the theory to the social media field; moreover, it offers an original analysis of the interconnecting framework of government-politics-social media through the lens of governmentality.

Findings From Case Studies

In China, one could conclude that the social media platform, Weibo, has brought the Chinese people unprecedented opportunities for public expression and debate, in more politically sensitive areas than ever before. Often there is the mistaken view that Weibo plays a democratizing role in Chinese society and genuinely creates a public sphere. However, while acknowledging that there is more space for free speech, this book argues that even such 'open' fields, are significantly instrumentalized by the government's regulatory strategies to achieve specific political outcomes.

If the Chinese authorities initially displayed an ambivalent attitude towards the internet, they have shown an arbitrary attitude to Weibo. Compared with the general impact of the internet, Weibo communication is more fragmented and unsystematic due to its technical structure (Tong & Zuo 2014). In the Weibo era, people are able to make more demands on the authorities than ever before, therefore, pressing the CCP to react to these demands. The government therefore needs to create a careful balance between the free flow of information and its own strenuous efforts to selectively control online content to shape public opinion, and since the development of technology is an unavoidable trend, the Chinese authorities have actively put in place a set of regulatory measures to minimize any damaging effects from undesirable information.

It is acknowledgeable that on some occasions, Weibo does provide a dynamic platform for the Chinese people to promote open discourse. The free speech platform has greatly sparked the Chinese people's collective wisdom, as contention from all walks of Chinese life appears on Weibo. But at the same time, the Chinese government derives more ideas and strategies to control it. For example, among the numerous examples and anecdotes about the internet, including Weibo-driven stories, the Chinese government categorizes the events and selectively ensures that some events become seen as typical cases, with the help of the mainstream press to highlight their importance, in order to fulfill its purposes.

This book explores the matching intentions and calculations of the Chinese government in this information environment—as stimulated by and in response to, Weibo. It argues that the Chinese authorities have gained more confidence and understanding in regulating Weibo, based on the fact that they have become more skillful and adept at dealing with it. Rather than the previous complete control of information in China, the authorities have permitted a certain degree of freedom on Weibo, targeted very strategically, to improve the leadership's governance and to strengthen its popular support. The case of "Ding was here" provides a view of an early version of governmentality in the twenty-first century, and shows the responsiveness of the government to the issues that concern its citizens. This is a less overt way of governing than has previously been the case in China.

The Chinese Version of Weibo as a Public Sphere. This book, first of all, established the background to the common assumptions of the role of Weibo in contributing to the creation of a genuine public sphere in the Chinese society. The public sphere has been examined as an ideal in Western liberal societies, first by Habermas. As a normative concept, the idea of the public sphere has provided a useful analytical framework with which to understand the political potential of Weibo in China.

A number of scholars saw it as inevitable that the arrival of the internet in China would lead to the opening up of the society in the direction of a public sphere. Other scholars have maintained that no new technology alone will create an ideal public sphere (Zhang 2011, p. 167). Weibo has proved to be its most provocative incarnation to date, and has certainly managed to create new public space for communication. However, greater participation in this space cannot guarantee a healthy and democratic public sphere, and therefore, it fails the Habermasian test. In the Chinese context, Weibo has, to a larger extent, offered an outlet for public resentment in a transformational period (Zhang 2012), but whether the public space ultimately transcends to become a public sphere is not simply a matter of technology (Papacharissi 2002). To enable a successful shift from public space to a public sphere requires specific conditions such as a relative autonomy of individuals from the state and the economy. It is obviously not possible for the Chinese government currently to allow this. Therefore, the role the internet-related technologies, including

Weibo, are playing in the realm of China's evolving political potential, is not decisive. The regulatory framework prevails, so from this perspective, Weibo is primarily a public space and does not serve as a platform for ideally deliberative discourses.

The two cases discussed in this book are among a growing number of such events in recent years where the authorities selectively highlight some events to influence the public. In both cases, Weibo created a public platform to generate vigorous discussions on the issues, which has shown Weibo's function of potentially contributing to a public sphere. Citizen engagement in online protests indicates that the public awareness of rights and accountabilities is evolving, although the extent to which it challenges injustice is limited. As demonstrated in the two case studies, however, Weibo offers an unprecedented platform for public debate which had been impossible in the past, even if the temporary version of a public sphere it offers is later managed and calculated by the government for its own purposes. The authorities skillfully control a new balance between freedom of speech and social and political control on Weibo.

However, in the current social media in China, voices on Weibo in particular, tend to criticize for the sake of criticizing, instead of expressing deliberative thought, so that the news objective, to some extent, declines when the purpose of most users is (above all) simply to attract more followers. While mass media tends to produce a homogeneity to meet its target audience, the advent of internet forums, blogs and other individual tools, produces a heterogeneity that "seems to have difficulties in controlling itself reflexively" (Rasmussen 2013, p. 98).

The Interaction between Mainstream Media and Weibo. Though different forms of the public sphere are operating on Weibo, which allow people to speak up and to question problems more freely than in the past, we have also seen innovative and adaptive governmental regulatory measures appear on Weibo. Particularly in politically sensitive events, netizens remain passive audiences who are subject to heavy monitoring. The new cooperative mode of interaction between the mainstream media and Weibo also works well to fulfil the official political agendas.

Therefore, despite the fact that scholars contend that the emergence of the internet and social media has profoundly opened China's public opinion structures, many Chinese still belong to the "silent majority", with Weibo itself in particular cases used for the government to realize its purposes. With its unique characteristics, it is impossible for the government to turn Weibo into the Party's mouthpiece as with the People's Daily in every case, but occasionally it does function in this way. Therefore, though Weibo offers a platform for citizens to influence the current system with their creativity, the government has also managed to stay one step ahead to influence or shape public opinion. In this way, control and freedom frequently crisscross or interweave on Weibo.

In the regulation of Weibo, the exercise of governmental authority can be understood as taking different articulations, including forms of pastoral power and forms of sovereignty. In the case of "Ding was here", public debate was initially stirred up on Weibo. However, when the debate reached a certain level, mainstream media such as the People's Daily became involved and made commentaries on this issue, with these commentaries later forwarded many times on Weibo. In other words, the traditional media reportage prompted more widespread coverage. The process of this interaction created a communication loop. The deliberate raising of this case to a higher level manipulated public sentiment into support for the official agenda for patriotism. Weibo then became a tool and a technology of governmentality, designed to guide the minds and manage the conduct of the Chinese to conform to desired cultural molds (Foucault 1991).

In the case of the Bo Xilai trial, Weibo was used by the government from the very first to take the commanding height. When the trial was underway, the Xinhua News agency published its first commentary and this also was forwarded on Weibo. This was a much more explicit version of the authorities using a medium as a technology of governmentality to fulfil the government's agenda and to successfully calibrate public opinion.

This book explores the procedures of how the events or cases involve both the formulation of governmental concerns and the ways of addressing these concerns. In the interaction between the official media and Weibo, a series of processes has been detected in the communication loop. Firstly, since government is considered as a problematizing activity (Rose & Miller 2010, p. 279), which is supposed to address problems and rectify ills, there must be existing problems which need to be fixed. In the case of "Ding was here", the travel etiquette of the Chinese people has been a serious and long criticized problem. With the increasing significance of China's overall strength in the world, it calls for a better international image and for social problems to be addressed in order to focus on social development rather than solely on the growth of GDP. In the case of the Bo Xilai trial, corruption has long been a social evil that undermines political stability and the CCP's legitimacy. In addition, there had already been a number of rumors about Bo Xilai's behavior before his trial which could cause a credibility crisis among political high-profiles and destroy the government's image. Therefore, in both cases, the Chinese government takes the initiative or is willing to address these two problems.

Secondly, Weibo offers a perfect platform to ignite discussion, and is able to shift the discussion from private to public. In the case of the Bo Xilai trial, the live broadcast trial on Weibo was extolled as "historically transparent" (Zhang 2013). The display of the trial on Weibo could achieve two purposes. On the one hand, the government showed its firm determination to fight corruption; on the other hand, it displayed a transparent image and eliminated rumors at the same time. In the case of "Ding was here", with the help of Weibo, an ordinary incident related to travel etiquette generated great debate, which was amplified to a higher level with the orchestrated involvement of the mainstream media.

Thirdly, the cases are selectively picked up by the government to fulfill its political will. In other words, it is the government that sets the agenda in particular cases to its advantage. In the Bo Xilai trial, it is obvious that the government has been the main actor in the trial, while in the case of "Ding was here", it was deliberately magnified by the government to fulfill its political agenda.

Fourthly, both cases received attention from the mainstream media to continue public discussion. However, the mainstream media in both cases focuses more on commentaries to educate or guide public opinion and to reinforce political will. Finally, the mainstream media commentaries were forwarded on Weibo to strengthen its influence. In these two cases, the Chinese government follows a cycle where it can be clearly seen that the state is playing an active role on Weibo, and it seems the state has found an effective way to deal with the overwhelming liberal tendency on Weibo.

However, there is a difference between the cases. In the Bo Xilai trial, the government takes control of the agenda at the very beginning, and then makes it a live broadcast on Weibo. In contrast, in "Ding was here", the incident took place first on Weibo, and then was picked up by the government. It showed that in sensitive issues, the government takes the commanding height at the very first opportunity, while in ordinary cases Weibo is first allowed to offer a public sphere for appropriate public discussion. When it is found to conform to the political will, the government will get involved to direct the trend. In this way, in the Bo Xilai trial, it is clearer to see a push-and-pull interaction between the netizens and the government. For example, when rumors about Bo Xilai spread online in 2012, it prompted the party-state to close down many prominent web portals and comment functions (Bandurski 2012). But in the 2013 trial, it showed greater freedom and openness than before. This push-and-pull interaction clearly shows the government's thinking and calculations behind the scenes.

The growth of social media constantly challenges the Party's capacity to exercise authoritarian control, bringing information that in the past would have been censored to the public eye, as shown in the Bo Xilai trial. But at the same time, the party-state is also managing the events and flow of information. Thus the interplay of highly interactive levels of information is "the product of the dramatic growth of the networked communications in China" (Lewis 2013, p. 679). Coincidently, the interaction between the mainstream media and Weibo reflects recent CCP thought on managing public opinion. In the fourth meeting of the Leading Group for Overall Reform on August 18th, 2014, President Xi Jinping pledged to build a modern communications system in which he called on the state to "integrate traditional media and new media to diversify its communication system" (Xinhua net 2014). Xi said traditional media and new media should complement each other in terms of content, channels, platforms, operations and management. Many scholars have given interpretations of this new reform. Song Jiangwu, Dean of the School of Journalism at the China University of Politics and Law, remarked that this is indicating new aspects among China's leadership about managing its public message (Clover 2014). Chen Lidan, a journalism professor at Renmin University of China, commented that integration not only means simple addition of new functions or channels, but "it is very significant that the President urged publicity officials to intensify 'internet thinking'" (ibid.). Such remarks indicate that the top leaders are fully aware of new trends in the media industry (Zhao 2014). Therefore, making good use the mainstream media to regulate Weibo becomes an important strategy for the government to regulate the communication platform of Weibo.

New Governmentality in the Weibo Era. This book is also set against the background of the transformation of the Chinese government. As the government has been criticized for its strict control of freedom of speech and corruption, it is also willing to show a more transparent side to the world. The Chinese government has regularly implemented a number of information containment strategies. In addition to specific regulations, technical solutions and self-censorship, it has designed more sophisticated and subtle strategies to attain their goals to regulate Weibo. These strategies are often invisible and therefore more effective. In contrast with the conventionally passive attitude, the Chinese government has shifted to a more 'cooperative' and active attitude to regulate Weibo. The seemingly open but actually regulatory behaviors are indeed characteristic of the current Chinese government's regulatory measures. However, this freedom on the surface is strictly limited within the political boundaries set by the Chinese government.

Lagerkvist (2006) has summarized this balance between greater freedom to maintain greater control as a zero-sum game with one increasing and the other decreasing, or with both control and freedom expanding or increasing simultaneously in the two cases. It is hard to discern the divergences between control and freedom, for these two are always running parallel. Although the party-state still has no official tolerance in the political field, such as in the Bo Xilai trial, it still enlarged its scope for wider public participation, which is a sign of shift from traditional crackdowns to new governing thinking. The relationship between Weibo and the Chinese government is vague and subtle. Since there is no clear boundary to test the bottom line of the government, there is always a balance between these two actors. Occasionally the government needs to adjust its level of tolerance to Weibo.

In many cases the Chinese government encourages Weibo users to monitor wrongdoings such as legal abuse or corruption as well as the uncivilized behavior represented in the case of "Ding was here". The reason for this encouragement is that the exposure of these bad behaviors is in line with the state's aims. Once such an event appears on Weibo and it reaches a peak of public contention, the authorities will get involved to give 'correct' guidance. In the case of "Ding was here", the echo of the mainstream media has re-emphasized the authorities' intentions to improve Chinese people's travelling behaviors. Therefore, in this light, Weibo was considered a tool for the authorities to fulfill their purposes. Under these circumstances, the Chinese government has displayed its intentions and action to guide people's thought.

The government intrudes into all walks of Chinese people's life, and it is in fact not exercised from one single controlling center—the state. Rather, the government refers to the manner of different agents to manage their own behaviors. A particular kind of philosophy or rationality has been taken up by the Chinese authorities in the practice of government to regulate social media. The CCP has started to actively use Weibo as a vehicle for its own propaganda or public opinion guidance, instead of simply restricting the information. In other words, the CCP has successfully claimed its agenda on Weibo. The CCP is looking for a middle ground between control and popular appeal, and to some extent, Weibo has been used by the government to further its related agendas and purposes. Despite the principle that the Party controls the media, the way the government manages Weibo is advancing with the times. Coercive measures are not abandoned; instead, they were expressed through a number of methods such as punishment and constraint.

Rethinking the Role of Weibo. With the rapid development of technology, there are many ways for people to seek credible information. Hence, people who are better informed than before have started to make new demands on government. However, many scholars have long debated the supposed democratizing power of the dramatic growth of networked communications in China. Scholars have argued that rather than the previous "blind optimism", authoritarian states have been successful in proactively using modern communications technology to shape public discussion (Kalathil & Boas 2003; Morozov 2011). How officials reacted to these demands to balance its risks and benefits can be seen in both case studies where the CCP has become adept at using Weibo to reach their purposes. In "Ding was here", when the public emotions fomented to a certain point, the government became involved in the event to guide public opinion and issue relevant regulations to solve certain problems. In the Bo Xilai trial, the central government directly set the agenda first and reasserted control over Weibo. It neutralized the public emotions and conveyed an image of competent and transparent government with strictness against corruption. The ambivalent attitude towards Weibo (openness on one side and control on the other) leads to a rethinking of the role of Weibo, considering its possible role as the executor of the Party's agenda, or as Party-based social media. The Chinese people are becoming more and more versatile and creative in the application of Weibo, which has posed new challenges for government control.

In China, where there is no reliable mechanism to detect the popular sentiment or to feel the public pulse on key issues, Weibo has indeed filled this gap. The two cases in this book have clearly demonstrated how the CCP used them to reclaim its agenda on the internet. With these official gestures in the direction of a public sphere, Weibo provides a forum for the provision of two-way political communication, helping the government to access different voices and to gain feedback, thus establishing a relationship between the government and the ordinary people. The party-state has enlarged the span of official tolerance of media freedom in some aspects, such as encouraging Weibo to monitor legal abuse, corruption and other wrongdoings outside the higher levels of the political system, but also in order to improve government accountability.

Although there is no doubt that Weibo has revolutionized the flow of information and information connectivity as well as expanded political opportunity, how this opportunity is exploited is up to users (Lewis 2013). The Chinese government has continued to maintain scrutiny and control over it. Though Weibo provides opportunities for public expression, issues are eventually covered by the mainstream press pushing events forward. Nevertheless, citizens' engagement in online protests indicates that public awareness of rights and accountabilities is evolving, although the extent to which it challenges injustice is limited. In the meantime, China's party-state is acutely aware of the effectiveness of Weibo (and other social media) as a communication tool and is responding to public events in ways that suggest a more tolerant and positive tone toward a transformative public sphere. For example, under the circumstance of the Bo Xilai trial, the role that Weibo plays is as Hassid (2012) suggests, a "safety valve", allowing citizens to voice their concerns on particular problems. Therefore, Weibo seems to provide a free speech platform, and even allows the government to better communicate with the public; this study argues that this is in fact the government's attempt to adapt media management to a more liberal public sphere. In other words, Weibo is the extension of government regulation of media to keep up with the information age. In this way, we should not draw a line between public expression and democratic potential; instead of merely looking at the popular expression; we should pay attention to the macro network conditions that enable it.

A New Typology of the Public Sphere on Weibo. The role of media and other institutions serves to produce multiple spatial and temporal publics that function in a mobile and flexible manner. It has been noted the public sphere cannot be viewed as a fixed spatial entity, likewise, the public cannot simply be considered as a gathering of groups (Rauchfleisch, A & Schäfer 2014). The government mentalities applied in the regulation of Weibo can be viewed as attempts to construct a number of spatial and temporal publics, such as the patriots in the case of "Ding was here", and the staunch supporters to fight corruption or even the Fifty Cents Party in the Bo Xilai trial. Each of them contributes to the interactions of the wider public sphere.

There is also a shift towards an "authoritarian deliberation" by the Chinese state from the perspective of political science (He & Warren 2011). Reflecting failures of command authoritarianism under the conditions of complexity and pluralism produced by market-oriented development, the Chinese government gradually adopts a variety of deliberative practices to shape public discourse. These practices exist within an authoritarian regime with no apparent interest in democracy, a phenomenon considered by Baogang He and Mark Warren as a form of authoritarian deliberation with "deliberative venues" used by the government to bolster regime legitimacy (ibid.). While the deliberation taking place within Chinese authoritarianism may bring about democratization, He and Warren believe that there could be another possibility, which is that the deliberative practices adopted by the government could stabilize and strengthen authoritarian rule.

Jiang (2010) applies the concept of authoritarian deliberation specifically to the Chinese internet context, illustrating four aspects of deliberative Chinese cyberspace. 1) "central propaganda spaces", referring to websites and forums built and managed by the government directly; 2) "government-regulated commercial spaces", referring to websites and forums which are owned and operated by private companies but are subject to government intervention for content censorship; 3) "emergent civil spaces", referring to websites and other digital platforms operated by nongovernment organizations, which are strictly subject to registration requirements and severe punishments such as arrest when if the requirements are disobeyed; 4) "international deliberative spaces", referring to websites and service that are operated beyond the Chinese government's jurisdiction, therefore, content and information not permitted on domestic websites can be found. Jiang (2010) goes on to mention that it is the first two categories that have the greatest impact on Chinese public opinion. The second perspective reveals how the Chinese state uses more proactive and sophisticated means to control the deliberative spaces, as Weibo is run by a private company.

As noted, Weibo has indeed facilitated open and critical public debates which have been impossible in the traditional Chinese media. However, in Habermas' original formulation of a public sphere, there is reference to a particular type of social condition that could enable a radical-critical debate about public issues conducted by private persons that further influences decision making by the leadership (Calhoun 1992, p. 1). In China, with the evolving media technologies, especially through the emergence of Weibo, the distinction between senders and receivers is blurred. Citizens can also become generators of public information, which has led to widespread discussion of Weibo's potential as a platform for creating a public sphere, as it allows a certain degree of public discussion or protest to take place regularly (Yang 2009). In this sense, the democratizing claim of Weibo is partly true. However, in response to this potential for a public sphere, the Chinese authorities, as always, "stay one step ahead of freedom" (Bandurski 2014), continuing to maintain a high level of scrutiny and control over Weibo.

Apart from the visible censorship of social media, there are new forms of invisible power being used in ways that deliver a positive outcome for government, such as strategically placed online commentary delivering the preferred status quo. Strategies for media regulation in contemporary China are softer and more subtle than in the past. Despite the appearance of new opportunities for greater public space, the social conditions in China are obviously not suitable for an ideal public sphere (which historically may never in fact have been achieved). Scholars describe multiple public spheres arising from Weibo, each embodying certain criteria of the public sphere concept (Rauchfleisch & Schäfer 2014). A study of online activism in China also shows that currently, there is neither the triumph of complete control on the part of the internet-controlling regime nor of successful resistance by internet users and activists (Yang 2009, p. 62). In this way, China is a particularly interesting case, with freedom and control co-existing. Therefore, despite the fact that Weibo communication is limited on many issues in many ways, there are still a number of instances or situations under which Weibo communication fulfills some of the core criteria of the public sphere. These include openness of discussion and wide participation. Therefore, between the public sphere and a non-public sphere, there is a middle ground from which public spheres may emerge, though certainly shaped to certain degrees at certain points. Moreover, the degrees of freedom and control vary, or are managed, under specific circumstances. In examining the prevailing degrees of freedom and control in different cases, a typology of three types of public sphere emerges, so contextualizing these outcomes. These types illustrate the existence of public spheres between the ideal and non-existent public spheres. Though there is no widely shared concept of the public sphere, there are some recognized fundamental aspects. Here, the Chinese government shapes the characteristics of the public sphere.

The first type can be considered as a real public sphere, in which public debate on Weibo is able to influence news and drive public agendas. There are a significant number of cases documented by scholars in which collective concerns have been discussed on Weibo with little censorship (Tai 2006; Yang 2009). Among these, Weibo plays a crucial role, for example in the recent 7.23 High-Speed train crash case in Zhejiang province, in which two high speed trains collided on a bridge and forty people died. Amateur video captured local government and military personnel burying entire train carriages, which was seen as an attempt to 'hide' evidence of the severity of the crash. Within a few days of this accident, Chinese Weibo users posted more than 10 million messages on the train crash, most of which attacked the government for a range of reasons, from the causes of the accident to the way the government treated the victims. Eventually this online circulation prompted a large public outcry and requested the government to handle the crisis. In addition, public debate over issues such as environmental problems and corruption scandals at local levels have been aired without too much state interference, as long as public debate over these issues on Weibo conforms to the political agenda of supervising the local levels of administration to improve their legitimacy.

The second type is what scholars identify as a non-public sphere, with a high degree of censorship and regulation. In these cases, authorities impose strict regulations on certain issues, such as the well-known Tiananmen Square protest in 1989. In fact, when the Bo Xilai scandal first occurred in 2012, key-words such as Bo Xilai and Wang Lijun were strictly regulated by the censors. Hence, there is no degree of public sphere in such instances.

The third type embodies a middle ground between great freedom and strict censorship, a less authentic, or questionable version of the public sphere, where the government allows some issues to be debated within a limited framework or where the government deliberately identifies certain cases and puts them forward for public discussion to fulfill its own purposes. Within this type, a significant number of cases with collective concerns can be discussed openly on Weibo, and even sometimes express criticism of the Chinese authorities by a large number of participants. As discussed in the case studies in Chapters Five and Six, this middle ground allows a relatively greater degree of freedom of speech than previously, within the context of the government's rationalities for regulation. Therefore, despite the fact that previous scholarly studies have documented many examples and stories where Weibo has played a significant role in greater public expression, pressing the authorities to respond, such examples are often accompanied by the strategic involvement and the deliberate arrangement of government. In these instances, the more attention the government demonstrates, the more likely it is to fulfill its purposes. In other words, the government deliberately gives national attention to particular events and allows targeted communications on politically sensitive issues or practices in order to better and more strategically respond to the Weibo age.

Social Media Power and Political Democracy

Many scholars question the state's monitoring and censorship role in the internet era, nevertheless, we should not jump to the conclusion that the internet is omnipotent and able to overstep too many boundaries. In China, media organizations must still obey the law or regulations. Borrowing from Lagerkvist (2010), since the Chinese state is always "waltzing" with the internet, it is often overlooked that the state continues to monitor and exercise control over the internet by exercising "soft control" (p. 222). As Lagerkvist (2010, p. 1395) expressed, some scholars "downsize the role and strategies of the state to contain internet use". Therefore, there is doubt as to whether the Chinese party-state is "bent on maintaining social and political stability" (ibid.).

This book argues that there is not necessarily a link between technology and democracy, though it acknowledges Weibo's great power offering an unprecedented platform for public expression with netizens able to use different genres, styles or forms to express or protest. The internet will not bring democracy to China simply because it is a technology, which is a tool, not a cause of political change (MacKinnon 2008). Pan (2006) also notes that being a tool should not be confused with being a cause of change, because the cause should be much broader in terms of social, economic and political factors.

China has developed its own version of cyberspace in the rapidly evolving micro sphere and in so doing, has successfully served the state's continuing economic development. In other words, learning the lessons of other countries, China's internet governance has its unique characteristics based on its own context. Zheng accurately described the interaction between the state and society over the internet-mediated public sphere that "is not necessarily a zero-sum game, and when conditions are 'right', it could be a win-win game" (Zheng 2008, p. 135).

Weibo is inherently democratic simply because of its wider range of access than earlier formations of the media. Nevertheless, in some aspects, Weibo enables the production and dissemination of views, some of which are not at all democratic. To some extent, it may even serve as a way of legitimating certain views and assisting in their circulation. The concept of the "demotic turn" put forward by Turner (2010) is a way of characterizing the increasing visibility of the ordinary people, to support a critical reappraisal of contemporary thinking in relation to popular media forms and of the increased participation of ordinary people in media production. This could accurately describe Weibo. Though ordinary people participate in public discussion on Weibo in diverse ways, as consumers or producers, it remains the case that Weibo produces and manages information which serves the government interests.

It could be concluded then, that the role of Weibo is primarily as a supervisory tool, rather than as an agent for the promotion of democracy. This book goes further, to argue that while Weibo is able to provide multiple public spheres to some extent, some of which offer more public space for citizen to citizen communication than was previously possible in China, in its current stage and for the foreseeable future, it also plays an important role in the administration of power and as a tool for the Chinese government to fulfill its agenda. Both case studies in this book are examples of both phenomena, taking place simultaneously. In contemporary China, the government's progress in response to the changing media ecology has been gradual, strategic and cumulative. The key message here is that the role social media plays in China should not be exaggerated in its impact as a democratizing force, but should be understood in all its multiple dimensions.

Remaking the Public Sphere in the Weibo Era

The paradigm of both allowing greater freedom of information, coexisting or alternating with new control measures, takes a new form on Weibo. In this way, what may appear to be fields of a public sphere are always designed within the larger framework of government deliberation and intention, employing multiform techniques to reach different determinations and specific finalities (Foucault 1991, p. 95). These results demonstrate that though there is more freedom shown on Weibo on some issues in some ways, they are structured within a larger framework of governmentality, in this way, forming distinctive types of public spheres.

The outcome of this precise management of Weibo is a group of well-disciplined microbloggers in a secure online environment which also constructs a seemingly transparent and more open image of the government. In comparison with the past, the emergence of Weibo and other social media has indeed provided more freedom for public expression and opportunities for social protest on many occasions, but it remains the case that the new freedom of speech is well-arranged within the existing political framework.

This study is concerned with the new dynamics of remaking the public sphere through new strategies of regulation on Weibo. The thinking and apparatus of governmentalities which are at work on Weibo have consequences for the ways in which Weibo users are constituted as actors in the public sphere. In this way, Weibo users are no longer considered simply as passive information consumers, but are invited by the state to participate in improving political security and public services. In this way, the public domain of participation and deliberation is produced and reproduced. This type of new governmentality constitutes the "empowered" Weibo users. Instead of making overt declarations of Weibo as providing a democratizing communicative space, the specificities of Chinese social and political circumstances should be taken into account as playing an essential and instrumental role.

Just as the Chinese government plays an essential role in the public sphere, the diminishing of the public sphere on Weibo has a number of consequences. The new forms of government thinking can be viewed as implementing new forms of power and authority, while enabling new forms of participation and freedom of expression. However, these forms may intensify new patterns of hierarchy and new forms of potential exclusion. Therefore, although the internet has enlarged a space for public expression; as MacKinnon (2008) contends, it may be a catalyst for long-term change, but will not directly lead to regime change. Thus, the role of the internet in China is more likely to improve political evolution instead of revolution (p. 31).

In summary, Weibo is not able to serve entirely as a platform for ideally deliberative discourses, with public space and the public sphere intermingling on many occasions. A study of online activism in China shows that currently there is neither the triumph of complete control on the part of the internet-control regime nor successful resistance by internet users and activists (Yang 2009, p. 62). In certain instances Weibo has opened new channels for civic/government communication which can be used for problem solving, such as assistance for saving begging children after photos of these children are sent to the authorities and publicly exposed on social media, as has been mentioned in previous chapters. This represents a distinct change from the purely top-down approach of the past to the current bottom-up response which is more in the direction of a public sphere. However, to a larger extent, this can be seen as a timely transformation of the state administration in the new media era. The government appears to be gradually extending some power to the civil society.

When assessing the power of Weibo to bring change, it should be remembered that much of the content is focused on gossip and celebrity. In comparison with Twitter, Weibo is deliberately intended to "maximize the cacophonous spectacle of entertainment and to minimize reasoned discussion and debate" (Benney 2013). Moreover, the examination of Weibo's accessibility and representativeness has shown that Weibo users are not a sufficiently large user base to represent the whole population, especially when taking its demographic profiling into account. It is likely that only when the contradictions in China's current socio-economic conditions are significantly eased, when people's media literacy is much stronger and netizens become sufficiently well informed to pay more attention to media ethics, will we be able to discuss the formation of a real public sphere on Weibo and in social media more generally.

Participation as a Conduit for Governance

The larger freedoms of expression on Weibo do not mean the disappearance of traditional power relations in China. Rather, the locus of power is shifting from control over content to the management of the circulation of content. Instead of the binary thinking of closed versus open communication, governmentality thinking offers the possibility of more sophisticated thinking and complex management in controlling information. This helps to illuminate the management of the "free" space of communication. In the Weibo era, rather than overtly deciding who can speak and who cannot, the government process devolves to the government agencies, the power to assign meanings and to attach importance to particular cases, in order to make them visible or to conform to its agenda. In addition, it strategically assigns cultural values to instances of public expression in order to use them to construct, or to reinforce, a traditional version of the identity of the people. Weibo becomes a conduit of governance as the Chinese government oversees the text and manages the circulation of information, through allowing less confrontational critical media through, while continuing to censor activities that are perceived to incite collective action; diluting the public's potentially negative reaction, by allowing a greater measure of freedom of speech than in the past.

Previous research has been focused on the alternatives of internet control or its empowerment potential. This study discusses the "adaptation" of the Chinese state in the changing internet ecology, which has hitherto been under-considered. However, this study does not focus narrowly on the regulatory practices of the Chinese state, but offers a nuanced view of online practices which sufficiently confirm the centrality of the Chinese state's role in contemporary Chinese internet culture. The research elaborates the multiple strategies used to maintain the state's authority in this new media space. Contrary to the previous "hard" regulatory measures, the Chinese state has evolved a range of subtle and almost neo-liberal strategies to regulate Weibo to its advantage. Therefore, this book focuses on whether, or to what extent, it forms a vibrant public sphere. The most important issue is, in the new digital space, who governs it, under what conditions and for whose benefit. Governmentality epitomizes the Chinese government's recent trend to utilize traditional methods of persuasion in the new arena of technology, for the purpose of better management of the people and the government.

Therefore, this book draws the conclusion that the Chinese government in the reform-era is undergoing a radical change in thinking. A more liberal tolerance of public expression in the social media field is a distinctive example of new versions of regulated freedom. The debate over the democratizing influence of Weibo in China, however, is rooted in a Western focus on individual liberalism—assuming that the participation in public discourse is evidence of a public sphere, while government control in public discourse fails to meet the criteria of the normative ideal public sphere. Such analysis often neglects the ways in which the Chinese regime shapes political outcomes, while allowing certain levels of freedom in some media spaces. In conclusion, the state's management and manipulation of public discourse in China is a complex, interactive, proactive and adaptive process by which the state selectively tightens and loosens regulation of public discourse online in order to facilitate ultimate control.

Some analysts are not predicting a strong future for Weibo, due to declining usage, fragmentation of information and a growing lack of interest by users in general content (Wu 2013), and they suggest that Weibo's "carnival era" of free play in social media space, may be ending. However, this book argues that instead of decreasing influence, Weibo has been considered as a battleground for the government in the process of public opinion management, an idea that has been highly emphasized in the 2014 China Annual Development of New Media Report. In this report, the questions of how to launch a scientific new media regulation system and how to establish an effective public opinion management mechanism have been raised to a national strategy level. From this point of view, this book has provided empirical and theoretical evidence and methodology with which to examine these issues, now highlighted as governmental intentions, so alerting new media security experts in China. As technology continues to evolve rapidly, the Chinese government will continue to devise new versions of management in the future, for cyber security would be the first priority for the Chinese government, as it is for the liberal democratic states. The Chinese state will certainly adapt to the changing new media environment for these purposes.

Further Implications

Research interest in the fundamental question of whether social media will bring the same great changes in China as in other authoritarian countries, has been growing for many years, particular for overseas observers and analysts. In the existing scholarship, there are two approaches to studying the political implications of social media in China: one focuses on the power of social media for dissident use or social protest; the other focuses on the Chinese government's strict censorship practices. Most scholarship considers the greater openness of public expression in contemporary China to be a sign of a growing public sphere, which is a core element of democracy. Taking the public sphere and governmentality together as a theoretical framework, this book focuses on the complex relationship between the apparent freedoms and ultimate control, especially within the Weibo era, through which the Chinese authorities map a new way forward.

Though the existing scholarship has moved beyond making overtly simplistic analysis of whether the internet and its relevant technologies will form or hinder the development of a public sphere in China, most studies take a positive view of the growing social media space and its capacity to enlarge the public sphere in China. This conclusion, however, is based on Western assumptions.

This book does not deny the power of social media in Chinese society, as Weibo's power to "change" the Chinese society has been shown in many studies. However, it argues that the power of social media ultimately depends on the state. With its increasing economic development and growing international significance, China is willing to communicate openly in conversation with the rest of the world, but without this conversation interfering with inner political stability. This is the fundamental reason for the logic underlying the contradiction of greater openness, matched by greater control of public communication in new social media and exemplified on Weibo.

Despite Weibo's shortcomings, such as its lack of representativeness and the triviality of much of its content, the Weibo era exemplifies the new power relations established between the government and the audience, requiring the Chinese government to devise new methods for responding to the public demand in China (and internationally) for greater freedom of expression, while at the same time maintaining control, and going further, instrumentalising the social media platform to achieve its political and cultural aims, all within a uniquely Chinese context. Thus, the advancement of technology continues, along with the higher demands of government, so creating the paradox of greater participation of ordinary people and growing consent to the political agenda.

Future research may focus on a number of currently under-researched areas which deserve critical attention. Firstly, comparative studies of a number of Weibo incidents from social, political and cultural perspectives might further validate and explore in more depth, an enriched typology of public spheres and parallel government response measures. It may also be possible to identify cases that are more contestable and more conflicted, by examining for example, government behaviors and strategies to deal with internet coverage of environmental issues, such as the Dalian PX chemical factory demonstrations in 2011. Secondly, research could explore the government's evolving governance strategies and how its regulatory techniques have refashioned the public response into different types. A new area to explore is the effect of such online governance on non-netizens. Finally, in analyzing specific events, it would be useful to investigate the tipping point in each incident, for example, when is the non-acceptable limit reached for the government to shut down specific Weibo information, and when is it acceptable for the government to allow more freedom.

To conclude, for scholars and policymakers interested in the effectiveness of state-directed patriotic campaigns and proactive cooperation with Weibo to ensure regime legitimacy, as well as the commitment of Weibo users to China's national development agendas, this book provides an empirical basis. It confirms that while the role the Chinese government plays in relation to Weibo provides opportunities for freedom and multiple public spheres, the Chinese government is still able to maintain and exert its power through careful management and guidance of public debates on social media platforms.

References

Bandurski, D. 2012, 'Control, with apologies to "users and friends"', China Media Project, 2 April, viewed 24 March 2013, <http://cmp.hku.hk/2012/04/02/21126/>.

Bandurski, D. 2014, 'Anti-social media: How China's censors stay one step ahead of freedom', Global Asia, vol. 9, no. 2, pp. 16–25.

Benney, J. 2013, 'The aesthetics of microblogging: How the Chinese state controls Weibo', Tilburg Paper in Culture Studies, viewed 23 May 2014. <http://www.tilburguniversity.edu/upload/e4ef741d-2c6a-4ad9-9b17-32e103332502_TPCS_66_Benney.pdf>.

Calhoun, C. 1992, 'Introduction', in Calhoun, C (ed.), Habermas and the public sphere, MIT, Cambridge, pp. 1–48.

Clover, C. 2014, 'China reveals media shake-up plan', Financial Times, 19 August, viewed 2 September 2014, <http://www.ft.com/cms/s/0/5c6474c0-277a-11e4-ae44-00144feabdc0.html#axzz3AuyVC3Qh>.

Foucault, M. 1991, 'Governmentality', in Burchell, G, Gordon, C & Miller, P (eds.), The Foucault effect: Studies in governmental rationality, Harvester Wheatsheaf, Hemel Hempstead, pp. 87–104.

Hassid, J. 2012, 'Safety valve or pressure cooker? Blogs in Chinese political life', Journal of Communication, vol. 62, no. 2, pp. 212–230.

He, B & Warren, ME. 2011, 'Authoritarian deliberation: The deliberative turn in Chinese political development', Perspectives on Politics, vol. 9, no. 2, pp. 269–289.

Jiang, M. 2010, 'Spaces of authoritarian deliberation: Online public deliberation in China', in Leib, E & He, B (eds.), The search for deliberative democracy in China, Palgrave Macmillan, New York, pp. 261–287.

Kalathil, S & Boas, T. 2003, Open networks, closed regimes: The impact of the internet on authoritarian rule, Carnegie Endowment for International Peace, Washington, DC.

Lagerkvist, J. 2006, The Internet in China: Unlocking and containing the public sphere, Lund University, Lund.

Lagerkvist, J. 2010, After the internet, before democracy: Competing norms in Chinese media and society, Peter Lang, Bern.

Lewis, OA. 2013, 'Net inclusion: New media's impact on deliberative politics in China', Journal of Contemporary Asia, vol. 43, no. 4, pp. 678–708.

MacKinnon, R. 2008, 'Flatter world and thicker walls? Blogs, censorship and civic discourse in China', Public Choice, vol. 134, no. 1–2, pp. 31–46.

MacKinnon, R. 2009, 'China's censorship 2.0: How companies censor bloggers', First Monday, vol. 14, no. 2.

Morozov, E. 2011, The net delusion: The dark side of internet freedom, Public Affairs, New York.

Pan, P. 2006, 'The click that broke a government's grip', Washington Post, February 19, viewed 23 September 2013, <http://www.washingtonpost.com/wp-dyn/content/article/2006/02/18/AR2006021801389.html>.

Papacharissi, Z. 2002, 'The virtual sphere: The internet as a public sphere', New Media & Society, vol. 4, no. 1, pp. 9–27.

Rasmussen, T. 2013, 'Internet-based media, Europe and the political public sphere', Media, Culture & Society, vol. 35, no. 1, pp. 97–104.

Rauchfleisch, A & Schäfer, MS. 2014, 'Multiple public spheres of Weibo: A typology of forms and potentials of online public spheres in China', Information, Communication & Society, no. ahead-of-print, pp. 1–17.

Rose, N & Miller, P. 2010, 'Political power beyond the State: Problematics of government', The British Journal of Sociology, vol. 61, no. s1, pp. 271–303.

Tai, Z. 2006, The Internet in China: Cyberspace and civil society, Routledge, New York.

Tong, Y & Lei, S. 2013, 'War of position and microblogging in China', Journal of Contemporary China, vol. 22, no. 80, pp. 292–311.

Tong, J & Zuo, L. 2014, 'Weibo communication and government legitimacy in China: A computer-assisted analysis of Weibo messages on two "mass incidents"', Information, Communication & Society, vol. 17, no. 1, pp. 66–85.

Turner, G. 2010, Ordinary people and the media: The demotic turn (Theory, Culture and Society series), Sage, London.

Wu, C. 2013, 'Weibozoudaoshengsicunwangjiaochakou (Weibo has come into an intersection between life and death', Beijing Business Today, July 17, viewed 2 April 2014, <http://www.bbtnews.com.cn/news/2013-07/17000000252410.shtml>.

Xinhua net. 2014, 'Xi says China to build influential new-type media groups', August 18, viewed 23 August 2014, <http://news.xinhuanet.com/english/china/2014-08/18/c_133566343.htm>.

Yang, G. 2009, The Power of the internet in China: Citizen activism online, Columbia University Press, New York.

Zhang, Q. 2011, 'Status and hierarchy', in Zang, X (ed.), Understanding Chinese society, Routledge, New York.

Zhang, T. 2012, 'Fangzhi "jiegouxing" yuanhen yinfa gaige weiji (Preventing structural resentment causing reform crisis)', Chinareform.org.cn, 29 March, viewed 20 March 2013, <http://www.chinareform.org.cn/explore/perspectives/201203/t20120330_138154.htm>.

Zhang, Q. 2013, 'Microblogging the Bo Xilai trial: Transparency or theatre?', BBC News, 23 August, viewed 22 March 2014, <http://www.bbc.com/news/world-asia-china-23806657>.

Zhao, Z. 2014, 'Pedagogisation of nation identity through textbook narratives in China: 1902–1948', Citizenship Studies, vol. 18, no. 1, pp. 99–112.

Zheng, Y. 2008, Technological empowerment: The Internet, state, and society in China, Stanford University Press, Stanford.

www.ingramcontent.com/pod-product-compliance
Ingram Content Group UK Ltd.
Pitfield, Milton Keynes, MK11 3LW, UK
UKHW021825130926
8597IPUK00004B/14

9 781433 152719